FOUNDATIONS OF EURASIANISM

Volume III

Translated and Edited by John Stachelski,
Jafe Arnold, and Charlie Smith

With an Introduction by Rustem Vakhitov

2024

PRAV Publishing
www.pravpublishing.com
prav@pravpublishing.com

Translation copyright © 2024 PRAV Publishing

All rights reserved. No part of this book may be reproduced or distributed in any form or by any means, electronic or mechanical, including photocopying, recording, or by any information storage and retrieval, without permission in writing from the publisher.

Cover image: "Alexander Nevsky" by Nicholas Roerich, 1942.

ISBN 978-1-952671-31-9 (Hardcover)
ISBN 978-1-952671-32-6 (Paperback)
ISBN 978-1-952671-33-3 (Ebook)

TABLE OF CONTENTS

	FROM THE EDITORS AND TRANSLATORS *John Stachelski*	7
	THE EURASIAN ANNALS: THE "OFFICIAL" HISTORY OF CLASSICAL EURASIANISM, AND THE REAL STORY *Rustem Vakhitov*	11
I.	AT THE DOORSTEP: REACTION? REVOLUTION? *Nikolai Trubetzkoy*	39
II.	THE TOWER OF BABEL AND THE CONFUSION OF TONGUES *Nikolai Trubetzkoy*	51
III.	TOWARD THE OVERCOMING OF THE REVOLUTION *Petr Suvchinsky*	67
IV.	IDEAS AND METHODS *Petr Suvchinsky*	87
V.	WE AND THE OTHERS *Nikolai Trubetzkoy*	135
VI.	THE TWO HEROIC FEATS OF ST. ALEXANDER NEVSKY *George Vernadsky*	155

VII. ON THE TURANIAN ELEMENT
   IN RUSSIAN CULTURE   179
   Nikolai Trubetzkoy

VIII. TO THE OPPONENTS OF EURASIANISM   205
   Yakov Sadovsky

IX. MASTER AND DOMAIN   231
   Petr Savitsky

X. THE MONGOL YOKE IN RUSSIAN HISTORY   273
   George Vernadsky

XI. THE PHENOMENOLOGY OF REVOLUTION
   (selected excerpts)   289
   Lev Karsavin

FROM THE EDITORS AND TRANSLATORS

John Stachelski

***

Perhaps even more so than in the first two volumes of the *Foundations of Eurasianism* series, this volume is as much an act of curation as it is an act of translation. In a general sense, each volume can be said to be organized around a particular Eurasianist tome – the first around the seminal *Exodus to the East* and the second around *Pathways*. However, volume three takes up the task of presenting much more than what the group themselves referred to as the third official Eurasianist tome, the first issue of *The Eurasian Annals*. The volume in your hands bundles together all three volumes published under the same title, and thus accounts for Eurasianist tomes three, four and five. This invites the question of how these particular texts were selected, and why several critically important texts have been omitted. In a certain sense, this decision might seem an odd one. If the goal of the *Foundations of Eurasianism* series is to present the most important texts that define the landscape of Eurasianist ideas to Western audiences, then how could any articles of the volumes described as "Eurasianist Dogma" be left out?[1]

The first response would be that not all of the works not found in this volume have actually been neglected, while others will eventually find a place in future volumes. A key example

---

1 N.S. Trubetskoy, *Pis'ma k P.P. Suvchinskomu. 1921-1927* (Moscow: Biblioteka-fond Russkoe zarubezh'e, Russkii Put', 2008), 228.

of the former is Savitsky's major text "Eurasianism", which we felt was critical enough to warrant inclusion in the very first volume of this series. An example of the latter is Karsavin's "Foundations of Politics", which is of such importance (and length) that it deserves more attention and space – either in a separate volume thematically devoted to political philosophy, or as a stand-alone publication. There are numerous examples to this effect, but overall, this volume attempts to include the most critical texts representing the Eurasianist tradition as a whole in tandem with the previous volumes, rather than treating each article on its own merit. While many readers would likely be curious to read Ivan Ilyin's "The Pillar of Spite Towards God", we felt that this text's inclusion in *The Eurasian Annals* alone was not necessarily an indication of its full agreement with Eurasianism, let alone its place among the pantheon of Eurasianist texts. Other texts, such as Sezeman's fascinating "Socrates and the Problem of Self-Knowledge", focus on particular historical or philosophical questions and thus speak less to the core tenets of the spectrum of Eurasianist thought.

However, the reader should know that the included texts were not simply hand-selected by the editorial team. The two-year process of crafting this ambitious volume began with a survey presented to a number of scholars and specialists on the topic of Eurasianism, who were asked to indicate the most important texts of the tradition found within the original tomes. While any true consensus here is excluded by the very nature of the question, we are confident that our selections are representative of a general agreement found among those who participated, further narrowed in combination with the criteria discussed above. Overall, this volume accomplishes the dual task of representing texts foundational to Eurasianism, while simultaneously showcasing the spirit and flavor of the *Eurasian Annals* trilogy and the moment(s) it represents in the history of the Eurasianist ideological course. For a detailed examination of the importance of these tomes for the tradition,

From the Editors and Translators

we are proud to refer readers to the original introduction written for this volume by Rustem Vakhitov, a lifelong researcher of Eurasianism, who has numerous published articles on the topic as well as a recently published monograph in Russian: *Eurasianism: Logos, Eidos, Symbol Myth*.[2]

In the coming pages, readers knowledgeable of the central aspects of the Eurasianist idea will notice the prominence of texts specifically addressing the question of the role of the so-called "Mongol yoke" in Russian history, an idea now synonymous with Eurasianism, as well as the presence of two thinkers who played absolutely pivotal roles in the development of the ideology, yet remained absent from previous volumes, namely George Vernadsky and Lev Karsavin. Other texts presented here suggest a fully formed conclusion on topics explored in the first and second volumes of our series, such as the Eurasianist view on the Revolution and their vision of "overcoming" it without surrendering to the utopian reactionary viewpoints of the White emigration. In general, it could be said that these texts represent the most complete representations of pivotal Eurasianist ideas at the heyday of its ideological ingenuity, leading up to the moment of the Clamart split which would see the movement fractured into multiple trajectories.

Taken as a whole, this volume represents the most difficult curation process so far, as well as some of the most challenging translation tasks our team has undertaken to date. On top of the sheer volume of texts that were read, chosen, and translated, certain texts presented formidable difficulties. Of particular note is Savitsky's "Master and Domain" [*Khoziain i khoziaistvo*], a text which extensively iterates and explores a word and concept that borders on untranslatable. How does one translate a term like *"khoziaistvo"*, a concept which simultaneously invokes the down-to-earth management of a small household or farm particular to Russia, and something

---

2 Rustem Vakhitov, *Evraziistvo - Logos, Eidos, Simvol', Mif* (Saint Petersburg: Vladimir Dal', 2023).

as broad as the economy in general? The meaning of this word is simultaneously so specific and yet used so broadly by the author, that nearly every instance of its use required a context-specific translation. This task is in a way reflective of the ordeal of translating Eurasianism generally, a struggle found to some degree in every text of the tradition. Eurasianism traces the correlation of concrete, cultural specificity (i.e. Russia/Eurasia) and broad, universal systems (i.e. culture or civilization as such). It attempts to bridge or, sometimes, altogether collapse, the distinction between part and whole. In the text in question, Savitsky attempts to take the often small, domestic, and culturally entrenched relationship of a master to his domain in the Russian countryside, and show how this microcosm could be reflected into the macrocosm of the economy in general in order to present an economic viewpoint distinct from both capitalism and socialism, and uniquely Russian. While undoubtedly a challenge both to translator and reader, such efforts cannot be shirked by any project hoping to represent or understand Eurasianism in its own words, a point which we strive to reach through the sways of translation.

It is with these considerations in mind that we, the editors and translators of the volume, must ultimately reject the notion that the *Eurasian Annals* represented a completed project. As the coming split would show, Eurasianism, as a train of thought that straddles the border(s) between philosophy, ideology, aesthetics, etc., was still in development and still experiencing its birth pains. While the central premises of Eurasianism are here laid out and can even be said to have reached a certain peak of maturity, this volume simultaneously reopens them for discussion, both amongst the translators and hopefully amongst our readers and future researchers.

THE EURASIAN ANNALS: THE "OFFICIAL" HISTORY OF CLASSICAL EURASIANISM, AND THE REAL STORY

Rustem Vakhitov

***

A Brief History of Eurasianism

The Eurasianist movement first appeared in the Bulgarian capital of Sofia between 1920 and 1921. It was there and then that fate brought five Russian political refugees together: Prince Nikolai Sergeevich Trubetzkoy (1890-1938), Petr Nikolaevich Savitsky (1895-1968), Georgy (Georges) Vasilyevich Florovsky (1893-1979) and Petr Petrovich Suvchinsky (Count Sheliga) (1892-1985). The fifth was Prince Andrei Alexandrovich Lieven (1884-1949), "the impresario of Eurasianism," as he called himself; while he did not make any of his own written contributions, he inspired his friends to write the first Eurasianist collection.[3]

All of them, with the exception of Florovsky, were nobles; Trubetzkoy came from a famous and ancient princely lineage. They were also all staunch anti-communists who saw the Bolshevik Revolution as a catastrophe and its ideology as

---

3   Letter from A.A. Liven to G.V. Florovsky dated 18 April 2022, *Transactions of the Association of Russian-American Scholars in the U.S.A.* vol. XXXVII (New York, 2011-2012), 25.

the apogee of atheism, and thus anathema to their own group, which combined their superb education with sincere Orthodox religiosity. Two of the founders of the Eurasianist circle in Sofia participated in the White movement: Savitsky was a deputy minister in the anti-Bolshevik Civil War era governments of Anton Denikin (1872-1947) and Petr Wrangel (1878-1928), while Prince Andrei Lieven fought in Wrangel's army in Crimea.

All of them (except for Lieven, who eventually became a modest Orthodox priest) would subsequently inscribe their names into the history of Russian and world culture in their respective fields: Trubetzkoy became a major linguist, the creator of phonological theory, Savitsky a famous geopolitician and geo-economist, while Florovsky became well known for his research in the field of Eastern patristics, and Suvchinsky found fame as a popularizer of avant-garde music and an important figure in the formation of French postmodernism. But in 1921, when they first met and formed a friendship in Sofia over discussions of Trubetzkoy's anti-Eurocentrist manifesto, *Europe and Mankind*,[4] they were young and energetic, propelled by the maximalism of youth into daring new ideas and projects. In August 1921, at the Russian-Bulgarian Publishing House (where Suvchinsky was the managing director), they published their first collection, which consisted of 10 articles devoted to understanding the revolution, relations between East and the West, and the search for religious truth against the catastrophic backdrop of war and revolution back in Russia. The title of the collection, *Exodus to the East*, parallels the biblical *Book of Exodus*, which tells the story of the Jewish people's flight from Egyptian captivity in order to return to their beloved homeland promised to them by God. The metaphor was transparent: the Eurasianists considered the 300-year period

---

4   His critique of Eurocentrism is sometimes compared to the anti-colonial concepts of the Western poststructuralists of the 1960s-70s. See Nikolai Trubetzkoy, "Europe and Mankind (selected excerpts)" in *Foundations of Eurasianism - Volume I* (PRAV Publishing, 2020), 57-88.

of Westernization in Russia, ignited by the reforms of Peter the Great, to be a form of captivity for Russia and the peoples of the "Russian world". Despite the irony of the argument in light of their emigre status, they perceived the revolution as an opportunity for Russians to return "home", "back to their roots." Of course, being staunch anti-communists, they were far from seeing Lenin as a "new Moses." The contributors to the collection and the founders of Eurasianism believed that Bolshevism was the last expression of the Westernism they hated (after all, the ideas of Marxism came to Russia from Europe) and believed that the socialist experiment would end in failure, after which Russia would finally reject all of the cultural forms of the West and take its own, original path of development. They conceived of Eurasianism as the ideology of the rebirth of post-revolutionary Russia (or, in Leon Trotsky's terms, the ideology of the future Thermidor).

Thoughts about a special path of development for Russia had already been expressed many times before the Eurasianists by the Russian Slavophiles and Pan-Slavists. However, the Eurasianists differed significantly from these groups (while still considering them as predecessors). The very name of their ideology was intended to show that they did not consider Russia to be part of Europe or the center of the Slavic world. Russia, in their opinion, is a non-European civilization that had absorbed various influences from the East, but stopped short of becoming fully Asian. Russia is not Europe or Asia, but a specific "middle continent" which they named "Eurasia". They considered the study of this "continent," the clarification of its borders and structure, and the study of the Turanian roots of Slavic culture, to be the main tasks of Eurasianism as a philosophical and scientific project aiming for the self-awareness of Russian civilization.

Orthodoxy was an essential part of Eurasianist ideology. Already in the first collection, the group stated that the victory of the revolution in Russia paradoxically meant the end of the era of materialism and a transition to an "era of faith."⁵ The communists, in their opinion, had awakened enormous religious energy in the Russian people which would eventually lead to the revival of Russian Orthodoxy. However, their vision of Orthodox revival was highly original and departed from the Orthodoxy of the White emigration. The Eurasianists united the Orthodox church with the style and ideas of modernity: they sympathized with Futurism (their first collection even had a Futurist design scheme) and, despite insisting on the "elimination of communism and the Communist Party," became apologists for the Soviet system, federalism, and industrialization.

The ideas of Eurasianism strongly resonated in the emigration (while Soviet philosophers responded to it with the expected curses of vulgar Marxist provenance). Bishop Antony (Khrapovitsky) even called the leaders of Eurasianism "the new Khomyakovs and Kireevskys," while the philosopher Fyodor Stepun called them the "Slavophiles of the era of futurism." Among Russian exiles, both harsh critics and ardent supporters of Eurasianism appeared almost immediately, as did patrons ready to finance new publications. The second Eurasianist volume, *Pathways*, was funded by Baron Alexander Vladimirovich Meller-Zakomelsky (1898-1971), the son of a factory owner and former White Guard who took an interest in Eurasianism. This collection was published in Berlin in 1922 by the Helikon publishing house and included two new authors: Kartashov and Bitsilli. The following year, with more money from Meller-Zakomelsky, the Eurasianist Publishing House was established. Later that same year, the English philanthropist, millionaire, philosopher, poet, and founder of the Department of Eastern Christianity at Oxford, Henry Norman Spalding, allocated such a large sum of money to

---

5   Petr Suvchinsky, "The Era of Faith" in *Foundations of Eurasianism - Volume II* (PRAV Publishing, 2022), 47-64.

the Eurasianists[6] (who had been introduced to him as a new Christian movement) that they were able to publish various publications such as *The Eurasian Annals*, *The Eurasian Chronicles*, and a weekly newspaper simply entitled *Eurasia*. They also used this money to hold meetings and congresses and pay royalties to authors. By the mid-1920s, Eurasianism was turning into a broad movement among the emigration (in Prague alone there were about 100 active Eurasianists)[7] with branches in numerous European cities (Sofia, Prague, Berlin, Vienna, Athens, Belgrade, Warsaw, Brussels, Paris), as well as Great Britain (London), the US (New York), and China (Harbin).

In 1924, the Eurasianists established a political organization with a governing body in Vienna, the Eurasianist Council, which included, in addition to the founders, the former monarchist officers Petr Semenovich Arapov (1897-1938) and Petr Nikolaevich Malevsky-Malevich (1891-1974), with the goal of spreading their ideas among the emigration as well as in the USSR. They issued collective manifestos, leaflets, popular brochures, and prophesied the imminent fall of communism in Russia and a return to their homeland to realize the Eurasianist political ideal: a Soviet but non-communist federal statehood. The eventual result was that numerous naive Eurasianist intellectuals came under the control of the Soviet intelligence services – the OGPU (United Main Political Directorate under the People's Commissariat of Internal Affairs of the USSR). Soviet agents convinced the group that there was a secret Eurasianist organization in the USSR (part of the mythical "Trust Cooperative"). Its representative "Denisov", the pseudonym of Cheka agent

---

6   More than 10,000 pounds sterling, which corresponds to around 40,000 dollars today. Sergei Glebov, *Evraziistvo mezhdu imperiei i modernom. Istoriia v dokumentakh* (Moscow: Novoe izdatel'stvo, 2010), 128.

7   From a memo by the assistant chief of the KRO OGPU, V.A. Styrne, to the head of the KRO OGPU, A.Kh. Artuzov, on the counterintelligence operations "Yaroslavets" and "Trust", 8 February 1925, in A.F. Kiselev (ed.), *Politicheskaia istoriia russkoi emigratsii. 1920-1940 gg. Dokumenty i materialy* (Moscow: Gumanitarnyi izdatel'skii tsentr, 1999), 251.

The "Official" History of Classical Eurasianism, and the Real Story

Alexander Andreevich Langovoy (1896-1964), joined the Eurasianist Council in 1926. Some of the Eurasianists (in particular, Savitsky) secretly visited the USSR through the Trust Cooperative, never suspecting that the "Soviet Eurasianists" guiding them were actually Soviet agents.

When the truth about the Trust Cooperative was exposed, it was a heavy blow for Eurasianism. Eurasianism was deeply compromised in the eyes of the emigration by its connections with the OGPU. This was soon followed by yet another major blow: the split of the Eurasianists into right and left. The left group (Karsavin, Suvchinsky, Svyatopolk-Mirsky, Efron, Klepinin) united around the newspaper *Eurasia*, which was published in Clamart, France in 1928-1929. This group grew increasingly pro-Soviet over time before finally breaking with Eurasianism altogether (many of them became communists and even agents of Soviet intelligence abroad). However, even the right Eurasianists continued to be accused of ties to Bolshevism despite the fact that they had publicly disowned the "left deviation" (Savitsky, Ilyin, and Alekseev even published a brochure entitled "The Newspaper *Eurasia* is not a Eurasian organ"). The caustic decadent poet Zinaida Gippius called Eurasianism "Bolshevism without communism", "Orthodox Bolshevism" and mockingly suggested that if the Eurasianists came to power in the USSR, the only change would be that the Cheka (an abbreviation for the "Extraordinary Commission") would be renamed the "Virtuous institution" or "Good Trusteeship".[8]

Trubetzkoy eventually cut ties with the Eurasianist organization alongside many other disillusioned members.[9] However, the tireless Savitsky managed to regroup and restore the group's publishing activities, putting out two more

---

8   Z.N. Gippius, "*Vtoroi koshmar*", *Poslednie Novosti* 170 (Paris: 2 March 1927), 2.

9   Trubetzkoy maintained a correspondence with Savitsky even after leaving the leadership of the movement. Savitsky later convinced him to contribute articles to the Eurasianists' publications in the 1930s, but Trubetzkoy did not return to any of the group's governing bodies.

collective volumes at the turn of the 1930s, *The Eurasianist Collection* and *The Thirties*, as well as a serial journal called *The Eurasian Notebooks*. In 1931, Savitsky and his associates created the Eurasianist Party in Brussels. The group attracted new members, and new cells began to appear in the Baltic states and Western Europe. The Eurasianists also began to collaborate with other post-revolutionary emigre organizations (the Young Russians, National Maximalists, Novograd). During this period, Eurasianism developed some of its most important and influential ideas, with Savitsky spearheading the creation of structural geography and Roman Jakobson pioneering the idea of the Eurasian language union.[10]

In the second half of the 1930s, Savitsky and Alekseev founded the anti-Nazi Russian Emigre Defence Movement. The group's political activities eventually died out at the beginning of the Second World War, but many of its former leaders and theorists (such as Savitsky and Vernadsky) continued to develop the scientific ideas of Eurasianism until the end of their lives.[11]

The Eurasian Annals: The Surface Level

This third volume of translations of essential works by the Eurasianists offered to the reader is devoted to content from the *Eurasian Annals*. The word "Annals", "*Vremennik*" in Russian, is a term used for periodic academic publications (for example, there was a scientific journal, *Vremennik of the Pushkin House*). As mentioned above, the three volumes of the *Eurasian Annals* were published (in 1923, 1925 and 1927 respectively)

---

10 On the connection between Eurasianism and Slavic structuralism, see the work of the Swiss historian of ideas, Patrick Sériot, *Struktura i tselostnost': Ob intellektual'nykh istokakh strukturalizma v Tsentral'noi i Vostochnoi Evrope, 1920-30-e gg.* (Moscow: Iazyki slavianskoi kul'tury, 1999). Revised English edition: *Structure and the Whole: East, West and Non-Darwinian Biology in the Origins of Structural Linguistics* (Berlin: Mouton/De Gruyter, 2014).

11 Savitsky died in 1968 in Prague, Czechoslovakia, and Vernadsky in 1973 in New Haven, US.

The "Official" History of Classical Eurasianism, and the Real Story

during the heyday of Eurasianism. They contain what can be considered the "Eurasianist classics". Trubetzkoy noted in one of his letters that the *Eurasian Annals* contained the "dogma of Eurasianism," that is, the programmatic provisions of Eurasianism accepted by all members, while their other nonperiodical publication, *The Eurasian Chronicles*, contained the "Eurasianist doxa," that is, opinions which reflected the positions of individual Eurasianists.[12] Perhaps this is why Sergei Glebov, a contemporary scholar of Eurasianism, has called the *Vremenniki* the group's "official publications". Ksenya Ermishina has an article that details and analyzes the contents of all three volumes of the *Eurasian Annals*.[13] I refer those interested to seek out this article, as I will only briefly be going over the main authors and their ideas here.

The first *Vremennik*, published in 1923 by the Eurasianist Publishing House, received the subtitle "Book 3", which indicates that the Eurasianists saw it as a continuation of their first two collections (1921's *Exodus to the East* and 1922's *Pathways*). In the preface, the Eurasianists speak of themselves as the successors of the Slavophiles, Gogol, Dostoevsky and Leontiev, but emphasize that "the content of Eurasianism is not read in books", that the "personal experience" of the founders played a decisive role in its emergence, meaning the experience of catastrophe, World War, and the Revolution and Civil War in Russia. The first collection contains nine articles.[14] In addition to the founders of Eurasianism (Trubetzkoy, Savitsky and Suvchinsky), the philosopher Nikolai Sergeevich Arsenyev (1888-1977), the historian Mstislav

---

12 In a letter from Trubetzkoy to Suvchinsky dated 13 January 1927, we read: "... ank and file Eurasianists saw everything contained in the *Annals* as dogma, subject only to assimilation and popularization, but not critical discussion." N.S. Trubetskoy *Pis'ma k P.P. Suvchinskomu. 1921-1927* (Moscow: Bibliotekafond Russkoe zarubezh'e, Russkii Put', 2008), 228.

13 K.B. Ermishina, "Evraziiskii vremennik" in O.T. Ermishin and K.B. Ermishina (eds.), *Materialy k 'Entsiklopedii klassicheskogo evraziistva* (Moscow: Dom russkogo zarubezh'ia im. Aleksandra Solzhenitsyna, 2010/2020), 474-481.

14 Petr Savitsky, P.P. Suvchinsky, and Pr. N.S. Trubetskoy (eds.), *Evraziiskii vremennik* (Berlin: Evraziiskoe knigoizdatel'stvo, 1923), 5-6.

Vyacheslavovich Shikhmatov (1888-1943) and the economist Yakov Dmitrievich Sadovsky (1861–1925) contributed to the first *Vremennik*. It should be noted that Sadovsky would only publish two articles to Eurasianist publications and died shortly after in 1927, while Arsenyev's article would remain his sole published contribution to Eurasianism. At the same time, the first *Vremennik* contained outlines of several important concepts of the Eurasianist worldview. In the article "Allegiance to the Idea", Savitsky introduces the concept of ideocracy and the "ruling idea."[15] Subsequently, these would become central terms in the Eurasianist dictionary,[16] which the group would begin using to characterize both the evolution of Western forms of statehood from liberal democracies to ideologically based autocracies, as well as their own state ideal ("Eurasianist ideocracy").

In the article "The Otherness of Russian Religiosity," Suvchinsky introduces another important Eurasianist term, "everyday confession" (*bytovoe ispovednichestvo*, which is sometimes associated with Paul Tillich's concept of "theonomous culture").[17] Later, the Eurasianists would point to this concept as a specific feature of Russian religiosity which brought Russians closer to the Islamic cultures of Eurasia.

It is difficult to overestimate the importance of Trubetzkoy's article "The Tower of Babel and the Confusion of Tongues." Here he introduced one of the most important concepts of modern linguistics - the "linguistic union" (as the antipode of the "language family"), which Savitsky later uses in his structural geography to point out another point

---

15 Petr Savitsky, "Allegiance to the Idea" in *Foundations of Eurasianism - Volume III*, 269-276.

16 Savitsky later suggested that the Eurasianist concept of ideocracy received detailed presentation in Trubetzkoy's "On the State System and Form of Governance" (1927). See P.N. Savitsky, "Idei i puti evraziiskoi literatury" in *Russkii uzel evraziistva. Vostok v russkoj mysli. Sbornik trudov evraziiev* (Moscow: Belovod'e 1997), 378-379.

17 A.A. Gritsanov, "Kul'turnaiaa shizofreniia" in idem, *Postmodernizm (Entsiklopediia)* [https://fil.wikireading.ru/41004].

of intersection between geographical and cultural boundaries in topogenesis. And yet, this is not even the main point of interest in Trubetzkoy's article. The article contained a theological justification for one of the central ideas around which Eurasianism was formed: the denial of the universalist philosophy of history and culture. The Eurasianists often faced reproach: how can intellectuals who declare their Christian religiosity deny the existence of a single humanity, a universal human and even a common Christian culture? Trubetzkoy writes that the tendency of cultures and languages to fragment is a consequence of God's punishment for the "Babylonian pandemonium" described in the Bible, that is, for their attempt to create a single universal culture based on materialism and atheism. The sin of the Eurocentrists, according to Trubetzkoy, is their attempt to impose European culture on all peoples, and in so doing destroy and level all other cultures. This goal is ultimately impossible and contrary to the will of God, and thus any artificially created Western superculture will collapse, but the process will also cause irreparable damage to non-Western cultures and bring much suffering to the diverse peoples of the world. Even Christianity, according to Trubetzkoy, is just a "grafting of the transcendental," but the task of every people that experiences this "grafting" is to create its own version Christian culture.

Finally, in his article "To the Opponents of Eurasianism", Sadovsky introduces the term "demotia," as noted by Savitsky in his 1931 article "The Ideas and Paths of Eurasian Literature."[18] The theory of demotia would be further developed by the Eurasianist philosopher of law Nikolai Alekseev (1879-1964) to contrast people's democracy with bourgeois, liberal democracy.

The fourth book of *Eurasian Annals* was published in 1925 in Berlin and contains 13 articles. In addition to Trubetzkoy, Savitsky, Suvchinsky and Shikhmatov, this volume also included articles by the theologian, philosopher and art critic

---

18 *Russkii uzel evraziistva*, 379.

The "Official" History of Classical Eurasianism, and the Real Story

Vladimir Nikolaevich Ilyin (1891-1974), the philosopher and historian Lev Platonovich Karsavin (1882-1952), and the historian Georgy Vladimirovich Vernadsky (1888-1973), all of whom would become major theorists of Eurasianism (Ilyin and Karsavin as religious philosophers and Vernadsky as a historian).[19] Conceptually, the fourth book of the *Eurasian Annals* deeply enriched Eurasianism. The most important theme explored in this collection was the Eurasianist concept of historiosophy (Ermishina even calls the fourth book of the *Vremennik* the "historiosophical" volume).[20]

Vernadsky's "The Two Heroic Feats of St. Alexander Nevsky" proposed a new understanding of medieval Rus' experience with the Mongol Empire (the so-called "Mongol yoke" in Russian history). This requires some explanation. In traditional Russian historiography, it was customary to perceive Rus' incorporation into the Mongol Empire as an exceptional tragedy, to portray the Mongols as cruel, "Asiatic savages", and the Russians as a highly developed European people who, having become a victim of the steppe people, saved Europe from the Asian invasion with their sacrifice. This view of the Mongol yoke was characteristic of traditional Russian historians (such as in the work of Karamzin and Solovyov); this is taught to Russians even today in schools as an "obvious truth." The Eurasianists proposed a different view, informed by their anti-Eurocentric orientation, that was more tolerant of the Mongols. Vernadsky recalled that in the 13th century, the Russians were threatened not only by steppe nomads from the southeast, but also by Catholic knights from the northwest. And if the former were indifferent to the religiosity of Russians and sometimes even supportive of the Orthodox Church, such as exempting it from taxation, the latter intended to eradicate Russian Orthodoxy and introduce Catholicism.

---

19 L.P. Karsavin would move away from Eurasianism after the "Clamart split," which he, in fact, initiated. V.N. Ilyin would remain with Savitsky during the split and leave the ranks of the movement only in the 1930s. Vernadsky continued to develop the ideas of Eurasianism until the end of his life.

20 See Ermishina, "*Evraziiskii vremennik*".

The "Official" History of Classical Eurasianism, and the Real Story

Since Orthodoxy, according to the Eurasianists, was and remains the core of Russian ethnic identity, Vernadsky argues that Alexander Nevsky's choice in favor of the Mongol Horde rather than the West should be celebrated and preserved. Viewing the "Mongol yoke" not as an absolute evil, but as an event that had positive consequences, is one of the Eurasianists' most well known innovations, which the majority of Russians, brought up on hatred of the Mongols as ruthless conquerors, perceived as scandalous and shocking.[21] For example, this is how the famous Russian nationalist Ivan Ilyin reacted to this argument: "We, thank God, are not yet subordinate to the 'Eurasianists'; the Komsomol does not yet fully 'believe' in Genghis Khan, has not yet transferred power over the Russian ulus to four inventive private assistant professors, and has not yet launched its upcoming Ural-Altai Genghis-*kh-a-m-s-t-v-a*..." (punning on the proximity of the title Khan with the Russian word *khamstva*, meaning "rudeness" or "crudity"), and further : "...was it for this reason that we overcame the Tatars and their 350-year-long invasion? (the last invasion of Moscow by Kazy-Girey took place in 1591), in order to seek salvation in its overpowered and dead elements?"[22]

A sense of "Asiaphilia" also peeks through Trubetzkoy's article "On the Turanian Element in Russian Culture", which analyzes the national character and culture of the Turanians (primarily the Turks) and points out the similarities with Russian culture and character.

Savitsky's article, "Master and Domain", attempts to metaphysically substantiate the economic theory of Eurasianism and search for a "third way" between socialism and capitalism.

Finally, in Shikhmatov's article, the concept of the "state of truth" first appears to designate the Russian political and legal

---

21 In his article "The Eurasianists", N.A. Berdyaev wrote about the group's Asiaphilia as a point of originality in their theory.

22 I.A. Ilyin, "*Samobytnost' ili original'nichan'e?*", quoted in *Nachala. Religiozno-filosofskii zhurnal* 4 (1992), 61.

The "Official" History of Classical Eurasianism, and the Real Story

tradition and its differences from the tradition of the West. This concept was subsequently developed by the Eurasianist jurist Nikolai Nikolaevich Alekseev.

Let us now turn to the third and last volume of the *Eurasian Annals* which was published in Paris in 1927 and received the subtitle "Book 5". It contains 10 articles, and its new authors include the aforementioned Alekseev (1879-1964), the orientalist Vasily Petrovich Nikitin (1885-1960), the historian Sergei Germanovich Pushkarev (1888-1984), and the philosopher Semyon Lyudvigovich Frank (1877-1950). Frank is a somewhat random figure for Eurasianism, as he did not share the Eurasianists' ideas and did not try to hide this; anti-communism was the only thing that brought him close to the group. The historian Pushkarev would also soon move away from Eurasianism and subsequently condemned his youthful passion for the idea (all the same, Savitsky later spoke highly of his contribution to Eurasianist historiosophy). Alekseev would remain a part of the Eurasianist movement until the end, becoming a specialist in Eurasianist jurisprudence and the creator of the theories of the guarantee state, legal obligations, and federalism (he served as a replacement for Shikhmatov, who left the group over his opposition to their Asiaphilia and historiosophy).[23] Nikitin continued (until 1930) to participate in Eurasianist publications as an orientalist (a Turkologist and Kurdologist), whose research interests revolved around the Middle East and China. In the fifth *Vremennik*, two articles by the philosopher Karsavin are of particular note: "The Foundations of Politics" and "The Phenomenology of Revolution". By the time of the third volume's publication, Karsavin had become the "official philosopher of the Eurasianist movement," incorporating Eurasianist ideas into his concept of the unity of personality. In "The Foundations of Politics," he defends the idea that the people are a collective personality and the main subject of history. He saw the state

---

[23] Alekseev's Eurasianist works are discussed in B.V. Nazmutdinov, *Zakony iz-za granitsy. Politiko-pravovye aspekty klassicheskogo evraziistva* (Moscow: Norma, 2018).

as a guarantor of the spiritual and personal unity of culture. In "Phenomenology of Revolution," Karsavin traced the natural phases of the revolution and came to the conclusion that after the anarchy and rule of fanatical revolutionaries, a new people would arrive - the creators of a new, post-revolutionary state. It is obvious that the Eurasianists saw themselves as the leaders of these new creators and state builders.

In the article "The Mongol Yoke in Russian History", Vernadsky develops a Eurasianist view of Russian history, according to which the incorporation of Rus' into the Mongol empire in the Middle Ages had a positive significance in bringing Rus' closer to the East.

Alekseev, in his article "Soviet Federalism," welcomes the federal structure of the Soviet state, but advocates for a transition from national to regional federalism.

These were the main ideas of the last *Vremennik*. The release of a planned sixth *Vremennik* was prevented by the split, which occurred in 1928-1929 and precipitated a new era in the history of Eurasianism.

The classical period of this history, which included the publication of the *Annals* (1923-1927), was the heyday of the movement, the period of the construction of the group's broad interdisciplinary program and ideology. Along with the *Annals* and *Chronicles*, the Eurasianists released two collective manifestos during this period: "Eurasianism: The Experience of Systematic Exposition" in 1926 and "Eurasianism (The Formulation of 1927)". A number of fundamentally important books were also released by the Eurasianist Publishing House during this period, including Trubetzkoy's *The Legacy of Genghis Khan* and *On the Question of Russian National Self-Knowledge*, as well as Savitsky's *Russia – A Special Geographical World* and *Geographical Features of Russia*, among many others.

In these works, the original, core concepts of Eurasianism (which had been formed between 1921-1923), including the plurality of cultural worlds, the unique world of Russia-

Eurasia, the revolution as the end of Westernized culture and an opportunity for Russian renewal, were expanded with several new critical concepts, including the Turanian element of the Russian character, the positive significance of the Mongol period in Russian history, federalism, and the collective personality of the people. Thus, Eurasianism turned from a set of several daring paradoxes into a comprehensive ideology.[24]

The Eurasian Annals: The Submerged Level

The contemporaries of the founding Eurasianists and the first new readers of Eurasianist texts when they were finally republished in Russia in the 1980s and 1990s saw the worldview as integral and internally logical. The crisis of Eurasianism that resulted from the "Clamart split" was thought of as a kind of accident, a consequence of external influence on the Eurasianist movement (primarily that of OGPU agents). Moreover, fascination with the "completeness" of the Eurasianist worldview led many in post-Soviet Russia to see it as a ready-made political ideology capable of solving the problems generated by the unsuccessful liberal reforms of Gaidar-Yeltsin. Thus, the politicization of the post-Soviet "Eurasianist Renaissance" proved inevitable.

However, in the 2000s, scholars of Eurasianism (Sobolev, Ermishina, Beisswenger, Glebov) delved into the epistolary heritage of the Eurasianists, and it immediately became clear that the printed works were only the tip of the iceberg. There was also a submerged level that the group had deliberately hidden in an effort to present a unified front to their adherents and readers. Meanwhile, behind the image of a "ready-made ideology" that emerged from the pages of Eurasianist collections and manifestos, there were hidden disagreements, disputes, and conflicts. This was especially evident during the "classical

---

24 For a breakdown of the schema of this ideology, see our work: R.R. Vakhitov, *Evraziistvo. Logos. Eidos. Simvol. Mif* (Saint Petersburg: Vladimir Dal', 2023).

The "Official" History of Classical Eurasianism, and the Real Story

period" when the *Annals* were being published. The release of the first *Vremennik* was bound up with an ideological conflict among the founders, which led to Florovsky leaving the ranks, while the cessation of the publication was a direct result of a dispute between Karsavin and Trubetzkoy, foreshadowing the "Clamart split."

In this preface to the third volume of the *Foundations of Eurasianism* series, we cannot ignore the latent disagreements and disputes reflected in the Eurasianists' correspondences and thereby risk depriving the reader of the background necessary for an accurate understanding of the *Eurasian Annals*' content as well as context.

After the release of the first collection, its participants, Eurasianism's founding fathers, dispersed to different cities in Europe (since it became clear that the Bolshevik regime in Russia was strong and was not going to collapse, while leftists hostile to Russian refugees were growing stronger in Bulgaria). Florovsky and Savitsky moved to Prague in December 1921, which was hospitable to Russians due to the policies of President Tomáš Masaryk.[25] Trubetzkoy found shelter in Vienna, where he received a professorship at the Department of Slavic Philology at the University of Vienna. For some time, Suvchinsky was kept in Sofia by his publishing affairs, but he too would move to Berlin in 1922, and then to Paris in 1925. However, the Eurasianists continued to maintain an active correspondence in which they discussed their ideology as well as issues related to the dissemination of existing collections and preparations for new ones. A look at their letters shows that in 1923, after the publication of the collection *Russia and Latindom*, a crack had formed between the former friends. The relationship between Savitsky and Florovsky deteriorated so much that the two leaders, despite having formed a familial connection (they married two sisters: Savitsky to Vera Ivanovna Simonova, and Florovsky to Ksenya

---

25 "Russian Help Action" was a program to help refugees from Russia announced by the Czechoslovak government in 1921 by Tomáš Masaryk (1850-1937), the first president of the Czechoslovak Republic (1918-1935).

Ivanovna Simonova), stopped communicating altogether. On 17 October 1923, Florovsky wrote to Trubetzkoy from the Savoy Hotel in Prague: "I will not deny 'personal motives' and 'personal ruptures'... I stopped trusting Savitsky, and on his part there followed a series of more than unrestrained, petty, stupidly proud attacks that made personal communication impossible and undesirable for us."[26] But Florovsky insisted that the problem was not only a result of "personal differences," but also "substantive differences." This is reflected in another quote from the same letter: "you cannot preach religious culture, you can only preach faith... otherwise you end up with demagoguery. Instead of the Orthodox faith, we get faith in Orthodoxy, replaced by damaging formulas: 'the Orthodox kingdom', 'Holy Rus', etc. And when this is combined with the sly optimism that Gardens of Eden will bloom in Eurasia and the Orthodox Tsar of all Eurasia from Cape Dezhnev to the Cape of Good Hope will exercise his despotic power, I become religiously afraid. Are we not like Shatov, who frantically believes in Russia, but still has yet to believe in God...?"[27] And further: "whether there will be a Great Russia or not, one must be Orthodox, one must revive church tradition for oneself, one must become a church member, without thinking about whether this will help drive out the Bolsheviks and take the stick to the Romano-Germanics."[28] Let us recall that Shatov, the hero of Dostoevsky's novel *Demons*, is a Russian nationalist for whom Orthodoxy is just a part of the ethnic culture of Russians, and not the highest Truth given from God and preserved in all its purity as the adherents of this confession themselves see Orthodoxy. Shatov declares himself Orthodox because he is Russian, yet he does not even believe in God. By the way, Florovsky, at the time of writing this letter, did not know that Shatov's prototype was Nikolai Danilevsky, the Russian nationalist philosopher and creator of the theory

---

26 *Transactions of the Association of Russian-American Scholars in the U.S.A.* vol. XXXVII, 123.

27 Ibid., 124.

28 Ibid., 124-125.

of cultural-historical types whom Savitsky himself would later call one of the predecessors of Eurasianism.

Florovsky reproached his fellow Eurasianists for shifting their interests to the field of culture, given that they had begun as religious philosophers and were perceived by the public as such. Metropolitan Antony (Khrapovitsky), having familiarized himself with the first collections of Eurasianists, even named the theorists of this trend "the new Aksakov and Kireevsky"!

Indeed, if we recall Florovsky's articles in *Exodus to the East* and *Pathways*, he had already expressed similar ideas. "It is not for 'Great Russia' that our heart should burn, but, first of all and above all, for the cleansing of the darkened Russian soul," he wrote in the article "Breaks and Ties."[29] Florovsky agreed with the other Eurasianists that the revolution, being a consequence of the unsuccessful Europeanization of Russia, destroyed the European-Russian culture created by Peter the Great and opened up a chance for the revival of Russian culture.[30] But Florovsky understood this revival not as the creation of a new Russian-Eurasian culture, and certainly not as the creation of an anti-European superpower, but as a revival of religious faith.

As a result, Florovsky called on his Eurasianist friends to abandon the idea of publishing the *Eurasian Annals*, which he called "demagogic", and proposed publishing a religious magazine called *Foundations* or *Eternal Foundations*, which, of course, was met with an unequivocal refusal. Trubetzkoy's answer in a letter to Florovsky dated 26 November 1923 is telling: without denying the importance of Orthodoxy or even belonging to and attending the church, he shifts the focus to the struggle between European and Eurasian cultures and sees the main task of the Eurasianists as connected

---

29 Georges Florovsky, "Breaks and Ties" in *Foundations of Eurasianism - Volume I*, 137-142.

30 According to the Eurasianists, the culture of the Saint Petersburg period was artificial and eclectic.

to cultural creativity. Trubetzkoy writes: "... the Orthodox worldview and Orthodox life in the conditions of European culture... are impossible... Therefore I am fighting against European culture... I am trying to create other concepts, a different psychological basis for culture..."[31] Trubetzkoy's idea is simple: the bourgeois European culture of his time is incompatible with Orthodoxy, and therefore its creation - the Westernized Russian culture that dominated in "Romanov, Petersburg Russia" - was incompatible with Orthodoxy, which constituted and continues to constitute the transcendental core of the culture of the Russian people. According to Trubetzkoy, the positive significance of the revolution lies in the destruction of this foreign culture. The nationally-oriented Russian intelligentsia was now faced with the task of creating a modern version of non-European Russian-Eurasian culture (developing the culture of pre-Petrine Rus' at a new stage). Hence the declaration of the cultural centricity of Eurasianism. Trubetzkoy states: "we continue to place the center of gravity not in politics or in the state system, but in culture and the ideological basis of culture."[32] Trubetzkoy even adds that "the state system only exists upon the support of culture,"[33] meaning that politics are a secondary concern and derived from culture. He rejects the accusation of "vulgar imperialism"[34], a clear response to Florovsky's accusation that the Eurasianists, like the National Bolsheviks, privileged "Great Russia" above all else, including religion.[35]

---

31 *Transactions of the Association of Russian-American Scholars in the U.S.A.* vol. XXXVII,129.

32 Ibid., 130.

33 Ibid.

34 Ibid., 131.

35 The National Bolsheviks were a group of non-communist Russian patriots (Yu.V. Klyuchnikov, N.V. Ustryalov, etc.), who in the early 1920s called for cooperation with the Soviet government, since, in their opinion, although it retained Marxist phraseology, had objectively revived and begun to fulfill the goals of Russian imperial nationalism. Their manifesto was a collection of articles, *Smena Vekha* ("Change of Milestones") (Prague, 1920), hence they are often referred to as the *smenavekhovtsy*.

The "Official" History of Classical Eurasianism, and the Real Story

If the stage of initial Eurasianism (1921-1923) can be characterized as religious and philosophical,[36] then the stage of the heyday of Eurasianism, which included the publication of the *Annals* (1923-1925), was the cultural and scientific stage characterized by the development of an interdisciplinary scientific project (Martin Beisswenger suggests calling these stages the "utopian, religious" and "scientific" respectively).[37]

As already mentioned, in the period from 1923 to 1927, new concepts were added to the Eurasianist core, strengthening the ideology into a broad and cohesive worldview.[38] In a 1926 letter to Suvchinsky, Trubetzkoy even stated that the construction of the Eurasianist worldview was completed and that only "applied tasks" remained: "... a certain period of our work has been completed... The completed period of our work was characterized by the development of the most general theoretical provisions... Quite clear, concise and definite formulas were crafted. They were crafted so comprehensively that, on the one hand, they can be condensed into a short cheat sheet, and on the other, into a foundation for serious, specialized scientific work."[39] Now, according to Trubetzkoy, all that remained was to develop Eurasianism as a scientific concept and disseminate the ideology created on its basis in the USSR. The Eurasianists believed that the "revolutionary ruling stratum" that dominated the USSR at that time would soon fall out of power and be replaced by young people who would abandon Marxism and the ideas of world revolution and focus

---

36 Trubetzkoy writes that even during the "Sofia period" Eurasianism was culture-centric, but it is enough to look at the content of the first Eurasian collections to see how large a share religious themes had there.

37 Martin Beisswenger, "*Nesluchainyi evraziiets: G.V. Florovsky v evraziiskom dvizhenii*" in A.V. Cherniaev (ed.), *Georges Vasil'evich Florovsky* (Moscow: Rossiisskaia politicheskaia entsiklopediia, 2014), 68. Savitsky also wrote that the meaning of the Russian Revolution was primarily religious in nature. See P.N. Savitsky, "*Idei i puti evraziiskoi literatury*" in *Russkii uzel evraziistva*, 371.

38 Of course, this was also not without controversy, but a full review of this issue goes beyond the scope of this article.

39 Trubetzkoy, *Pis'ma k P.P. Suvchinskomu*, 196.

The "Official" History of Classical Eurasianism, and the Real Story

instead on statecraft. For this, they would need the ideology of Eurasianism. It should be noted that the Eurasianists turned out to be right, as many among the original Bolshevik core were killed and replaced by Stalinists.[40] Although Stalin did not abandon Marxism, he began to do approximately what the Eurasianists called for, albeit masked by Marxist vocabulary: he began to build a strong, authoritarian, ideocratic state.

But it was precisely in 1926, when it seemed to Trubetzkoy that Eurasianism was more or less complete, that a dispute broke out which ultimately led to a split. It began with seemingly the most notional and abstract questions - questions of the philosophy of personality.

At the end of 1926, Karsavin – by that time the "official philosopher of the Eurasianist movement" (he had already written his manifesto "Eurasianism: The Experience of Systematic Exposition", which was published anonymously as a document of the entire group)[41] – prepared a text devoted to the metaphysical aspects of the relationship between the Church and the state (in the correspondences of the Eurasianists it appears under the title "Karsavin's Note on the Church" or simply "the Note"). Initially, it was to be published in the journal *Bulletin of Orthodoxy*, then in book five of the *Eurasian Annals*, but in the end it was published in the form of a brochure entitled *Church, Personality, and State* and signed by its author. This is significant, as it indicated that the position expressed was his own, and not the general position of the Eurasianists as his previous manifesto had been.

---

40 Many of Lenin's comrades in the Communist Party, Trotsky, Bukharin, Rykov, etc., were killed during Stalin's "Great Terror".

41 This text was published in 1997 in P.N. Savitsky, *Kontinent Evraziia* (Moscow: Agraf, 1997), which erroneously attributed its authorship to Savitsky. A.K. Klementyev writes of Karsavin's authorship: "It was L.P. Karsavin who, on the orders of the Eurasianist organization, compiled what was the first and would remain the most accessible presentation of the new doctrine: 'Eurasianism: The Experience of Systematic Exposition.'" A.K. Klementyev, "*Materialy k istorii deiatel'nosti L.P. Karsavina v evraziiskoi organizatsii (1924-1929)*", *Vestnik Ekaterinburgskoi dukhovnoi seminarii* 36 (2021), 400.

This decision came about as a result of Trubetzkoy's disagreement with some of the content of Karsavin's text. In his review, "N.S. Trubetzkoy's Considerations regarding L.P. Karsavin's 'On the Church, Personality and State'", Trubetzkoy sharply objects to Karsavin's understanding of the state as a personality.[42] An explanation is needed here. The Eurasianists belonged to the line of Russian religious philosophy which teaches that individuals are not only individuals, they are also parts of their associations or social groups, such as family, clan, class, people, and finally of humanity as a whole as well as, of course, the Church. This line goes back to the Russian Slavophiles,[43] and first of all Kireevsky and his idea of *sobornost'*. In Russian, the word "*sobor*" is related to the words "gathering", "assembly" (*sbor, sobranie*). It has two main meanings: (1) a large church as an architectural structure and (2) a meeting of representatives of one local Orthodox church or all churches.[44] It is the latter meaning that is used when talking about the Ecumenical Councils at which, from the 4th to the 8th centuries, the most important dogmas of the Church were adopted. In Orthodox theology, these dogmas are recognized as the product of the Church, the "conciliar intellect" (*Sobornyi Razum*), which is guided by the Holy Spirit – the third hypostasis of the Divine Trinity. The recognition of this intellect, that is, the consciousness and self-awareness of the Church, allows us to

---

42 Karsavin wrote in his notes: "the state is a necessary form of personal existence for every conciliar [*sobornyi*] subject, since it unifies itself in the empirical and sinful sphere and opposes the Church in its own truly and completely personal existence. The last, but not empirical and empirically inaccessible, goal of the state is to transform it into a church personality." L.P. Karsavin," *O Tserkvi, lichnosti i gosudarstve*" [https://litresp.ru/chitat/ru/K/karsavin-lev-platonovich/sochineniya/12].

43 The Slavophiles were a group of Russian philosophers and publicists from the first half of the 19th century who opposed the Western path of development which the country had embarked on starting with the reforms of Tsar Peter the Great. The Slavophiles believed that Russia should preserve its originality, which they saw in the Orthodox monarchy and peasant commune.

44 There are also other meanings: "the council of saints" (*sobor svyatikh*) and "the council of ethereal forces," (*sobor besplotnikh sil*) that is, the angels.

understand it as a collective personality. This line developed in the bosom of the "philosophy of all-unity" created by Solovyov. Karsavin eventually became one of the idea's most prominent representatives. Even before joining the Eurasianists, he had developed a detailed and well thought-out doctrine of "symphonic personalities". However, Trubetzkoy, while not a professional philosopher, had a predilection for metaphysics and an excellent philosophical education (his father, Sergei Nikolaevich, and his uncle, Evgeny Nikolaevich, were famous philosophers of the "Solovyovian school"). He had his own doctrine of collective personalities which he referred to not as symphonic, but choral.[45] Trubetzkoy considered peoples and multinational formations, such as Russia-Eurasia, to be choral personalities. At the same time, he denied the existence of a collective personality of humanity. He also denied the personality of the state, contrary to Karsavin. Trubetzkoy writes the following about the state: "The state is not a person and is not a Creation of God, but an earthly boon created by human hands."[46] Trubetzkoy refers here to the Holy Scripture, wherein God cares about the salvation of peoples, punishes them, admonishes them, that is, treats them as personalities who need salvation; it is ultimately unimportant whether they have their own state (kingdom) or not (for instance, the Jews were deprived of their state during the Babylonian captivity). Trubetzkoy calls the state "a category of geographical volition" and sees its goal as "the organization of earthly, material life on a certain piece of land."[47] Personalities have an immortal soul, which means they need salvation after death. This, according to Trubetzkoy, also applies to peoples, while states are deprived of immortality: they are social instruments which are created for certain purposes, break down and fall apart. One and the

---

45 For more about the meaning of the Russian word *khor*, "choir", in this context, see Ermishina's preface to the previous volume.

46 B.E. Stepanov, "*Spor evraziitsev o cerkvi, lichnosti i gosudarstve*", Issledovaniia po istorii russkoi mysli. Ezhegodnik za 2001–2002 g. (Moscow, 2002), 132.

47 Ibid., 133.

same people can have several different states over the course of its historical life.

This is not as abstract a discussion as it might seem at first glance. Recognizing the state to be a person raises its ontological status to the status of a people and multinational entities. For Eurasianism, this meant disregarding the secondary nature of politics and the primacy of culture, which is precisely what Trubetzkoy had insisted on in his polemic with Florovsky in 1923, using this argument to counter accusations of "vulgar imperialism." It does not seem an accident that it was the Paris group of Eurasianists, whose ideological leader was Karsavin, that took extremely pro-Soviet positions. The point is not the penetration of Soviet agents into the Parisian circle (pro-Soviet agents also had influence on the Prague group). If we recognize the state as a collective personality with a unique, immortal soul, then it will no longer be possible to perceive the fate of Soviet statehood with such indifference: we must side with the USSR completely, which is what the Parisian group eventually did.

Of course, this does not exhaust the internal disputes of the Eurasianists in the 1920s. The real evolution of the ideas of the Eurasianists, a course which is radically different from the ostensible unanimity of their textual collections, is just beginning to be studied and awaits its further researchers.

The Eurasianists and Americans

As already mentioned, in 1924, the Eurasianists planned to publish a collection of translations in English for American readers. The project was supposed to be financed by the American artist Henry Clews Jr. (1876-1957), the son of millionaire investment banker Henry Clews Sr.[48] Savitsky even wrote an article simply titled "Eurasianism" for the collection, wherein he attempted to comprehensively explain

---

48 Glebov, *Evraziistvo mezhdu imperiei i modernom*, 126.

the Eurasianist worldview. Since the plan for the American collection was never realized, Savitsky's article was later published in book four of *The Eurasian Annals*.

However, exactly 100 years later, the dream of the Eurasianists has finally come true. PRAV Publishing is already on their third volume of the selected works of the Eurasianists in English. Now, general American readers have the opportunity to familiarize themselves with these important works, which until now were only available to specialists. The question then arises: who are these American readers and what can they learn from the teachings of the Russian Eurasianists?

The most obvious answer is that these texts will be useful for those who are interested in Russia, its intellectual history, culture, philosophy, and science. Eurasianism was a critical phenomenon in Russian culture during the first half of the 20th century. Moreover, Eurasianism was a further development of Slavophile, neo-Slavophile, and Pochvenik (Native-Soilest) thought (Kireevsky, Danilevsky, Lamansky, Dostoevsky), as well as the tradition of Russian scholarship at large (Lomonosov, Mendeleev, Shchapov, Klyuchevsky, Dokuchaev). Without knowledge of Eurasianism, a complete picture of the Russian Revolution and its influence on Russian culture is impossible. The Eurasianists, especially the "leftists," along with Nikolai Ustryalov and the "Smenovekhovites", were important participants in Stalin's "Soviet Thermidor".

However, even those who are not interested in distant historical events, but rather immediate Russian history and Russia today, must know about Eurasianism. The Eurasianists of the 1920s influenced Lev Nikolaevich Gumilev (1912-1992), a well-known Russian ethnologist whose views have significant influence among Russian patriots today. Various Eurasianist ideas can be found in the programs of Russian parties and movements – from the revolutionary conservative Eurasia movement of the neo-Eurasianist Alexander Dugin to the left-wing "Russian communism" of Gennady Zyuganov.

The "Official" History of Classical Eurasianism, and the Real Story

But there is another important aspect here for English-language readers. The word "Russia" in European languages (German *Russland*, English "Russia", Spanish Rusia) means "the country of the Russians". However, in addition to ethnic Russians, about 200 peoples and ethnic groups live in the country. Many of them are peoples of Turkic and Finno-Ugric origin who lived in the territories of their current residence even before Russians arrived. In this sense, paradoxically, Russia is similar to the United States. Just as white migrants from Europe, having arrived in the New World, found tribes of Native Americans there (who, by the way, are also descendants of Asians, meaning that America, as it turns out, was once also a "little Eurasia"!),[49] East Slavic settlers from Kievan Rus' found Finnic and Turkic tribes when they arrived in Northeast Eurasia in the 11th century. Even the names of the rivers and settlements in northern and central Russia are often of Finnic origin, although Russians have lived there for about a millennium: Oka, Sura, Vyazma, Ukhta (just as places in the US often have names of Native American origin: Manhattan, Idaho, Michigan, Mississippi). The scientific study of non-Russian peoples and their cultures began in the Russian Empire only in the 18th century, and became systematic only at the beginning of the 20th century. The Eurasianists not only intensified this process, they were the first to challenge the colonialist discourse which saw the Russians as civilized Europeans and the Tatars, Bashkirs, Mari, and Kalmyks as "backward barbarians". The Eurasianists proclaimed the equality of all peoples of the "Russian space". The Eurasianist Savitsky inaugurated a revolution in Russian nomad studies, substantiating the thesis that nomadic cultures are not at all backward compared to sedentary ones. The Eurasianists drew attention to the cultures of the nomadic, steppe peoples of Eurasia, to the problem of the "Mongol yoke"

---

49 Despite the obvious element of irony here, as the Russians say: "every joke has a grain of truth."

and its consequences, and to the phenomenon of "Turanian psychology". Researchers of the non-Russian peoples of Russia cannot ignore the achievements of the Eurasianists.

However, the significance of Eurasianism goes beyond the scope of Russian studies. For instance, Patrick Sériot has shown that the Eurasianist ideas of Trubetzkoy, Jakobson, and Savitsky influenced the formation of structuralism in Eastern Europe. One can also note the influence of the Eurasianists on academic science in the US. In the 1920s, the Russian emigre historian George Vernadsky (1887-1973) lived in Prague and corresponded with Savitsky and members of the Prague group of Eurasianists, publishing several articles in the *Eurasian Annals*. His seminal work, *The Eurasian Outline of Russian History*, was published by the Eurasianist Publishing House. In 1927, Vernadsky received an invitation from Yale University, after which he and his family left Europe forever and lived in New Haven until his death in 1973. Even a researcher as biased against Eurasianism as Charles Halperin, Vernadsky's first biographer, admitted that Vernadsky remained faithful to many of the Eurasianist ideas of his youth until the end of his life (and for many years he maintained friendly, scientific correspondence with Savitsky). At the same time, in 1969, at a celebration in honor of Vernadsky's life and work, then Yale President Kingman Brewster told him: "You have inspired students to follow you as the leading expert of our time on Russian history."[50] It should be noted that this inspiration contained Eurasianist overtones. Vernadsky's textbook, *A History of Russia*, which has gone through many reprints and has been used by several generations of American history students, was based on Eurasianist methodology and traced the unique features of Russian history back to the specifics of Eurasian topogenesis.

---

50 See Charles J. Halperin, "George Vernadsky, Eurasianism, the Mongols, and Russia", *Slavic Review* 41:3 (1982), 477-493; idem, *Rus' i Step': Georges Vernadsky i evraziistvo*, ed. Iu.V. Seleznev (Voronezh: izdatel'sko-poligraficheskii tsentr 'Novaia Kniga', 2018), 97.

The "Official" History of Classical Eurasianism, and the Real Story

This concludes my story about the classical period of Eurasianism. I can only congratulate American readers who now have the genuine intellectual pleasure of getting acquainted with the paradoxical yet extremely interesting hypotheses and ideas of the Eurasianists. I must also express my gratitude to everyone (especially Jafe Arnold and John Stachelski) who helped prepare this book.

***

AT THE DOORSTEP: REACTION? REVOLUTION?

Nikolai Trubetzkoy[51]

***

In both political and cultural life, "left" and "right" are relative concepts. Everything depends on one's point of departure. The leftist ideal always propels itself from the current ideological status quo, which in relation to the given leftist ideology is the ideology of the right. This original ideological status quo may continue to live even after the leftist ideal has seized its victory and incarnated into a form of sociopolitical routine; the relationship between left and right does not change because of this. In transitioning from the role of conservation to that of opposing the existing order, the right remains nonetheless reactionary. Strictly speaking, the right is always bolstered by the immediate past, and is only supported by the contemporary moment insofar as this moment is an immediate continuation of the past. The right is inimical to innovation, not only when it is called up in the imaginations of "leftists," but also when it has already been realized within the forms of real life. Those ideals which were once held by leftists and which have been manifested in life remain leftist only as long and insofar as they are perceived as something new: as long as the feeling of innovation exists, the defense of these ideals is a matter of the left; and the struggle against them, as against innovation, is a matter of the right. But there may come a moment when the feeling of a given ideal's newness

---

51 Originally published in *The Eurasian Annals*, book 3 (Berlin, 1923).

becomes so faded and dissipated that its defenders from the left become conservatives and its opponents begin to attack it not for its novelty, but for its obsolescent archaism, calling for it to be replaced by another ideal that is more appropriate to the contemporary age. Since this new ideal will not constitute a return to the *immediately* preceding status quo, its defenders will be leftists and the previous leftists will become people of the right – conservatives.

To this day, the accumulation of new ideals in European life, in displacing the old ideals into the realm of an obsolete status quo, have progressed in a generally straight line. The terms "right" and "left" were for this reason successfully applied every step of the way. Each new ideal was indeed "farther left" than its immediate precedent, as it had progressed beyond the previous ideal in the same direction, diverging even more dramatically from the original status quo. The trajectory of politics may be mapped as follows: "democracy – socialism – communism," "constitutional monarchy – democratic republic – Soviet Federative Socialist Republic"; these are all idealistic trios arranged on a straight line from right to left. But one can imagine the result once this movement has been driven to its final extremity, to the dead end from which there will be "nowhere left to go." In this instance, the new ideal, propelling itself off of the immediately preceding ideological status quo, will not turn out to be farther left (for "there is nothing farther left than this"), but rather will find itself somewhere outside of the straight line on which leftist and rightist ideals had previously been located. This idea can be applied not only to socio-political doctrines, but also to those which determine national relationships, religious convictions, etc.

In analyzing the contemporary political, social, and cultural life of Europe on the one hand and Russia on the other, one arrives at the unavoidable conclusion that the "leftist" ideologies which have determined those lives until now have not only lost their freshness, but have utterly dissipated and corroded; they have been covered over by some kind of inertia and protective obscurantism. We observe this not only in countries which have long ago realized "leftist" political ideals and have always been considered "leaders," but also in the young republics which have only recently progressed to the "front of the pack." Laws concerning "the defense of the republic" and constant fears of "counter-revolution" are phenomena characteristic of modernity, evidence of the extent to which once leftist ideologies have lost the youthful freshness that endowed them with strength. In modern leftism, one finds a kind of inertia, a fear of novelty – traits of conservative and reactionary ideologies. Leftism has begun to reek of conventionality and, most significantly, old age. The person who sincerely believes in leftist ideologies is usually either already aged or he belongs spiritually to the previous generation. In the mouth of authentically modern man, leftist speeches come off as a state-mandated lie of "supreme affirmation," in which even the speaker himself does not believe.

The dilapidation of previously leftist ideas ought to have led to the emergence of new ones even further to the left. However, those far-left ideas arrived at in the minds of men which have been partially realized (in Russia, for example), show themselves precisely to be the limit of leftism, beyond which there is nowhere further to go in that direction; one senses in these extremities an arrival at absurdity, an approach toward the point at which positive infinity becomes negative infinity. It is unsurprising, therefore, that modern man, in seeking an exit from his dead-end, turns his gaze more to the right than to the left. We live in a strange time when "children" are either already bereft of principles or have gone farther right than their "fathers."

Nonetheless, a simple turn toward the right can in no way extricate us from the contemporary situation. This is to say nothing of the fact that history knows no backward movement as such; one must not lose sight of the fact that the previous ideological status quo from which leftists once propelled themselves is now made up of obscurantist ideologies which have utterly outlived themselves and have lost all viability. If people have now lost faith in those "leftist" ideals which formerly seemed so attractive – if the theoretical basis for these ideals now gives off a rotten scent of conventionality, busted phraseology, and philistinism – then the same is even truer for those "rightist" ideologies toward which the modern faithless, disillusioned with the left, turn their gaze. The simple fact that, in their time – a time not so long ago, when the cultural environment was not so different from our own – rightist ideologies were unable to satisfy the progressively minded and keep them from moving leftward, tells us all we need to know about the inviability of these rightist ideologies. It would be an absurdity to ascribe this to the blindness of "advanced society," which either could not or would not recognize the value of the right's salvific essence: if these rightist ideologies had indeed been strong and viable, their fundamental rejection by every layer of society would have been unthinkable. The recent past can only be idealized by people with a short memory and, since the average human memory is not that short, the deceit of such an idealization becomes rapidly apparent. The fact remains: when it was the rightist ideologies that governed life, many enjoyed better lives than they do now. But the majority was unsatisfied, not only with life, but (which is far more important to our current case) with these very ideologies; and, in searching for new, more satisfying ideologies, the majority went leftward. Now, people have equally lost faith in these leftist ideologies and many are living in even worse conditions than before. It follows from this that the path taken by the majority was poorly chosen. But this in no way implies that they should return willingly to the unsatisfying situation which compelled them to seek a change of ideologies and forms of life to begin with. One can countenance such a deliberate return to the unfavorable "rightist" status quo only as an attempt at "maneuvering," or of returning to the starting point (having discovered the errors of the "leftist" path) in order to find a different direction. But, in this instance, the

At the Doorstep: Reaction? Revolution?

rightist ideology turns out not to be an "ideal" in the authentic sense – moreover, in order to lead people out of the ditch into which they have fallen, the blatant acknowledgement that they have fallen into the ditch is of no use; it is precisely an ideal which is called for.

The primal move "to the right" – the instinctive striving of modern man to return to "the good old days" – is but a sign of desperation. In this cast of mind, a combination of keen malcontent with the contemporary situation and, in contrast, exaggeratedly idealized reminiscences of the recent past plays the most obvious role; here, there can be no question of authentic, considered, and deliberate ideology. The ideological poverty of the contemporary right is striking to any disinterested observer. Moreover, the theoretical concepts which lie at the basis of certain phenomena of this rightist movement are in full contradiction with the very spirit of any ideology that can be truly considered of the right. The "rightists" have rubbed against leftist ideologies and the leftist worldview for so long that it is as though they themselves have been infected by the mindset which subtends all leftist ideologies. One must bear this in mind at every step of analysis. The monarchist Russian emigrants are filled with the same faith in the magical salvation of juridical formulae that has always distinguished the leftist ideologues: the only difference is that leftists believed in the immediate enshrinement of universal happiness with the help of a democratic republic, universal suffrage, etc., while rightists expect the same immediate and automatic enshrinement of universal benefit from the restoration of the monarchy. Because the monarchy is understood as a rightist ideology precisely because of its complex of juridical norms, in themselves possessed of a magical salvific power independent of time, place, or living person, it is natural that monarchism should turn into legitimism. It is here that the ideological incoherency of this approach grows apparent. The view which holds the head of state to be the sum of juridical rights to succession changes the monarch from a living personality, in

At the Doorstep: Reaction? Revolution?

whom the will of the nation is concentrated, into some kind of algebraic sign. Such a view would be natural in the mind of a republican, or that of a staunch parliamentarian and defender of the people's rights, for whom the head of state is no more than a signature machine that only incidentally bears a human image; but it is difficult to combine such a mechanization of monarchy with the true monarchic spirit. The mechanical legalism that has penetrated the thinking of those who lead the contemporary rightist movement says more than can be imagined about the ideological helplessness and impotence of reaction, being purely a movement *backwards*: there is nothing in the ideological baggage of this movement's leaders besides an overwrought and idealized memory of the "benevolent days of yore," which they experienced only a little while ago. It naturally follows that the leaders are primarily those for whom it is particularly easy to idealize the immediate past – those who had previously enjoyed an especially high quality of life and have now lost an especially great deal; and in such conditions as these, it is equally natural that those who are insufficiently inclined towards idealizing the recent past (either due to the sharpness of their memory or because they did not particularly enjoy good conditions in the past) should take up against the rightist movement, perceiving it a movement of pure avarice.

And yet, despite the ideological emptiness and fruitlessness of those molds from which the rightist movement has been cast at the hands of its leaders, there is something healthy and authentic in the very fact that the younger generations are moving rightward without meditating on the theoretical foundation of their predilections. This intuitive rightward turn secretly contains the unconscious presentiment of a truly new ideology which alone can lead us out of the left's dead-end. Those by no means novel reactionary ideologies and formulae which are de facto evoked in this development are merely a surrogate for an unexpressed and unrecognized ideology which is authentically new and making its arrival. This is happening out of inertia and amidst a general inability to distract oneself from the habitual surface of political thought, in which rightism and reaction are set in opposition to leftism and "progressivism." Instinct suggests that an unconsciously sought ideology lies somewhere quite distant from the extreme left end of the chain of possible socio-political and socio-ethical ideologies; and because only this chain of ideologies exists in a ready-made form, one involuntarily casts his gaze rightward, even toward the extreme right end of the chain. But this is an error caused solely by the familiarity of that chain or straight line along which all expressible ideologies and formulae calling for a normativity of sociopolitical life, culture, and the everyday have been situated from right to left. In reality, the intuitive movement on the part of the youth toward the right is a fruit of the unconscious drive toward the new as opposed to the old, and those belonging to the old guard who live only through reminiscences of the recent past are organically incapable of either understanding or governing this movement. The new ideology – the one to which the future belongs – does not lie on the usual straight line. Perhaps if one were to project this ideology onto the usual straight line, the point of projection would end up somewhere in its right-leaning regions – this would explain the optical illusion experienced by those who have grown accustomed to looking at things only in terms of this line. But the essence of the new ideology – that which makes it authentically new, viable, and mobile – consists not in the fact that it is projected to the right of the extreme left point of the outmoded ideological chain; rather, it consists in the fact that this ideology itself lies *on a different plane*. It is precisely for this reason that the new ideology is not reactionary; it does not herald an about-face toward the recent past, but calls its adherents toward dramatic revolution, to leap onto a different, utterly new plane. The sentiment that the recent past can never be returned has gained currency. People of every political stripe – left and right – are repeating this. But in the mouths of these people, having grown accustomed to thinking only within the limits of the outmoded ideological chain, such a sentiment acquires some painfully banal content: they imagine their desired future as some sort of compromise between the various old ideologies, as a new combination of elements, assembled out of the previous obsolete "programs" and trends. It goes without saying that this combination remains within the boundaries of the very same outmoded ideological line. But the conviction that a return to the recent past is unthinkable gains an entirely different significance for those who reject this ideological line as a whole: only on this condition can the future be painted as an authentically new way of life. One can only hope to find an exit from the dead-end of modernity by taking this route. Everything old has outlived itself, has been picked over and hopelessly compromised. What we need is something authentically new, not a new combination of old elements; we must introduce substantively new elements.

Nothing in history is ever absolutely new. Historical development is unthinkable without historical memory; it is precisely from this memory that one culls inspirations and models for any new creation. But to exit the old paradigm of "rightist" and "leftist" ideologies that has been followed to its conclusion is in no way to reject this historical memory. On the contrary, it is none other than those who continue to stomp around in the old ideological categories who deserve censure for their dearth of memory; their memories go no further back than the beginning of this ideological line – in Russia, this was the 18th century. In any radical innovation or revolutionary ideology,[52] one always finds a conjunction with extensive historical memory. What is essentially important is that this memory is a highly antiquated one, that it relates to times that have long ago elapsed, as opposed to the recent past to which actually conservative ("reactionary") ideologies –

---

52 [Trans.]: Here, Trubetzkoy employs the adjective "*perevorotnyi*," which refers, in a literal etymological sense, to an "overturning," and which is often a synonym for "revolutionary." But Trubetzkoy prefers this linguistically Russian phrasing over the foreign adjective "*revoliutsionnyi*." In the original text, he adds parenthetically that the "*perevorot*" or "overturning" is the authentic meaning of "revolution."

At the Doorstep: Reaction? Revolution?

i.e., those which pull backwards – appeal. The French Revolution – that classic model of overturning – was utterly saturated with the living memory of the Roman Republic. Innovation does not consist in a rejection of the past, but in propulsion off of the immediate or most recent past, in leaping over that immediate past in ideological conjunction with more remote epochs. These *ancient elements*, drawn from the depths of historical memory, turn out to be new and revolutionary precisely thanks to their transplantation in a new context. We are speaking here not of a simple restoration or reinstatement of the remote past, as this past is too old. The elements of the remote past which have been uprooted from their historical perspective and transplanted into the novel context of modernity begin to live a completely new life and are then able to inspire those who perceive them toward authentically new creativity. It follows that one must distinguish the old from the ancient. In regarding the banal and sentimental icon painting of the previous century, the contemporary artist perceives it as no more than useless scraps, as an *"überwundener Standpunkt"*[53] [2]; but, in gazing upon an ancient Russian icon, he may be ignited with the fire of true inspiration and create something authentically new, in which case this new thing must by no means be a restoration or even a stylization. A modern artist will never be able to paint like an old-Russian master; this is not so much because he is a man of a different culture, but simply because, in looking upon an old-Russian icon, caught up in exultation and inspiration, he simultaneously takes 19th-century painting as his point of departure, which would be an impossibility for the old-Russian master; this would result in an utterly different, substantial perception and experience of old-Russian icon painting. Similar psychological processes can be observed both in other realms of creativity and in the realm of ideologies. A new ideology, propelling itself from the long line of ideologies immediately preceding it, may glean inspiration from the far depths of historical memory and

---

53 [Trans.]: German: "A point of view that has been overcome".

nonetheless remain something essentially new, for the elements of antiquity will find a totally new aspect of expression within it (even if this expression should be historically inaccurate, it would still hold value from the contemporary perspective). "Revolution" (in the sense of an overturning of worldview) is propelled from the immediate past. It cannot be a "restoration," but can be a "renaissance" of deep antiquity – and more often than not, it strives to.

And so, those ideals which are capable of delivering us from the modern dead-end lie beyond the surface along which, until now, "rightist" and "leftist" ideas, have been arrayed. The sensation that these ideals are located somewhere to the right of leftist ideas currently known to us is founded on an optimistic act of self-deceit – on the habit of projecting everything onto a single straight line. The instinctive drive to move backward is the fruit of a misunderstanding: there is no salvation to be had in the recent past. One can only leap over the recent past in order to derive inspiration from the remote past, which in turn will allow for the creation of something authentically new. What is required here is not reaction, but revolution in its real sense, i.e., an overturning of consciousness.

The European ideological road, a straight line from right to left, has been passed through to the end: not only does it all lead to a dead end, but there is not a single point on it at which one might be able to stop. One must discard this line altogether, for good, and seek a new one. We Russians must first of all refuse all European forms of political thought; we must cease our prostrations before the (foreign) idol of "governmental form"; we must stop believing in the possibility of ideal legislation mechanically and automatically guaranteeing general welfare; in so many words, we must abandon our view of human society as a soulless mechanism – a view upon which all modern socio-political ideologies are based. We ought not to seek the coming ideal in a perfected model of legislation, but in the spirit, which creates and bolsters the state through everyday life and a resilient ideology. The task of our time is not to be

At the Doorstep: Reaction? Revolution?

found in juridical speculation, but in the creation of a sturdy spiritual base and its embodiment in everyday life.

The thirst for a new, salvific ideal is fatiguing and strained. To satisfy oneself with a surrogate in the form of reaction's worn-out formulas is both impossible and harmful. One must clearly recognize that this is not what is to be desired. Instead, we must concentrate our hearing; with all our being, we must prick up our ears so as to make out the new word. This word must be – and will be – spoken. Collective presentiments do not deceive and, with God's help, our collective efforts can work miracles.

We stand at the doors. Knock, and they shall be opened unto you.

***

THE TOWER OF BABEL AND THE CONFUSION OF TONGUES

Nikolai Trubetzkoy[54]

***

Aside from Adam and Eve's punishment for the first fall of mankind, Holy Scripture mentions a second punishment for the collective fall of all mankind, namely, the confusion of languages that followed from the punishment for the pandemonium of the tower of Babel.

The confusion of tongues, i.e., the establishment of a plurality of languages and cultures, is depicted in the Holy Scripture precisely as a punishment, as a Curse of God, similar to the curse of laboring "by the sweat of one's brow" once imposed on humanity through Adam. Both curses are expressed in the establishment of a natural law against which mankind is powerless. The physiological nature of man and the entire surrounding world were arranged in such a way that the procurement of food was now bound up with the cost of physical labor. The laws of the evolution of peoples were arranged in such a way that they inevitably entail the emergence and preservation of national differences in the field of language and culture. No matter how many machines man invents to reduce the need for physical labor, he will never manage to abolish such labor altogether. And no matter how much

---

[54] Initially published in *The Eurasian Annals*, book 3 (Berlin, 1923), later republished in Trubetzkoy's *The Legacy of Genghis Khan* (Berlin, 1925).

people strive to oppose the fact of the multiplicity of national differences, these differences will always exist. But more than that, physical labor is so connected with the normal functioning of the human body that its complete absence is harmful to our health, and people who are not obliged to physically work to earn their daily bread are forced to artificially replace practical manual labor with gymnastics, sports, and exercise. In the same way, the dialectical fragmentation of language and culture is so organically connected with the very essence of the social organism that any attempt to destroy national diversity would lead to cultural impoverishment and death. Taken by itself, labor in its purest form is never pleasant. Only the feelings and moods accompanying work, the consciousness of one's strength and dexterity, one's interest in the direct result of work, the sense of competition, the anticipation of rest, etc., are pleasant. The fewer such accompanying feelings and moods, the clearer the true nature of labor as suffering comes to the fore. It is well known that wherever labor is turned into a punishment, they try to deprive it of everything that could brighten it up, and the true nature of workers' labor is hidden from them — penal servitude is labor in its purest form. As a special act of mercy, God grants individuals physical strength or success in work. But even these gifts of God only alleviate the pain of labor if the worker recognizes them as gifts and rejoices in them, while the labor itself remains labor, i.e., suffering.

Thus, labor in itself is always suffering, and the law of the necessity of labor remains an eternal curse, God's punishment for the fall of man. On the other hand, the law of dialectical fragmentation and the inevitable multiplicity of national cultures is not associated with any kind of suffering in itself. This law serves as an obstacle to the implementation of many human intentions and ideals; it often entails wars, national enmity, oppression of some peoples by others, but in itself, in its pure form, it is not associated with suffering. The difference between the law of fragmentation and the multiplicity of national cultures on the one hand and the law of the obligation of physical labor on the other is connected with the fact that, while the latter is simply a punishment imposed on humanity for its first fall, the law of fragmentation, according to the Bible, is not so much a punishment as it is God's response to the Babylonian pandemonium, a divine decree aimed at preventing future attempts at something like the construction of the Tower of Babel.

Questions about the historical background of the biblical story of the Babylonian pandemonium aside, it bears recognizing the deep, inner meaning behind this story. In this narrative, Holy Scripture depicts all of humanity speaking the same language, i.e., as linguistically and culturally completely homogeneous. It turns out that this singular, universal culture, devoid of any individual, national characteristics, is extremely one-sided: with the enormous development of science and technology (as the existence of such a plan indicates!) comes complete spiritual emptiness and moral savagery. As a result of these cultural conditions comes the exorbitant development of complacency and pride, the embodiment of which is the godless and, at the same time, senseless plan to build the Tower of Babel. The Tower of Babel is a miracle of technology; it is not only devoid of religious content, it also has an explicitly anti-religious, blasphemous purpose. In order to prevent the implementation of this plan and to put a limit to the blasphemous self-exaltation of humanity, God imposes the confusion of tongues, i.e., he establishes the law of national fragmentation and the plurality of national languages and cultures for all eternity. In this act of divine Providence lies, on the one hand, the recognition that the godless, self-exalting technology clearly manifest in the plan to build the Tower of Babel is not accidental, but an inevitable and natural consequence of a uniform, nationally undifferentiated universal human culture, and, on the other hand, an indication that only nationally limited cultures can be free from the spirit of empty human pride and lead humanity along pathways pleasing to God.

The Tower of Babel and the Confusion of Tongues

The internal connection between pandemonium and the concept of a homogeneous universal culture is clear. Any given culture is a continuously changing historical product of the collective creativity of the past and the current generations of a given social environment. Each individual cultural value aims to satisfy certain (material or spiritual) needs of the social whole or the individuals within it. Therefore, every culture within a given social whole levels out the individual differences of its members. Cultural values which gain general recognition erase the imprints of the overly individual traits of their creators and the overly individual tone of the needs and tastes of the given socio-cultural organism's individual members. This happens naturally, due to the mutual neutralization of polar, i.e., maximally opposite, individual differences. As a result, the entire culture bears the imprint of a certain average mental type for members of a given social environment. The greater the individual differences among the members of a socio-cultural whole, the more vague, indefinite, and impersonal the average type embodied in the culture becomes. If we imagine a culture whose creator and bearer would be all of mankind, then it follows that its impersonal vagueness would be at a maximum. Such a culture would embody only those psychological elements that are common to all people. The tastes and beliefs of all people are different, and individual fluctuations in this area are extremely strong — but everyone has the same logic and everyone has more or less the same material need for nutrition, means of saving labor, etc. Therefore, it is clear that in a homogeneous, universal human culture, logic, rationalistic science, and material technology will always prevail over religion, ethics, and aesthetics. In such a culture, intensive scientific and technological development will inevitably be associated with spiritual and moral savagery. When logic and material technology are not ennobled by spiritual depth, they leave man spiritually dry and undeveloped, frustrating his path to true self-knowledge and hardening his pride. Thus, a homogeneous, universal culture inevitably becomes godless, theomachic and susceptible to the temptations that lead to pandemonium.

On the other hand, in a nationally distinct culture, everything which fosters intimate spiritual needs and predispositions, aesthetic tastes, moral aspirations — in a word, the entire unique moral and spiritual image of a given people — is given a place of honor. In a culture imbued with a distinct national psyche, the spiritual element is intimately and organically close to its bearers. The embodiment in culture of a certain spiritual image and spiritual experience facilitates the work of personal self-knowledge for the members of a given national organism. Therefore, it is only within the confines of such a culture that morally positive values can arise which spiritually elevate a person.

Understanding the positive aspects of national culture, one should, however, have a negative attitude toward national fragmentation beyond a certain organic limit. It is necessary to emphasize in every possible way that national fragmentation is by no means equivalent to the anarchic dispersion of national-cultural forces, i.e., fragmentation in this case does not entail total disintegration. That this is exactly the case can be felt especially vividly when considering the darker sides of national fragmentation. The law of the diversity of national cultures limits a person: human thinking turns out to be limited not only by the special nature of thinking itself, by an inability to escape from the space, time and "categories," by an inability to completely overcome the blinders of sensory experience, but also by the fact that each person is only able to fully perceive the creations of that culture to which he himself belongs, or the cultures closest to it (which particularly takes it toll when the fragmentation of cultures degenerates into their disintegration). By virtue of the law of the diversity of national cultures, communication between the representatives of different nations is complicated and, upon a certain degree of difference, becomes completely impossible. But along with these negative consequences, the law of the diversity of national cultures (since national-cultural fragmentation does not go beyond a certain organically necessary limit) also has positive, beneficial consequences for humanity, because, as is clear from the above, it creates the possibility for the emergence of morally positive and spiritually uplifting cultural values among different peoples. Recognizing this fact, all peoples must put up with the negative consequences of this law and consciously endure their national limitations without complaint.

While the pursuit of easing physical labor and reducing its necessity is totally natural and not inherently sinful, efforts to destroy the diversity of national cultures and create a single universal culture are almost always sinful. This leads to the establishment of the conditions that immediately preceded the pandemonium of Babel in Holy Scripture, conditions that will inevitably lead to mankind making a new attempt at building such a tower. Every "International" is essentially godless, anti-religious, and full of the spirit of human pride: it is not a matter of coincidence.

This is the main and fundamental sin of modern European civilization. It strives to level and annihilate all individual national differences, to introduce uniform forms of life, social and governmental structures, and identical concepts everywhere. It breaks the unique spiritual foundations of life and culture of each nation, but does not and cannot replace them with other spiritual foundations. Resting only on material-utilitarian or rationalistic foundations, it can only implant external forms of life. As a result, European civilization wreaks unprecedented devastation in the souls of Europeanized peoples. It sterilizes their spiritual creativity and incites indifference and savagery in their morality. At the same time, an exorbitant awakening of greed for earthly goods and sinful pride becomes this civilization's faithful companion as it inevitably heads toward a new Babylonian pandemonium. From the moment that Romano-Germanic culture began to strive to become a universal civilization, material technology, purely rationalistic science, and an egotistically utilitarian worldview gained decisive preponderance over everything else, and their cultural importance is only increasing over time. Nothing else can exist: the Japanese and the German can only agree on logic, technology, and material interest, and as a result, all other elements and driving forces of culture must gradually atrophy. But it is a mistake to think that it is possible to break down barriers and facilitate communication between cultures simply by leveling their differences and destroying their spiritual side. A "brotherhood of nations" purchased at the price of the spiritual effacement of all peoples is a vile fraud. No brotherhood is possible when selfish material interests are placed at the forefront, when technology itself drives international competition and militarism. The very idea of an "international civilization" gives rise to plans for imperialism and world domination. Far from abolishing the challenges of communication between peoples, the abolition or relegation of the spiritual side of culture leads only to moral savagery and the development of selfish egoism, which deepens hostility between various social groups even internally. This is the inevitable consequence of the desire for an international, universal civilization, and these consequences clearly prove that such desires are theomachic and sinful.

The diversity of national cultures and languages is a consequence of the law of fragmentation. The effects of this law are most clearly manifested in the sphere of language. Every language can be broken down into regional languages, regional languages into dialects, dialects into subdialects, and so forth. Moreover, each dialect, in addition to its own idiosyncratic features, has features common to all others of the same region; it has certain features in common with one neighboring dialect, others in common with another, and so on. Between neighboring dialects there are transitional dialects that combine features of both. Language is thus a continuous chain of dialects, gradually and imperceptibly turning into one another. Languages, in turn, are united with each other into families, within which we can distinguish branches, sub-branches, etc. Within each of these units of division, particular languages exist in relation to one another in the same way as the dialects within them, i.e., each language of a given branch, in addition to the features characteristic of it alone and the features characteristic of the branch as a whole, also has features that bring it closer to other specific languages within the branch; very often, there are transitional dialects between related languages. Just as languages within a branch are related to one another, so are the individual branches within a family. There is no fundamental difference between the concepts of branch, language, dialect, and subdialect. When all units of division of a given linguistic whole are so close to each other that their speakers understand each other freely without resorting to the help of a translator, these units are called subdialects, their groups are called dialects, and the linguistic whole itself (i.e., their totality) — language. When representatives of individual dialects cannot freely understand each other, the dialects are renamed into languages, their groups become branches, and the collection of branches becomes a family. As a result, disputes often arise over whether a given unit of division is a language or a dialect, or which of two neighboring related languages belongs to a given group of border transitional subdialects. For the most part, such disputes cannot be resolved by the means of linguistic science alone. This is how the relationships between linguistic units are formed and united genetically, i.e., they go back historically to the dialects of the once common proto-language of a given genetic group (family, branch, sub-branch, etc.). But in addition to this kind of genetic grouping, languages that are geographically adjacent to each other are often grouped irrespective of their origin. It sometimes happens that several languages located in the same geographical and cultural-historical region exhibit features of similarity not as a result of common origin, but rather due to historical proximity and parallel development. For these groups, which are not based on a genetic principle, we propose the name "linguistic unions."[55] Such language unions exist not only between individual languages, but also between language families. Several families, otherwise genetically unrelated to each other but widespread in the same geographical and cultural-historical zone, are united by a number of common features into a union of language families. Thus, the Finno-Ugric-Samoyed (otherwise known as Uralic), Turkic, Mongolian and Manchu families are united by a number of common features into one union of Ural-Altaic language families, despite the fact that modern science denies the genetic relationship between all these families. The division of nouns into grammatical genders and the ability of the root to change, insert, and discard the root vowel in the creation of new forms (e.g., in Russian: *soberu*, "I'll gather", *sobrat'*, "to gather, to equip", *sobirat'*, "to be gathering, to harvest", and *sobor*, "assembly, council, cathedral") unite the Indo-European, Semitic, Hamitic, and North Caucasian families into a union of Mediterranean language families, to which other extinct languages of the Mediterranean basin probably also belonged. Such unions of genetically unrelated linguistic families exist across the globe. Moreover, it often happens that the same family or language belongs to two unions at once or fluctuates between two neighboring unions, thus playing the same role as transitional dialects in a genetic classification.[56] Thus, taking into account both possible groupings of languages, genetic (by families) and non-genetic (by unions), we can say that all languages represent some continuous network of links

---

55 A striking example of a linguistic union in Europe is the Balkan languages — Bulgarian, Romanian, Albanian, and modern Greek: belonging to completely different branches of the Indo-European family, they are nevertheless united with each other by a number of common features and detailed similarities in grammatical structures.

56 Thus, the Indo-European family, belonging to the Mediterranean union, in some ways (for example, in the absence of prefixes) comes close to the Ural-Altaic union and in some particular cases is strikingly similar to the Uralic (Finnish-Ugric-Samoyed) languages. The lonely languages of Eastern Siberia (Yenisei-Ostyak, Gilyak, Yukaghir and the so-called Kamchatka, i.e. Kamchadal, Chukchi and Koryak) are like a transitional link between the Ural-Altai and North American (Eskimo-Aleut) unions, etc.

that mutually transform into each other, like a rainbow. And it is precisely because of the continuity of this rainbow-like linguistic network and the gradual transition from one segment to another that the general system of languages of the globe, in all its motley diversity, still represents a kind of unified whole, even if only in our perception. Thus, in the field of language, the operating of the law of fragmentation leads not to anarchic dispersion, but to a harmonious system in which every part, down to the very smallest, retains its clear but repeatable individuality, and the unity of the whole is achieved not by depersonalization of the parts, but by the continuity of the rainbow-like language network.

The distribution and interrelationship of cultures does not coincide with the grouping of languages. Speakers of languages not only of the same family, but even of the same branch can belong to different types of cultures: an example illustrating this situation is the Hungarian (or Magyar) people: the closest relatives of the Magyar language are the Vogul and Ostyak languages (in northwestern Siberia), while the Hungarian and the Vogul-Ostyak cultures have absolutely nothing in common. And yet, the distribution and interrelationships of cultures are generally based on the same principles as the relationships of languages, the only difference being that what corresponds to families in a culture has much less significance than what corresponds to unions. The cultures of individual peoples neighboring each other always present a number of similar features. As a result, well-known cultural and historical zones are designated among these cultures, for example, in Asia we have the zones of Muslim, Hindustani, Chinese, Pacific, steppe, and Arctic cultures, etc. The boundaries of all these zones intersect each other, so that cultures of a mixed or transitional type are formed. Individual peoples and parts of peoples represent specifications of a cultural type to which they bring their particular characteristics. The result is the same rainbow-like network, unified and harmonious due to its continuity while at the same time infinitely diverse due to its differentiations.

These are the results of the law of fragmentation. Despite the seemingly anarchic diversity, individual national cultures, each retaining their own unique individual identity, represent in their totality a continuous, harmonious unity of the whole. They cannot be synthesized, abstracting from their individual uniqueness, for it is in the coexistence of these clearly individual cultural and historical units that the basis of the unity of the whole lies. Like everything natural and innate that arises from the laws of life and development established by God, this picture is majestic in its incomprehensible and immense complexity and at the same time complex harmony. Any attempt by human hands to destroy it, to replace the natural organic unity of living, lively individual cultures with the mechanical unity of an impersonal universal human culture, which leaves no room for manifestations of individuality and is wretched in its abstraction, is clearly unnatural, theomachic and blasphemous. The fact of the universal significance of Christianity seems to speak against such a sharp and unconditional condemnation of attempts at the cultural unification of humanity and the creation of a homogeneous universal culture as attacks on God. For those who see Christianity as just one of many religions on the globe, a product of certain historical and cultural conditions, this problem, of course, does not arise at all. In this view, Christianity, as a product of a certain culture, is placed on a par with other products of certain cultures and is introduced as an element into the general scheme of the diverse cultural manifestations of humanity. In this case, it cannot be recognized as having any universal human significance.

But for those who in Christ recognize the Son of God who came in the flesh and in Christianity the only true religion, the words of Christ — "Go and make disciples of all nations, baptizing them in the name of the Father and of the Son and of the Holy Spirit" (Matthew 28:19) — seem like a refutation of the position that the cultural unification of humanity is an ungodly matter. However, in actuality there is no contradiction here. After all, in recognizing Christianity as an absolute truth based on divine revelation and taught to people through the direct intervention of God in the historical process, we thereby abandon the view of Christianity as a product and an element of a particular culture. Preaching Christianity is not the introduction of some new cultural element into culture.

In contrast to Judaism, which is associated with a particular race, and Islam, which is associated with a particular culture, as well as Buddhism, which is in principle hostile to any cultural division, Christianity is above races and cultures, but it does not abolish their diversity or originality. The adoption of Christianity entails the rejection and transformation of a number of elements of national pagan culture, but the specific forms of this transformation can be very different depending on the cultural and historical soil on which Christianity falls, and uniformity in this area is not only not necessary, but also impossible. Christianity is a "leaven" that can be put into a variety of types of dough, and the result of the "fermentation" will be completely different depending on the composition of the dough. Therefore, the above-discussed rainbow-like network of the globe's uniquely individual national cultures should retain its structure even if all the peoples of the world were to adopt Christianity.

Christianity does not require any leveling of national and cultural differences, nor the creation of a homogeneous universal culture. Christianity as a divine institution is unchanging. In the historical process, Christian dogmas do not change, but are only revealed. Culture is, essentially, the work of human hands. It is subject to historical changes, the laws of evolution, and above all the law of fragmentation. A uniform Christian culture is a *contradictio in adjecto*. Not only can several differing Christian cultures exist — they must exist. Every nation that has adopted Christianity must transform its culture so that its elements do not contradict Christianity, and so that in this culture there is not only a national, but also a Christian spirit. Thus, Christianity does not abolish the unique national cultural creativity, but, on the contrary, stimulates this creativity, imparting it with new tasks. All Christian peoples have been given the task of harmonizing their culture with the dogmas, ethics, and canons of the true Church of Christ, creating churches and forms of worship and implements capable of evoking Christian sentiments in the praying representatives of a given people — and each nation not only can, but must also resolve these tasks in their own way, so that Christianity will be perceived organically and intimately merge with a given national psyche. Of course, this in no way excludes the influence of one Christian culture on another. Such influences are also observed between non-Christian cultures; these influences are connected with the very essence of the development of cultures and, in the natural course of this development, do not in any way lead to the leveling of national differences. It is only important that the influence of one culture on another is not overwhelming, that cultural borrowings are organically processed, and that a new unified whole is created from one's own and foreign elements, tightly fitted to the unique national psyche of a given people.

The Church of Christ is one. Its unity presupposes living communion between individual local churches. But this communication is possible even without cultural unity. The unity of the church is expressed in the community of Holy Scripture, Holy Tradition, dogmas and canons, but not in those specific everyday, artistic, and legal forms by which dogmas, canons, traditions, and writings are adapted to the life of each given people. Attempts to fix these forms and to destroy the differences between peoples belonging to the same church, but not exactly the same culture, are based on superstition and ritual belief and do not lead to any good. We Russians suffered severely from such an attempt, that undertaken by Patriarch Nikon, which led to a schism in the ecclesiastical sphere, to the weakening of the Russian cultural-national organism's resistance in the everyday sphere, and paved the way for Peter the Great's debacles.

The Tower of Babel and the Confusion of Tongues

So, for a Christian, Christianity is not associated with any one specific culture. It is not an element of a specific culture, but a catalyst that can be introduced into a wide variety of cultures. The culture of Abyssinia and the culture of medieval Europe were completely different from each other, despite the fact that they were both Christian. If we take a closer look at the history of the spread of Christianity, we will be convinced that this spread was successful precisely wherever Christianity was perceived as a catalyst and not as an element of a ready-made foreign culture. Christianity was organically and fruitfully accepted and inculcated only where it contributed to the national culture without abolishing its originality, and vice versa. One of the most powerful inhibitors to the spread of Christianity has always been the erroneous identification of Christianity with some foreign culture specific to a given people. If in many cases the rejection of Christianity by a given people had and has its own deep, perhaps mystical and providential reasons, then in a number of cases, perhaps even in the majority, the reason lies in the fact that the missionaries did not spread Christianity as such, but a particular Christian culture. Orthodox missionaries also sinned in this way: it is no secret to anyone that missionary work within Russia was often an instrument of Russification, and outside Russia was a weapon for the spread of Russian political influence.

But this applies to an even greater extent to non-Orthodox missionaries — Catholic, Protestant, Anglican. Romano-Germanic missionaries see themselves primarily as cultural leaders. All their missionary activities are connected with "spheres of fusion," with colonization, Europeanization, concessions, trading posts, plantations, etc. Missionaries are not preachers of revealed truths sent from God, but agents of colonial policy or representatives of the "interests" of one or another power. Preaching not Christianity, but Catholicism, Protestantism or Anglicanism, i.e., those divergences from Christianity that took root in the conditions of Romano-Germanic culture and which are closely connected with it, these missionaries actually preached this culture itself. Naturally, the success of their preaching has depended on the degree a given people is able to "join European civilization." And since this civilization has long relegated Christianity to the background, where it has been drowned out by pandemonium, it is natural that the newly converted "natives" who perceive Christianity as just one not necessarily important element of European civilization, turn out to be very poor and creatively barren Christians. With this method of missionary work, it is not entire peoples capable of organically reworking their national culture in the Christian spirit who are converted to Christianity, but only individuals who, by the very fact of their conversion, are cut off from their native national culture's trunk and become collaborating agents in carrying out the economic and political plans of a foreign power.

Thus, Christ's commandment to teach all nations, to baptize them in the name of the Father and the Son and the Holy Spirit, essentially remains unfulfilled. It has not been fulfilled to a large extent precisely because missionary work was turned into a tool of Europeanization, into a means of establishing a homogeneous universal human culture, the ungodly essence of which we have tried to reveal in the preceding. The desire to level national differences cannot be justified by references to the need for Christian missionary work. On the contrary, this missionary work ends up being fruitless and unsuccessful precisely because of its alliance with forces that are anti-Christian and *Kulturträger* in essence.

***

TOWARD THE OVERCOMING OF THE REVOLUTION

Petr Suvchinsky[57]

***

The longer the era of revolution, the wider and deeper the revolution's scope, the more responsibility falls to the reaction (in this case, meaning a creative revolution, which is essentially a path to the new and which, if successful, would become a true revolution in Russia instead of a false one). The catastrophic form and dimensions of the Russian revolution, the "organized torment" of the Bolshevik yoke, first of all, draw attention and effort to the problem of understanding the causes of the revolution and evoke an immediate thirst for the active overthrow of communist power. However, since reality points to the undeniable prolongation of the Bolshevik period of the revolution, there is time to understand the depths and root causes of the Russian catastrophe and, in direct connection with this, to pose in full breadth the question of the future and inevitable Russian reaction.

The revolution cannot be overcome by mere emotions. It is already evident that the revolutionary darkness and the evil of rebellion will be defeated in Russia only through a long trial of the people's consciousness and conscience. Therefore, the reaction will have sufficient time frames to comprehensively understand the experience of the Russian disaster and proceed to act not out of blind vengeance, but with a mature,

---
57 Originally published in The Eurasian Annals, book 3 (Berlin, 1923).

creative awareness of the future spiritual-empirical Russia, an awareness developed out of the thick of the passions of destruction.

The problem of the future reaction is a matter of extreme responsibility and profundity, for the revolution singed and shocked all aspects of Russian life. Of course, it would be a pathetic pretense, no matter who it comes from, to try from afar to direct the processes of Russian history. The reaction, like a revolution, will break through and take shape spontaneously and unexpectedly. However, as a constructive beginning determined by the pathos of the struggle against revolutionary ruin, the reaction is, to a certain extent, also a conscious overcoming of the dark, chaotic instincts of the revolution, the result of the creative tension of conscience, thought, and will. If revolutionary tactics can consciously calculate and methodically create devastation, can any attempt to establish the future foundations of the construction and restoration of the disintegrated existence of the people and the country be considered fruitless fortune-telling or an unnecessary hint to the history of its paths and reversals?!

In order to outline and establish the supporting principles of the future, it is necessary to look closely at the revolutionary reality of Russia, for the very process of the revolution has already outlined those aspects of the people's giftedness, the very essence of the Russian nation, that either resist the revolutionary onslaught and influence in a peculiar way or remain ultimately and organically incompatible with communism despite having surrendered to it. This must be the basis for overcoming Bolshevism and the establishment of future reaction.

First of all, some part of Russia has already seen the light spiritually.

This is especially clear if we compare the current spiritual and ideological mood of Russia and the West. The religious awakening of Russian consciousness, after all, is a mass phenomenon. Meanwhile, the global disaster of world war has not yet resulted in a genuine religious reaction in Europe on a scale equivalent to the level of destruction. The increased importance of Catholic clerical parties in some countries can be taken into account as a politico-reactionary fact, but of course this does not entail a genuine return to mass religious confession. Still, it should be recognized that Europe lives with the memory of Christianity imprinted in the code of its civil ethics and morality.

The assertion that some part of Russia has come to its senses and seen the light does not disregard the sacrilege or blasphemy of modernity. Of course, at present, the masses are leaving religious life, madly excommunicating themselves from it, but at the same time, the poison of communism and the touch of true evil has raised a passionate impulse of religious awakening and re-established the central problems of religion, faith and the church as an antidote in response, at least for a minority. The catastrophes and happenings of our era now appear for many to be religious fulfilments. There is no need to downplay the significance of this. But there is something else: the experience of the catastrophic implementation of extreme socialism has revealed and exposed its primary essence, which in tactical and gradual socialism remains hidden and unexposed. The Russian Revolution showed that true socialism is not only formalistic, but also ontological. From now on, it is clear that socialism derives its tenacity and pathos not from the implementation of its unrealistic ideals of social existence and equality, but from the very depths of a genuine anti-God and anti-Christ essence.[58]

---

58 Socialism is opposed to Christianity and fights against it primarily in its conscious confusion, in its establishment of a false synthesis of the principles of spirit and flesh. Christianity, as a divine-human [*bogochelovecheskaya*] religion, categorically separates these principles and establishes an immutable legitimacy in the relations between them. Socialism, on the one hand, by denying the creative primacy, autonomy and ontology of the spirit, materializes it, and on the other, by sublimating material existence and proclaiming it the ultimate and sufficient goal of human life, thereby imparts to matter and flesh a certain semblance of spiritual quality, i.e. it pneumatizes them. Because of this, a degrading osmosis between spirit and flesh is established, which in its deepest essence is contrary to the revelation and teaching of Christianity.

Toward the Overcoming of the Revolution

The experience of evil that befell Russia and which is its *privilegium odiosum*, in its essence is, of course, an experience of a religious order.

It can be said that the "quenching of the spirit" on which the entire plan of the communist takeover of Russia was built has failed. In dying, Russia has come to life in spirit. Here one cannot measure in quantities and masses. Of course, the majority of the Russian people have been seized by a thirst for material wealth and passion for their bourgeois future. But since popular inspiration and spiritual expansion are not governed by laws, the ignited religious consciousness of the minority will find a response in the shrouded religious element of the entire country; the obvious trampling of the divine world order must to some extent lead to a true vision of the boundaries of the divine and human, a religious vision of the ultimate boundary between the sphere of the world order and the limits of human creative possibility.

To the extent that the first stage of the revolution played out mainly in the socio-political sphere, the revolutionary process has come to be concentrated in the spiritual and religious sphere. This is easy to verify, in the very least by the Bolsheviks' consistent attention to anti-religious propaganda. The very fact of the revolutionization of the church, testifying to the greatest darkness of the people's consciousness and conscience, is a direct encroachment on the most sacred treasures of the people, and, perhaps, this extreme blasphemy will best show Russia where the revolution has led it and what it is being forced to give up.

But great temptations also confront those who have already seen the light and are already trying to rely on the foundations of spirit, faith, and the church. It is necessary to avoid using this conversion for evil, but instead for the creative and faithful freedom of spiritual activity. Otherwise, trust in faith will be replaced by new accusations and doubts among those of little faith. And who would dare to say they are of more than little faith?

Toward the Overcoming of the Revolution

If the revolution has not managed to destroy the exceptional gift of the divinely-inspired Russian element and its religious memory, then it has also not extinguished real feeling for the empirical image of Russia. In all the disasters and humiliations of the revolution, Russia, both in its own eyes and in the eyes of the world, invariably appears as an insurmountable, uniquely powerful, cultural and political world, impervious to pan-European neutralization and unification and engaged in overcoming some of its fate. Being at the apogee of socialist Europeanization, Russia has nevertheless found itself opposed to Europe. In fact, paradoxically, the revolution has sharpened consciousness of Russian cultural and political peculiarities and led Russia to once again feel the full force of displacement and the self-sufficiency of its empirical array. The feeling of cultural sovereignty is here combined with the feeling and aspiration of state-political sovereignty.

In the decades preceding the revolution, Russia's loss of spiritual and cultural face was reflected among the masses as a darkening of the sovereign self-awareness of the people as a whole. There was a general feeling of great-power fatigue and a sense that Russia had grown aimless in its existence as a great-power, that this existence was no longer an organic incentive for unity and power. The revolutionary breakthrough was revealed in the unprecedented political fact of the voluntary sanctioning of the collapse and disintegration of the entire great-power statehood as the form of the Russian Empire. This was a clear sign of the fall of all the forces that brought together the disparate entities of the great state. One can, of course, attribute the self-betrayal of Russia in 1917-18 to the will and initiative of revolutionary elements, but it would be more accurate to see in this fact the discovery of a deep, nationwide process of the impoverishment of sovereign self-awareness, the roots of which stretch back to the historical fates of Russia in the 18th and 19th centuries.

By the beginning of the world war, Russia did not have a sovereign historical mission or self-understanding. It was already lost before the war began. The loss and helplessness of the Russian government and the Russian "guardians" in directly instilling in the people their historical dignity and mission played, among other things, a fatal role in the long struggle of the authorities against the revolution. The Russian Revolution was not an unexpected catastrophe: one part of society had long set it as an open goal, Russian creative genius prophetically predicted it, while the government and Russian conservatism recognized its inevitability only to fight against it. The mindset of the Russian intelligentsia was precise, and its tactics were consistent: the Russian faith, culture, and way of life were labeled as savagery, barbarism and obscurantism. The common goal was European enlightenment and total-equalizing progress.

As for the government-protective ideology, it crafted declarations about the identity of the Russian people and their callings in defense (starting with Magnitsky and Uvarov and ending with Katkov and Pobedonostsev); however, it did not present any specific, independent historical task to the Russian state. On the contrary, yielding to the general course of events, Russia was increasingly drawn into pan-European political entanglements and thus the government actually refuted its ideological premises about creating an independent destiny for the Russian state.

One can easily trace how often Russia appeared in the international life of Europe and became intertwined in its destinies without any of its own essential or organic need. Having several times had the opportunity to neutrally assert itself as a great and self-sufficient whole, Russian statehood fatally reduced its significance to the level of an individual political factor compelled to be a part of a complex pan-European equilibrium. In this regard, the political history of Russia, the "reason" and "justification" for its wars (including the last world war), require special attention, especially at the present moment.

Toward the Overcoming of the Revolution

The revolution, having isolated the Bolshevik continent and withdrawing Russia from all international relations, somehow brings, against the will of its leaders, Russian statehood (currently hidden under the guise of communist power) closer to finding its own independent historical and empirical task and forces them to take inspiration from it. One of the signs indicating the accumulation of state consciousness in today's Russia is the "National Bolshevik" doctrine. However, since this current stabilizes the revolutionary-transitory order in the state system and, turning a blind eye to all the abominations of the revolution and not setting itself any spiritual tasks of revival, builds its ideology on revolutionary paradoxes (i.e., through the international it hopes to create the national construction of Russia), it cannot be called anything other than another ugly product of the revolution. However, it must be admitted that some kind of tragically fatal and, of course, temporary and partial substitution in the Russian popular consciousness is indeed still present: the blind "defense of the revolution" is, for some hitherto unaware Russians, in essence, an unconscious defense of the national-state sovereignty of Russia.

But sooner or later, Russian self-consciousness will have to fully understand the true spiritual-empirical form of Russia. This will shed new light on the problems of international political self-affirmation. Signs of a correct reaction to the betrayal of 1917-18 can already be found in national consciousness, in the fact that questions about true national being and dignity are being felt, at times sharply and acutely, in circles where these questions had not been considered at all until now.

If the symptoms of this understanding are already present in Russian consciousness, then it is all the more urgent that they should be developed into a broad and integral ideology that can evoke that popular passion that the revolutionaries were able to instill in certain elements of the Russian people for the idea of the international. Here, elements of the religious awakening and a loving vision of the earthly form of Russia must come together in some kind of unity. Of course, the rapprochement of the religious sphere with the empirical sphere is fraught with many dangers and temptations. History knows many examples of this union being used for evil. But anyone who believes in Russia's creative endowment must take this risk. Perhaps this combination will bring the expectant reaction in Russia as it often has in the past, or perhaps the art and experience of revolution will direct the Russian future "towards the unprecedented." In any case, combining the problem of Russian spiritual revival and confession with the problem of the empirical flesh and the historical form of Russia into a single ideology and goal has a greater chance at the present moment of helping overcome the Russian collapse and outlining the paths of construction than all the baseless ideologies and schemes of formal politics in the meanwhile. In general, all attempts to heal Russia by imposing ready-made political formulas and regimes on it have so far turned out to be blind, unbearable scholasticism, the pathetic psychologisms of people who have forever lost their sense of Russia.

But, most importantly, the imagination is ghostly hot with immediate tasks and active political plans that are not destined to be realized, and the majority of the emigration thereby loses its understanding of the real, albeit more distant prospect; and, not seeing the implementation of its feverish and confused calculations, the emigration undermines its faith in its own strength, giving rise to painful impatience and leading into the temptation of cowardly compromise. The emotional counter-revolution still cannot become a conscious-volitional reaction, that is, it cannot acquire a new mindset or new spiritual-psychological content.

It is useless to hysterically denounce the revolution. While staying aware of its sins and the evils of its violence, it is nevertheless necessary to be inspired by creative, constructive optimism. Otherwise, it will be impossible to settle accounts with what has happened, because the longer people mentally

Toward the Overcoming of the Revolution

remain in an atmosphere of revolutionary evil, the more tenacious the revolutionary poisons will be..

The emigration, busy with its feverish and chaotic denunciations, gives little thought to the problem of what a truly creative reaction would look like.

It is necessary to understand that modern Bolshevism has ceased to be an exclusively social and political phenomenon; it has sprouted with innumerable roots and currently permeates and entangles all of the soil and subsoil of Russian existence. If not everyone has recognized communism, and even if there are sectors of Russian life that oppose it and will resist it, then everyone and everything in Russia has still been deformed, poisoned, or distorted by it in one way or another.

The fact is that, along with fatigue of great-power statehood and the loss of a sense of self-understanding, Russia, by the end of the 19th century and at the beginning of the 20th century, had a general thirst for self-manifestation, a vague consciousness that "history is calling Russia to take her turn," which the "reaction" and the government did not understand and were unable to make use of. Without a proper outlet, the people's tension blindly and ill-fatedly surrendered to that strong-willed and imperative principle, which managed to further agitate and bring together all sides and levels, confusing both positive and negative elements of Russian existence, in order to seize Russia and, in a fit of blind rebellion, force it to renounce itself and surrender to the alien and hostile. It is useless to go against Bolshevism with only politics or moral denunciations, or in general with any isolated slogan of struggle. It is necessary to put up against the Bolshevik front a front that is equal in scope and breadth, which, having turned around, would be able to launch a more accurate network of offense to recapture Russia simultaneously and conjugately on all sides, in all directions and to every depth captured by the revolution. It is necessary to deeply plow the Russian fields in order to break the entire underground network of thin overgrown roots of Bolshevik chaff. Only a clear and comprehensive vision of the future can make Russia come to its senses, only this can convince and attract a Russia that has lost faith and lost itself.

Meanwhile, the political doctrinairism of some sections of the intelligentsia continues to wreak harm. On the other hand, attempts are being made to idealize the pre-revolutionary past, which, in comparison with everything being experienced today, naturally arises in our memory as unappreciated perfection. In both cases, the effect of the two central and interrelated factors of pre-revolutionary Russia that most immediately led to the catastrophe continue to be felt. Leaving aside the pan-European crisis and the deep causes of the revolution, one should not (as is sometimes accepted now) place blame solely on the intelligentsia, although they, indeed, treacherously retreated from understanding the sovereign existence of Russia and thereby undermined its foundations. It must be resolutely acknowledged that the pre-revolutionary government in recent decades had clearly lost its direct, yet living, connection with the people, culture and modernity, and that it alone is responsible for this. The main evil was not in the shortcomings of the system, but in the fact that, starting from the very heights of power, Russian great-power statehood had become spiritually impoverished and degenerated, losing its meaning, imperative, and even style.

After all, there is nothing unexpected in the current catastrophe: everything that has come to be was written about and predicted (take, for example, the passionate and persistent warnings and prophecies of Konstantin Leontiev). And if "Russian conservatism" and the "Russian guardians", clearly aware of everything that was to come, could not prevent the death of "original Russia", it means they did not have the organic support, convincing will, or self-confidence needed in order to convey their religious and state task to the country and the people, to convince the "commoners, liberals and intellectuals" who were "undermining the foundations", and, in spite of everything, to defend the correctness of their position and implement their plans in reality. After all, the government was still strong and autocratic! This must be recognized in order not to idealize Russian conservatism beyond measure. Appearing in various aspects in different decades of the second half of the 19th century, the Russian "conservative guardians", generally speaking, failed to inspire long-term and sustainable trust in Russia for the beginning of a national-cultural movement with the goal of the original development of the Russian religious-cultural and state-social organism. It did not live up to its idealistic slogans and aroused suspicion in its selfish adherence to class and property interests. As for the heights of the Russian public, they could not become a stronghold of cultural "protection", since they themselves uncontrollably gravitated along the path of de-nationalization and Europeanization (inevitably associated with a bias towards liberalism). As a result, this conservatism turned out to be only political, and not national-cultural, and thus became decidedly unconvincing for the entire nation.

If the catastrophe of the Russian Revolution has deep and distant causes in the historical past of Russia, then the end of the 19th century was the decisive moment. It was then that Russia's social and governmental horizons grew so dark that it became clear to the most diverse and attentive people of the 1880-90s that in a half century, no more, the Russian people would little by little, without even noticing, go from being a people of "God-bearers" to one of "God-fighters". This era was already tragic for Russia because the external growth and great-power policy of Russia did not have any ideological, national-spiritual expression or leadership. Slavophilism had almost been eliminated by this time, and all that remained of it was the overbearing pseudo-Russian style, especially during the reign of Alexander III, who left his mark on all aspects of "official" life in Russia. (The national-Slavophile exaltation associated with the Turkish campaign turned out to be fatally unviable. The reasons for this constitute one of the deepest problems of Russian statehood and culture).[59] The "guardians" themselves essentially became Westernizers. They nevertheless defended a reaction, but a politically narrow one. And since "Westernism" has always been identified with liberalism, it is natural that this "Westernization" reaction was unconvincing and only resulted in a confusion of concepts and extreme irritation in the consciousness of Russian society.

In some sense, Russian society had the right to be essentially dissatisfied: if the reaction and the government failed to create an original era of universal prosperity for post-reform Russia, and they themselves took the path of "Europeanization," then following this path further to a constitution and civil freedom meant "truly and exclusively breathing the nitrogen of complete stagnation." And life actually fell out of step with statehood and ceased to charge the national accumulator of Russian sovereignty with its energy. On the contrary, it began to feed currents and moods that tore asunder or "undermined the foundations." This created that oppressive atmosphere of

---

59 The Slavophile idea was no longer presented or developed by anyone in any form close to its fundamental principles (I.S. Aksakov died in 1885); later, the peculiar Slavophilism of K. Leontiev was perceived in wide circles as an anachronism and obscurantism; Katkov was odious as an official spokesman for government reaction. Strakhov's influence remained limited. The theocratic utopianism of Solovyov at that time, although rooted in the teachings of Kireevsky and Khomyakov, significantly modified the basic elements of old Slavophilism and gave them a different ideological and emotional meaning. In the seductive concept of Russian "national self-denial", the transubstantiated Rome and the world theocracy of Solovyov (which conditionally influenced Dostoevsky), the sharp Slavophile criticism of the "division and rationality" of Europe completely disappeared. Solovyov's break with Aksakov also dates back to the early 80s, and the immediate reason for the divergence was Solovyov's Catholic temptations and his preaching about the central authority of the Roman throne. Somewhat later, Solovyov spoke negatively and critically about Danilevsky's "creeping" theory of cultural types: having previously believed that the world should be saved "by Russian thought alone, by the Russian God and Christ," in 1880, he declared in his Pushkin speech that "all our Slavophilism and Westernism are just one great misunderstanding among us..." But the most important thing to note is that the widest circles of Russian society and even the non-advanced intelligentsia, in a purely philistine and practical sense, began in these years to blindly and unreasonably "worship the West", and understanding the prospects for the Russian future turned out to be as obscured in these passive social circles as their historical memory of the past was dulled...

hopelessness and embitterment, boredom and fear, in which the darkest and most justified prophecies about the Russian future took shape; in the same atmosphere, Chekhov, Andreev and Blok, Ropshin's *The Pale Horse* and Bely's *Petersburg* were born. Meanwhile, there were people who insisted that "the world in its present form is already passing over Europe", and that Russia could find salvation only by forming an original state and following its own socio-economic path. But the reaction did not heed this notion. Of course, it was possible to fight against the fashionable European liberal public, but, in this case, it was necessary for Russia to create its own developmental prospects on a national scale, first of all, by highlighting a number of vitally necessary reforms in order to build the independent and creative protection of the religious and state essence of Russia, preserving its internal structure and historical face. Especially important were those reforms related to the land structure of the peasants, which would have been a psychologically satisfactory and an economically expedient resolution to the age-old "land dispute" from the odious sphere of political liberalism. But this did not happen...

There is no place for political accounts, biased accusations and incriminations after the fatal death of Russia's religious way of life and statehood. Many facts of the revolution, of course, will still find redemption in the religious conscience of future generations. But still, the blind reaction of the 1880-90s and the dead end of 1917, the convulsions of that time, the metaphysical emptiness, the pangs of hopelessness and emptiness, must be remembered no less than the horrors of the revolutionary era.

The late historical period of the Russian revolution, which occurred when humanistic and socialist idealism was exposed and began to lose its seductiveness, and the actual need for a comprehensive reconstruction of Russia, imposed a special responsibility on the era that followed the revolution. If the Russian reaction does not reveal a renewed religious, cultural and sovereign face of Russia, then all the passions and sacrifices of the revolution will remain unredeemed. Returning to a feeling and understanding of the form and fate of the homeland and the resurrection of one's love for it must be recognized as a religious category. How darkened the Russian pre-revolutionary consciousness had become can be judged by more than the malice and betrayal of Russia's open enemies; the degeneration of the true sense of homeland also made itself felt in Russian creativity (most clearly in Blok and Bely). These authors' works are filled with love and passion for Russia, but this love belies impending catastrophe. The ongoing disasters and horrors in Russia became immanent in the personal fate of each author and evoke a painful "joy of suffering" for them, as well as almost sadistic reflections and an egoistic thirst for death and decay rather than volitional resistance to the coming disaster.

This reflected the powerlessness of the people of the era of Russian spiritual and social decadence to understand the homeland personally and ideally at the same time, that is, religiously; to understand that everyone should merge their fate with the fate of their homeland, but at the same time, that one cannot equate personal biography with the existence of one's country and one's people, no matter to what extent personal life in certain eras was determined by this existence. The attitude toward the homeland must be incommensurable with all internal-social relations; the loss of this attitude leads to the death of patriotic pride and the establishment of helpless individual pride, excluding the possibility of patriotic service. To serve is to understand the fate of one's homeland and to create it with one's will...[60]

There are eras when the historical task fades in the very consciousness of the people. Despite all of Russia's decomposition, the people's memory of themselves and

---

60 This does not mean that socialism is not destined for major victories in the near future, for now it is inextricably linked with industrial civilization, and the possibilities for the growth of the latter are limitless, since modernity has learned to artificially create thousands of unnecessary needs in order to immediately serve and satisfy them.

the main features of Russian national giftedness still live. They must be clarified and strengthened. To do this, we should try to create, on the irrevocable foundations of the organic, Orthodox-Russian worldview, a system of conjugate contemplation upon all currently developing processes and events in Russia. Only through keen observation and comparisons of facts can we obtain a correct, unbiased judgment about the Russian present and future. However, it is impossible to assess what is happening without having solid foundations for a future reaction that would center, form, and bring together all the data of experience and observation. But, in choosing these foundations, it is necessary to responsibly establish the real principles of Russian religious and empirical self-affirmation, without which the construction of the spirit and state of the future Russia is unthinkable. Clarification of the integral tenets of Russian life must go hand in hand with the creative experience of modern reality. One without the other is unthinkable, leading to the danger of either lifeless doctrinairism or unprincipled opportunism.

Ideology must also become methodology.

Returning to the recent past with jealous memories, thoughts, and desires is useless and even harmful. This memory is painful for everyone: a feeling of late repentance, the fatal meaning of everything that has happened, and an understanding of common guilt are mixed with a keen awareness that the catastrophe could have been avoided and a thirst to denounce the "generation of fathers", who, having divided into two camps, on the one hand, openly and with evil will, attacked Russia and finally took possession of it and, on the other, failed to stand up for it. The memory of the last half-century is also difficult for the people. Not because the regime was violent, as it is customary to say, but because the general spiritual, moral, and state-class decomposition penetrated to the very depths of the masses and created a sick, agitated atmosphere, constantly irritating the nerves and passions of the people, who understood well that they were the object of someone else's dispute.

It is necessary to remember and recognize the recent past as a terrible experience, but it is not this past that should be used as the basis for the ideological and empirical revival of Russia. It is necessary to awaken the historical memory of Russia in all its sharpness and depth (of course, not just aesthetically and without artificial archaization), which over the past centuries has grown shallow, has lost the ability to synthetically embrace the past fate of its faith, culture, and statehood, and has ceased to resurrect the past in the present.

At some fateful time in the existence of Russia, there was a break in the successive chain of national-historical memory, and the organic Russian past was cut off and died for subsequent generations. "The heights of Russian culture" grew ugly with their impoverished ideals by the 18th and 19th centuries, and the people transferred all their historical memories into everyday life, and now, in leaving this everyday life, they are at the same time leaving the consciousness of their history. But religious-historical memory must now be combined with modern vision in order to clarify and reaffirm what is an immutable, original tradition in the fate of Russia and what is now revealed as a creative task for future generations. It is not to the near past, but to the distant past and far future that the coming "reaction" must call!

The shock of the revolution gave Russia the greatest acceleration, charged it with rapid and heavy inertia, both evil and positive at once. The reaction must pick up this movement and dynamically assert itself, replacing the frenzied fanaticism of the international with passion and the creative, original ideal of Russian faith, culture, and sovereignty.

The reaction must concentrate, express, and use the entire multifaceted experience of the revolution; it must confront Russia with maximum responsibility for the problems of religious-state and cultural-sovereign self-determination and creativity. When, if not after her terrible revolution, will Russia be able to creatively strain all of its national forces and, through a nationwide impulse, establish truly updated forms of its internal existence? It cannot be otherwise than that the fire of the revolution has tempered in Russia "the bold springs of a new citizenship." But in order to be successful, the political reaction must become an act of nationwide, religious, and cultural self-restoration. Otherwise, instead of a self-creative reaction, Russia, having thwarted its ardor in overthrowing communism, might very quickly take the path of ready-made European political schemes and regimes and thereby prepare for itself a reaction that is even less national than the Bolshevik international.

Of course, it is simpler (and this, of course, will be the goal for many) to rush to introduce into the usual channels that national excitement, which, one must foresee, will spread in a wide wave following the collapse of communism. But this cutting of the wings of the national impulse is not what all those who seek to use the experience of the revolution deeply and significantly should desire. In its catastrophes, the revolution revealed in a collected and aggravated form the entire historical form and all the historical sins of Russia, it went through all the tones of the spiritual and mental structure of the Russian people, which had long ceased to be clearly recognized by the intelligentsia due to two extremes: partly due to the inauthentic idealization of the people, partly out of blind contempt for them. This terrible summation needs to be understood; it testifies not only to the rebellious and godless element of the people; in it one can also see a fierce impulse (unconscious, perhaps) to throw off alien and foreign forms and the privileges of a culture that is not one's own, as well as a religious desire to find one's own truth of social and state existence. However, socialism took advantage of this Russian mood to such an extent that it gave its deceitful and ugly forms concrete manifestations. But in the still hidden depths of the Russian revolution a grain of national genius is concealed, which only in the future and under better circumstances will be able to bear fruit, which, perhaps, will justify all of the evil, violence, and abomination of the revolution.

After all, the revolution gave rise to undeniable heroes of evil and destruction.

In order for the reaction to be heroic, of course, in the opposite sense, one must, first of all, want it to be so. One must understand all the responsibility, significance, and meaning of the era that will come after the Bolshevik overthrow. All those who are not hypnotized by dead political doctrines and rules, all who want a great and creative future for Russia, must now set themselves a firm and strong-willed task in all its breadth, because if the colossal scale of revolutionary destruction was tragic, then a reaction that is not on a grand scale and does not lead to the great goals of nationwide repentance, self-knowledge, and disclosure may turn out to be even worse.

The Russian intelligentsia experienced a terrible crisis of its ideals and beliefs. And still amazed by the failure of its past, it cannot come to its senses and reorganize its faith, thoughts, and feelings into harmonious and firm goals. Sometimes it seems that the "organized torment" of Bolshevism, which was supposed to unite the intelligentsia, did not squeeze it enough in its grip, and the crumbling upper cultural layer of Russia has not yet been cemented into a single strong social layer. Without even mentioning the politicking part of the emigration, for whom everything is simple and clear, because its plans do not extend beyond the restoration of the monarchy or the establishment of a democratic system, it must be admitted that in broad circles the entire experience of recent years has not yet been realized and formalized. The upcoming goals of religious construction, state restoration, and, in general, the entire concrete future of Russia, are very vague prospects for the majority. Meanwhile, it is easier to be disappointed by vague ideals and dreams. Sooner or later, when faced with any reality (which will never be able to satisfy their vague aspirations and plans), all those who are not using the experience of the past and what they have experienced as the basis for the real tasks of the future will inevitably find themselves the same as they were before revolution, on the side of the principled opposition, and thereby deprive the future Russian restoration of the necessary unanimity. The Bolsheviks surprisingly managed to give vitality to their dead doctrine, to put it under the signs of perverted religious fanaticism and heroic false idealism. It is scary to think that true national inspiration, which sooner or later will awaken all of Russia, can be reduced to common political templates and reactionary formalism.

Many often talk about various historical mistakes, but in addition to mistakes, there are also historical sins; and not understanding the true form, essence, and historical mission of Russia after so many disasters and misfortunes, and thereby not atoning for the sins of the past, means committing a great new historical sin for which future retribution is inevitable. Over the past centuries of European history, Russia has more than once found itself opposed to the West. If modern Russian generations do not come to their senses, do not take into account the current isolated position of Russia —when fate itself, perhaps for the last time, has opened up the opportunity for the Russian people to find their own original and independent paths and opportunities in order to overcome their ill-fated "Westernism" in the face of the revolution and begin to create in a new way, albeit in some accordance with their oldest, spiritual and empirical destiny — and if the unprecedented experience of the revolution does not lead to an understanding of the falsity of the foundations of the modern "advanced" system of life, then it will be necessary to admit that all the passionate dreams and prophecies of Russian seers about the destiny of Russia were a vision of a great historical opportunity which Russia itself consciously rejected, preferring instead to devote itself to the common fate of European civilization.

Toward the Overcoming of the Revolution

In some respects, great upheavals establish a mutual assessment of events and build collective will, but a conscious sensitivity to the needs of the time is also required, a readiness for common action; until now, such cannot be found among the leaders and masses who set themselves the goal of overcoming the revolution. Without this, it is impossible to find unity in conscience, inspiration, and will in the circle of conflicting interests and private judgments. This confluence is an indispensable condition for finding a common way out of the revolutionary catastrophe; without it, it will be impossible to gain the strength to lift the spirit and flesh of Russia out of darkness and destruction.

***

IDEAS AND METHODS

Petr Suvchinsky[61]

***

I

Despite the international and diplomatic successes of the Soviet authorities, Russia internally continues to exist in a state of dramatic revolution; one may state with full assurance that every attempt on the part of the Bolsheviks to transition from a revolutionary rule of Russia to a regulated stabilization (even by their standards) of communist order will yield nothing whatsoever. Indeed, in recent times, it is as though the Russian people's organic desire for material prosperity is intensifying at the expense of their national self-understanding; at times, this state of affairs noticeably reduces their spiritual resistance to communism. Nonetheless, in submitting to dictatorship – in perceiving and even adopting certain distinct elements of the Soviet regime – the majority of the Russian people continues to view the communists as hostile, alien occupiers who, sooner or later, will be overcome and quelled. We could, of course, accuse today's Russia of national disorder and passivity; however, we would do well not to disregard the fact that the spiritual-ideological and active struggle against communism is no light task. On one hand, leading up to the moment of revolutionary cataclysm, the Russian values of religion, nation, the state, the people, and everyday life were partially forgotten, partially disparaged; the readymade foundations for a concentrated, organic, and

---
61 Originally published in *The Eurasian Annals*, book 4 (Berlin, 1925).

favorable worldview that might have been set in opposition to the burgeoning fanaticism of revolution was nowhere to be found and, in essence, is absent even now. On the other hand, every year the pressure of the purely economic forces of the people coming from below makes itself felt more and more strongly; the people strive to express themselves in a new social situation, eager, regardless of the general forms and principles of statehood, to realize their economic energy. Besides this, the degree to which the communists are refining and flaunting their skill at governing is the same degree to which the anti-Bolshevik masses of the Russian people are growing coarser and more elemental. (This is plainly seen in the current chaos of the church; in many instances, the actions and habits of the "pawns" are reminiscent of Russian mores of the sixteenth and seventeenth centuries.) One can negatively evaluate this situation only conditionally – only to the extent that this Russian "savagery" serves as a factor in blunting the blade of struggle against communism. As far as the essence of this phenomenon goes, it naturally does not lend itself to precise evaluation, because the development of new internal values might be hidden behind this external coarsening. If we recall the cultural crisis in which pre-revolutionary Russia found herself due to the break between the rarefied heights of the intelligentsia and the lowly level of the people, we might even say that the partial coarsening and simplification of Russian life will, in the future, yield a desirable influence. Already now, in observing the contemporary moment in Russia, we may arrive at the paradoxical conclusion that if Russia has never before been captured by a principle so foreign to her as the ongoing yoke of communism, it has nonetheless been a long time since she has manifested the autarchic essence of her elementality as explicitly as she has done during certain episodes of her terrible revolution.

In light of the situation that has arisen, one must wield a great self-mastery of spirit and will so as not to give oneself up to the general process of elemental degeneration and

Ideas and Methods

passive simplification — and so that, in certain situations that are parallel and perpendicular to this one, we may attempt to return ourselves and those close to us to an understanding of the religio-spiritual and governmental-historical callings and aims of Russia. In evaluating everything that has come to pass, and in taking stock of the reasons for such prolonged success on the part of the Bolsheviks, we must acknowledge that the forces required to resist them — the seemingly unnatural ideas and ideals[62] which contradict and undermine themselves every step of the way — are found by the current Russian authority primarily in the ability to combine abstract, theoretical fanaticism with concrete actions and tactics. A fateful meeting has taken place between the doctrinaire activities of the intelligentsia, nihilism and atheism, popular revolt, and the limitations of the black earth, which have altered the entire structure of Russian agrarian and socio-juridical relations to its very roots. Moreover, the Bolsheviks, with the cunning of their politics, have managed to inculcate the people with a notion of the integration and even total identification between these two qualitatively different phenomena. The shift of social classes and the relocation of values and property from the hands of the former privileged class into those of the peasants have combined in the people's understanding with a militant atheism, a negation of patriotism for the motherland, and an anarchism that rejects civil law. As a result, Russia has seen the formation of a sort of median *worldview* of the masses, difficult to overcome, in which the most heterogeneous and fragmented

---

62 The very idea of social-communism must, of course, be considered an easily adopted and accessible phenomenon of something which is a *solely* human Principle. However, it is important to note that, in the process of its realization, this principle encounters an insuperable reaction precisely from the field of empirical reality and the specific human essence which is one of its constituent parts. This reality is by no means indicative of the social environment's inability to realize its dubiously natural and inevitable idea; on the contrary, the presence within man of a certain other nature which expresses itself — imperiously and in opposition to all arbitrary surmises and artificial conclusions — by means of organic, inescapable destruction and the removal of anything that should attempt its realization on the basis of false and unlawful pretenses. It is for this reason that communism is unrealizable: not because people are bad, but because they are still far too good.

ideas have fused with contradictory psychological attitudes (e.g., the combination of economic materialism, godless atheism, the psychology of rebellion, and an elementary sense of thrift in agricultural matters) into a monstrous and complex whole.

It is precisely for this reason, as one attempts to establish a different order of ideological positions and creeds against the contemporary median psychology of the Russian people, that one must realize this intention through the creative synthesis of an *organic system* and worldview which, taking its roots in the depths of spirit, would lead to direct action and tactics. One must naturally begin with the deepening of this worldview's foundational pillar. In the face of today's Russian catastrophe, when all fundamental values of spiritual and secular governmental life have been crushed or subjected to reevaluation, it is not enough to base one's creation of an anti-revolutionary ideology on such concepts as political equality, civil freedom, democratic republic, monarchy, and so on. Because none of these categories are any more than the derivative values of a particular type of worldview, their internal meanings are not comparable to the first principles of communist ideology, which today have been directly laid bare and exude an immediate influence on society with their false ontology. Moreover, the very tone of the contemporary Russian psyche and the awakening of consciousness covers up and drowns out that emotionality which is contained in contemporary norms of formal politics and "enlightened" civil duty. In order to find a true method, tone, and style in our evaluations of what is occurring, and to find authentic paths into the future, we must, first and foremost, have no fear of becoming religiously candid and patriotically sincere. This is not the simplest task, for the entire pre-revolutionary epoch had morbidly distorted and stifled the very foundations of the organic Russian worldview.

Every person possessing an inner consciousness of the fact that he is Russian must understand that, before the terrible

Ideas and Methods

picture of his motherland's destruction, in his attempt at restoring certain reviled or annihilated values, he must deepen his spiritual strength to the greatest degree possible; he must raise the very problem of Russia to the height of her historical and metaphysical meaning. And, in assigning himself the task of exalting a volitional system of ideas and actions, the Russian must concern himself least of all with the possibility of overstepping the bounds of linearity and a certain kind of simplification in the process of carrying it out. Since every heroic act is always a willful disclosure of inner openness and immediate sincerity, that act, to a certain extent, inherently bears the stamp of verbal singularity[63], emotional nakedness, and provocative directness. First, one must overcome his false shame at the use of simple words and concepts, and he must see that the fundamental national-religious values of human being disintegrate and take on a hypocritical, sanctimonious sense and tincture only as a result of spiritual weakness and the moral decay of people themselves. Until a true platform is found for the dogmatic pillars of the extra-temporal values belonging to Russian historiosophy, one may directly assume that the very problem of Russian restoration has yet to be posed.

Every reduction, schematization, and irresponsible simplification of one's approach to the events of the Russian Revolution, with each passing year, is beginning to take on the character of a malicious profanation; for there is no time for jokes, smooth dialectical expositions, or youthful invectives when Russian reality continues its involutions into complexity in connection with the various phenomena of Russian and European life – when it is becoming clear that, after seven years of Bolshevik rule, that fundamental axis has yet to be found in Russia, around which the forces fit to overcome revolution might rally and solidify. Without in any way minimizing the significance of economic and practical considerations related to the problem of the Russian restoration, it must nonetheless be understood that the urgency of ideologically replacing

---

63 [Trans.]: literally, "monosyllabicity [*odnoslozhnost'*]"

Ideas and Methods

the current reigning stimuli in Russia and establishing authentically spiritual provisions of law capable of constituting the foundation of the entire post-revolutionary epoch to come must take priority. We must realize that it is precisely this approach to the revolution and modernity, this fundamental erection of a new, organic worldview in counterbalance to the system of communism, which constitutes the sole form of profound resistance to and struggle with communism for Russia; for, if the Soviet authorities have birthed a terrible hatred of themselves, they have also instilled in many Russian people a deep and internally concentrated relationship to everything surrounding them; they have instilled an understanding of the entire depth and complexity of reasons for Russia's fall. We ought not to obscure our vision with ghostly illusions and plans; even less ought we to simplify our understanding of the facts and processes of revolution; but, standing face-to-face with the mission of the Bolsheviks, understanding the utterly alien nature of this mission to Russia, and seeing with our own two eyes the discontinuities of historical successions, we must understand with particular clarity the true face of Russia. And, on the basis of that experiential knowledge which, in the current conditions, can and must be intuitively grasped by all Russians and become a return to their long-forgotten organic truth, we must create both a contemporary front of ideas and a method for their realization.

Before all else, we must establish that, in evaluating the Russian revolution, the moment of its cause (strictly speaking, the meaning of the conditions under which the Revolution was able to break through) plays a secondary role. What is important is clarifying *the very structure of the phenomenon of revolution* which, in turn, reveals its true foundations and its meaning. There was, of course, a genetic line leading to the revolution, but this fact in itself tells us little, as the processes of Russian cultural decay have acted in a variety of ways, often in contradictory causal orders, altering its aspects during

Ideas and Methods

different epochs. Only now, having fully unraveled the fact and phenomenon of the Russian Revolution – in its "completeness" and "stability" – does the possibility of close analysis and definition, of elucidating the entire complex structure of Russian deformation, present itself.

On first glance, two conditions would seem to refute a similar pretension to understanding the revolution as the sum total of profound cultural rebirths of the Russian organism: 1) war has served as an immediate facilitator for the revolution (i.e., the external fact), and 2) after 1905, a socio-economic renaissance could be observed. But, of course, it would be false to view the war as an externally imposed catastrophe: Russia's participation therein[64], as well as the very possibility of a pan-European war, were conditioned by the most tortuous complex of cultural-historical facts, extending far into the past. As for this pre-revolutionary economic renaissance, it cannot be interpreted outside the context of the ideo-cultural situation of the period, in which a corresponding ascent did not take place.

The idealistic and aesthetic reaction to the long years of persistent nihilistic blindness and philistine bad taste that emerged in the 90s was not friendly; it broke down into a number of morbid and fanciful tendencies, incapable of laying the foundational current in the ideological social life of the day. The multifariousness of the ideological "renaissance," lasting from the 1890s to the 1900s – its vagueness and fractured character – belied a misguidedness and lack of firmness in the fundamental principles upon which it was necessary to consolidate Russian consciousness anew, perverted and obscured in the fog of long-past deluges. Remaining unhealed, it was with unelucidated ideas and without a firm social worldview that Russia accepted the

---

64 Count Rostopchin's conceit (which he voiced in his report to Emperor Pavel in relation to the war of 1799, which had cut nearly all ties between Russia and other lands) that "Russia should have no relations with foreign powers other than those of a commercial character" was ultimately never realized in "Petersburgian" politics during the period of European imperialism.

news of mobilization in 1914; the patriotic upsurge of the war's first years was hysterical and semi-conscious and, almost unnoticed, transitioned into a delirious, epileptic agitation toward revolution, civil war, and Bolshevism.

It is only natural that the internal unity of the abovementioned stages and changes in Russia's social attitudes in no way overcame but, on the contrary, confirmed the idea of the profound crisis in which Russian culture found itself at the outset of the war and the revolution; this fact nullifies the significance of the "renaissance" of the 1900s.

If it is at all justifiable to attempt, in a few words, to express the meaning of profound and complex historical phenomena, one might characterize the essence of the Russian revolutionary process – both over the course of prolonged and varying phases of preparation and in the real forms of its manifestation – with the following three words: *self-apostatizing*, *self-loathing*, and *self-combatting*.

These terrible distortions of Russian self-consciousness, possessing their own long-running tradition, have at the same time always been capable of transforming into the most variegated and often contradictory forms and appearances. It is precisely now – equally to find a real way out of the current situation and for spiritual and ideological self-restoration – that it is necessary to deepen the understanding of those phenomena of Russian culture, which have long been and continue to be sources in relation to the Russian essence revolutionary poison.

II

The Russian Revolution was primed and unleashed on two apparently different, yet immediately mutually conditioning levels: that of the socio-political and that of the religio-cultural. Only now, when the old Russia has collapsed, as we approach the subsequent events broadly, perceptively, and dispassionately, is it possible to uncover the roots and scope of her terrible revolutionary disease; as it turns out, we can now observe the full degree and multiplicity of the distortion that took place in pre-revolutionary Russian being. This is precisely a distortion, and it prevented the majority of Russian society from understanding the reality of the impending horrors to come; it is because of this distortion that the circles of social authority lacked the comprehension and decisiveness necessary to sacrifice the small and the personal in order to save the whole and the common.

If one interprets historical events from the perspective of practicality, adhering to purely material evaluations as one does so, then the second Russian Revolution indeed presents itself as a stupid and senseless act of self-destruction and regression. However, the entire picture into which the Revolution has now developed, its distinct facts, manifestations, and appeals – its very being and inclinations – bear unmistakable witness to the fact that, beginning as an agrarian social movement, it became more complex on the way to broadening itself with some other meaning and content, which to this day is derided by communism and, therefore, is still not fully understood.

The agrarian revolution itself did not predetermine the horrible war that the people then declared against its whole cultural class without understanding that, in many cases, this approach implied the people's self-destruction. The socialists immediately obscured the original meaning of this cultural struggle with their own fanatical party slogans of destruction; and, as strange as it sounds, we must acknowledge that, in destroying the authentic values of Russian culture, the Bolsheviks were in many respects fulfilling the direct will of the people. The Revolution revealed the Russian popular masses' hatred toward and lack of adaptability to a host of facts and phenomena proper to pre-revolutionary culture. The people, therefore, were able to accept the slogan of class struggle so easily and elementally precisely because they sensed in it not only a chance to settle accounts with the property-owners, but also the possibility of delivering themselves from the yoke of

Ideas and Methods

an alien culture which had long been in the process of creating an incomprehensible type of person and had long supplied this alien type with property inaccessible for others.[65] This fateful idea in the people's consciousness about the prerogatives of the ruling cultural class[66] – and consequently about the foundations of power, in which the fact of property endowment and the legal exclusivity of the "upper classes" was inextricably merged with the alien nature of their internal culture and external image – testified to the deep decomposition of authentic and healthy principles of governance. And, to a certain extent, this popular understanding was not wrong: the imperial authority and reigning circles of power had long before headed onto a path of dissociation with their "primitive" component (to be understood here as the primordial essence of a worldview dictated by the elemental nature of Russia, bearing its own ontological sources and determining the fundamental meaning, way of life, and style of both religio-national being and the everyday life of Russia). By the same token, psychological and day-to-day governmental conditions were created under which the people began to feel *uncomfortable*; they found themselves in a state of "moral alarm" – indeed, in a "great

---

65 One may say with full justification that, in the style and mode of life among the pre-revolutionary petty-landowner class, the people saw something culturally hateful that had long incensed them which, in turn, imbued the agrarian revolution with a particularly cruel and, at first glance, mindlessly destructive character. This should be especially emphasized, as the first onslaught of rebellions against the provincial agricultural estates was decisive in the entire further development of the revolution; we hear echoes of it up to today in hateful slogans against the "master [*barin*]" and the "lord [*gospodin*]."

66 In the context of the current essay, the concept of the ruling class is to be understood in its fullest possible breadth as the culmination of all individual forces directing and actively regulating the state and social life of the people. When the life of the state is healthy, the principle of *governing tradition* is inseparably bound up with the selection of an indeterminate, external governing milieu – with *organic cooptation*. Only the moribund conditions of Russia could have led to the situation during the period of the final tsars, when both "tradition" (here to be understood as historical power) and "selection" (the nobility and, in general, the privileged elements of the country), having been stripped of all coherence or memory of mutual interests, declared the cruelest imaginable war upon one another, as a result of which both sides ended up equally annihilated.

Ideas and Methods

state of isolation" – and could not organically integrate into the system of political life and its dynamics.

It would be a false folk idealization to think that, while the landed class and intelligentsia were giving themselves up to worship of the West without circumspection, the Russian people continued to stand rigid guard over their self-essence. The decay impacted the people as well, but, of course, it is strictly the tempters and exemplars, incapable and unwilling to set governmental and cultural sanctions and develop the raw "primitivity" of the people, who are to blame.

Whatever the historical crossroads and deviations of the people, no matter how capricious their fate, the tradition of power and the selection of rulers – as defining elements of the nation for themselves and for the common benefit of historical action – must provide and watch over affairs, so that the people's memory and consciousness does not lose its ability, even if only in rare and decisively critical cases, to appeal for the sake of self-verification and self-location to their primordial historical principles, and so that they might renew their link to them by way of the past. In order to ensure this, the most important requirements are a sound intuition of state, durability, and an organic directedness, at least in relation to active historical transformations. In the general balance of the people's historical values, which are being summed up at any given moment, unconsciously, immutably and symbolically, it is crucial that significant values concretely govern the ways in which national entelechy is observed, forcing a reconciliation with the entire mass of inescapable historical sins, errors, and malicious acts. The positive foundations of national historiosophy must be recognized intuitively and steadfastly in order to overcome the origin of historical evil, which has its own memory and the ability to genetically transform and pass in different forms from generation to generation, from era to era. Therefore, we may clearly comprehend the full degree of responsibility set upon the shoulders of the leading cultural minority, whose duty it is to actively acquaint new generations with the religio-historical values of their past. Violations of this process of assimilation always lead to a conclusion in which the elemental forces of the people cease to understand themselves and are drawn into a wrathful self-loathing and self-destruction. It is precisely this event which has occurred in Russia with her ruling elite and her people. There have been great misfortunes, fateful failures, and sins in Russian history, as there has been a chain of mutually determinant negative historical facts reaching far into the past. But there has naturally been, and continues to be, a procession of sacred, great, and immutable historical values as well. However, the chain of favorable inheritance has been broken in several places and for varying durations by the culturally dominant class; and, at a critical moment when the imperial power was being crushed, the link to the historically primitive, necessary for rediscovering the national self, has proved unrecoverable, and it was by then impossible to draw strength and knowledge from Russia's organic depths. As a defining component of the "White movement", the voluntarist impulse to defend those values that the revolution had attacked was both sacrificial and heroic, but historically it was doomed, if only because it was based solely on impulse and noble reflexes. Therefore, being in possession of all ethical and logical data relating to the rightful succession of Russian state power, the White movement was nonetheless crushed by the Revolution, which managed in short order to accumulate within itself all of Russia's evils, both present and past, thereby attaining a seemingly organic resilience and false legitimacy. At the same time, as the volunteers were forced to act as "their own ancestors" and to exposit without confidence their sometimes ill-founded slogans of struggle, drawn from a fallen and oblivious governmental-social milieu, acting more like a military organization than a heroic militia composed of the people bearing an authentic idea and the will of the nation, the Bolsheviks, to their own advantage, concentrated all of Russian history into its negative meaning and, in so doing, took command of that history's living center; with the greatest reality, they stamped themselves not only with

Ideas and Methods

the traits of contemporary social-communism, but also with elements of the movement of Bolotnikov, Shakhovsky, Razin, and Pugachev.

From an external perspective, from the first moment of the conflict, the situation of the belligerents proved to be highly significant: the Revolution immediately took control of the center and forced those acting in defense of rightful state succession to fortify themselves on the outskirts. This situation decided in advance how the conflict would end. The capture of the center at the hands of the revolutionary forces immediately created a set of conditions that were substantially different from those in which Razin and Pugachev carried out their rebellions, during which the center had remained in the hands of the government and the landed class.

Along with the end of the White movement came the end of the leading role played by the noble-bureaucratic ruling class of the old Russia; for, in the form of the White armies, they suffered defeat, were internally unmasked, and not only were the generations of the current era and the recent past condemned, but so was the entire 200-year tradition of Russian cultural and state leadership in the spirit of Europeanization.

Several decades before the revolutionary defeat, at the end of the 19th century and the beginning of the 20th, the Russian authorities and ruling circles were faced with a difficult, but not fatal task: it was necessary to again delimit the sphere of reforms and evolution from the sphere of intransigent state-religious dogmatism, in order to be able to combine protection with broad state-social work.

The salvation of the Russian future depended on this redrawing of boundaries, for the increasing complexity of Russia's socio-economic structure had begun to combine unnaturally with the growing ideological struggle against the very foundations of Russian statehood. And only under the condition of a broad and creative initiative on the part of the government in the sphere of economic development did it seem possible to split this ugly fusion and oppose the revolutionary excitement with firm protection. Generally speaking, the evolution of the state may only progress fruitfully when its very normative, national, foundation-laying worldview stands behind it, as when a state religious dogma is bolstered and lives only through the flexibility and mobility (the evolution) of the governing apparatus which, in renewing everything in a conditionally living and changing state and adapting itself to the changing forms of life, all the more unshakably affirms the authority of its first foundations without profaning them in the course of day-to-day, pressing politics.

The government did not comprehend just how indispensable this redrawing of boundaries was and, quite rapidly, under the pressure of events, mistook complacency toward real reforms for preservation; and, in its caution, not wishing to upset the very prerogatives of the social order on the path of "applied" development, it undermined precisely those prerogatives. The concepts of revolution and reaction, evolutionism and conservatism, had become so mixed up that, at every turn in the course of the final tsarist reigns, the state waged a struggle against its own ruling class and saw enemies where there were still faithful subjects (it is an absurd fact that even Khomiakov, in his time, was suspected by the police of "disbelief in God and a lack of patriotism"; cases like these remained typical in perpetuity and had numerous analogues). The state feared precisely those reforms which could have reinforced the most destabilized social pillars.[67] Frequent cases in which the spiritual forces of Russian communality

---

67 In this sense, the fear of major transformation in church leadership and the return of her sacred rights is characteristic. Of course, this was an indication of the sinful caesarist-papist power tradition introduced by Peter which at times took on a malevolent aspect of blasphemy against the church (beginning with the reforms of Peter I himself, progressing into the reign of Catherine II, and ending in the church politics of empress Aleksandra Fedorovna). The government's perspective on problems of church renewal were officially voiced in a fully explicit manner in K. P. Pobedonostsev's response to S. Yu. Witte's note "On the Modern Situation of the Orthodox Church," disseminated to the members of the Ministers' Committee in February 1905. This response, dated 12 March 1905 and titled "State Secretary Pobedonostsev's Views on Questions Concerning Desirable Transformation in the Structure of Our Orthodox Church," is striking for its spiritual deafness and

Ideas and Methods

have been inadequately and, in some cases, totally unutilized bear brilliant witness to the non-correspondence between the practical and ideal requirements of state development in relation to governmental structure. A malicious "worldview liberalism" in society was, to a point, caused by governmental doggedness, as the government had no desire to understand the

---

its deadening of all religious feeling, paired with a nihilistic desolation. The themes which Witte discusses in his "Note" go essentially unmentioned in Pobedonostsev's text. In response to its fundamental thesis concerning the non-canonical character of the church reforms which took place under Peter I, Pobedonostsev writes, with pure formality, that "the Synod is a constant council." Further on, he draws the reader's attention to the fact that the consular principle [*sobornoe nachalo*] of the church leadership cannot be realized in Russia in light of the inconvenience of communicative channels – because of Russia's "vastness" and "dissipation" (!). Without the slightest wavering, Pobedonostsev demonstrates his willingness to consider the incidental convening of certain bishops as local councils. In response to the allusions of the "Note" to the fact that the Consistory, in taking the place of the canonical "council of presbyters," acts as a bureaucratic chancellery where the workers are suffocated by paperwork, Pobedonostsev calmly suggests that one cannot do without bureaucrats, for official "correspondence, as it proliferates, grows in other consistories up to 20,000 outgoing documents per year." Pobedonostsev describes the closed, caste-like nature of the clergy in a rather cynical manner as the consequence of their abundance of children, the majority of whom are predestined to secure sustenance and work for themselves in the very same office.

In general, the fundamental ideological positions of Pobedonostsev, as found in his abovementioned "Views," can be reduced to an acknowledgement of the full validity of "Spiritual Regulation"; and, in some of his surmises of this kind, we find the traits of a typical positivist "man of the sixties" and a blind, juridical dogmatist who sees in the past of Russian religion (the "period of the patriarchy") nothing more than "the lifelessness of ritual formalism and church routine," "superstitious habits," and "the ignorance of the pastors." He openly admits that "the events which took place at the end of the 17th and beginning of the 18th centuries showed that patriarchal leadership is dangerous for the government and, therefore, in the interests of the government's self-defense, there remained no other option than to annihilate it" (!?).

It is interesting and extremely typical that Pobedonostsev's conservatism is combined with his specific conviction that it is impossible to leave the "new world" and return to the interests of Rus' as it was in the 16th and 17th centuries; in his eyes, a contemporary "qualified priest," in comparison with the illiterate priest of the old times who "repeated the church services from memory in order to give sacrifice," undoubtedly harbored the new value of enlightened development and was an undeniable indicator of progress. We must search within this spiritual and historiosophical bankruptcy for an alignment and even fateful coincidence of ideas and methods belonging to the surviving conservatism with the tactics of violent revolution.

Ideas and Methods

full indispensability of a *methodological* and *applied* liberalism. This dimming of governmental self-awareness and concrete historical vision attests to an unprecedented and fatal internal impoverishment at the site of the very "ancient roots" on which Russian authority rested. Lacking within itself a living image of Russia, governmental power itself essentially had no faith in the real meaning of its sacred sources and, therefore, lacked the authority necessary to make others recognize that meaning. The very sacred words, concepts, and principles expressed by the government sounded like empty rhetorical formulae – like gold-leaf sentimentality – and only provoked a feeling of irritation which inevitably undermined the structural support and authority of the entire edifice of the state.

Meanwhile, the period following 1905 was objectively the time to comprehend the full imminence of a real, liberational revolution, and its initiative at the cost of any sacrifice for the sake of saving the psychological foundation upon which the statehood which circumscribed the being of the people was affirmed.[68] But instead of a "second epoch of great reforms," which was to be observed only in the activities of Stolypin,

---

[68] Even if one were to abstain from a strict and responsible evaluation of such phenomena as the state "legalization" of the workers' movement in the time of Zubatov and Gapon, the participation therein of the police department, the "union of the Russian people," and various other political "brotherhoods," and even if one were to ascribe the most favorable view possible to all of these, one would nonetheless be obliged to recognize that, in all of the state's methods of struggle against the first revolution, we find indications of degradation in that "moral force" of which Benkendorf spoke in his day at the foundation of a corps of gendarmes; it is this fact which speaks of the total, moribund impotence of the authorities, who knew neither how to lead the young movement nor how to create a path of legality for it. Given a more precise analysis of all the conditions and events of that time, the judgments and actions of certain individual state representatives are shocking for their foresight and rectitude. However, history places not only individual figures on trial, but does so also with collectives, and only *collective* ingenuity – the instinct of the masses and of all authoritative groups and circles – is in a position, during critical moments, to deliver the people from the danger of self-induced disintegration and ruinous temptations. It was this collective reason and instinct that the ruling class from 1903-1905 (and in the period to follow) failed to evince; and the instinct of the common good and self-preservation (at the time, these concepts coincided), in the decadent complexities of competing interests and opinions, was unable to prevail and emerge the victor.

Ideas and Methods

who was not employed to the full capacity of his capabilities and went unsupported by the authorities themselves, the government went down the weak-hearted and insincere path of half measures and an uncertain "self-defense." The order and peace that had been restored after the events of the first revolution afforded the luxury of silence, both in relation to the danger of a new revolution, and to the necessity of a broad, sweeping wave of state creativity. As a result, the time during which it was possible to heal Russian statehood was irreparably squandered. So that weak people can find within themselves the strength for sacrifice, one must inculcate in them a lucid understanding of that in whose name the sacrifice is to be made; and, toward the end of the "critical" 19th century and the beginning of the insurrectionary 20th, the ruling circles of the country had lost their ability to partake in the living mystery of what was "primitively" Russian to such an extent that, in addition to their obliviousness to the common fate of the people, they lost not only the idea of sacrifice, but also the instinct of personal self-preservation.

This degeneration was all the more horrific for the fact that Russia has an exclusively great basis for possessing a strong and living feeling for the people's primitive nature and auto-legislative historiosophy, capable of defining her fate on governmental and spiritual levels, determining folk-historical tasks, and providing inspiration to her cultural vanguard.

Of all the peoples to have accepted true Eastern Orthodoxy, only the Russian people have been endowed simultaneously with a great gift and a most burdensome, inescapable yoke which demands that they historically manifest themselves on the scale and in the high style of an authentic great power.

Russia's historical being and even the very fact of her existence are determined by a certain unity-in-duality of the socio-ethnographic element with the religious, Orthodox one. This unity-in-duality should be viewed as a molecule, the primordial moment of Russia – of the Russian entity.

Therefore, in one's understanding of Russia and in the historical memory of her first foundations, these two principles must inevitably cross paths. Indeed, it is in the combination of Russia's religious chosenness and empirical endowments that we find the most terrible temptations of her history; though, on the other hand, only this affinity of *faith* and *spatial vastness, universality* and *national typicality*, provides an authentic ontological and historical form for Russia. It is for this reason that Russian imperialism bears as its responsibility and mission the imperative of being adequate to the objective meaning and value of its nation's metaphysics, in which the sole possible resolution of Russia's historical dialectic (those of an Orthodox great power) becomes possible.[69]

It is precisely Russia's historical endowment, combining a unique wealth of qualitative and quantitative values, Russian religio-national rudiments, and primordial, formational ethnographic forces in which the characteristic spiritual-ideological structure of Russian historiosophy finds its origin, which has ceased to serve as the real determinative foundation for state culture and for the politics of the ruling elite. Now that many facts of Russian history, along with their causal chains, have been revisited and reevaluated in the face of the Revolution, it would seem quite easy to imagine the essence of those processes that have lead to this fateful degeneration, even when considered in a condensed schema.

The disintegration and depersonalization of the ruling class has progressed along two streams: the first stream was

---

69 The meaning and metaphysics of Russian great-power statehood was deeply comprehended by Khomiakov when he said, "A power greater than others presents the soul with a manifestation of that high and, until now, unreachable aim of the peace and good will among men to which we are called; because, when realized, a spiritual union among millions raises the soul of man higher than even the very closest of connections between a few thousand; because visible and unceasing enmity always rears its head near the narrow borders of minor societies, and because the abolition thereof ennobles and calms the heart; and because, finally, by means of the mysterious (and, perhaps, comprehensible) sympathy between the spirit of man and the full scope of society, grandeur of mind and thought itself belongs only to great peoples." (In response to an essay by I.V. Kireevsky, 1852).

Ideas and Methods

determined by the state authority's irreversible drive to create a techno-bureaucratic apparatus for the formal and formulaic satisfaction of requirements imposed by a police state modeled after an uncritically adopted Western form. The second stream followed the line of cultural degradation as a result of the artificial adaptation of ancestral nobility and governmental bureaucracy to Western cultural-ideological principles which, at times, made no good sense even in their original homelands. Then came the emergence of those social elements which gradually formed into the revolutionary intelligentsia, beginning from the 1840s and ending with the Russian Communist Party, in correspondence with the process of disintegration which occurred among the national ruling class; for, between the two above-mentioned streams of development, bereft of the flow of real Russian life, a Russian people formed who lacked both a spiritual and everyday settlement, for whom the state which had given them birth either could not or would not find a creative application. From this class, over a span of generations, especially beginning in the 1860s, came about that configuration of Russian *raznochintsy*[70] and revolutionaries who were inimical in equal measure to both the Westernizing faction of the Russian nobility and bureaucracy, and to the Russian people. For a number of fateful reasons (and, most of all, to the unity of the ideological source which nourished these changes), a sort of interpenetration, mutual exchange, and conditionality was established among the landed class, the bureaucracy, and the *raznochintsy* belonging to the intelligentsia; and it was precisely this circumstance which bolstered and magnified the accumulation of that specific poison known as Russophobia in all three groups; at the same time, the opposing constructive forces were prevented from reinforcing themselves and realizing some kind of state and

---

70 [Trans.]: A term literally meaning "people of varying ranks," *raznochintsy* refers to a specific Russian social estate which incorporated the lesser court and governmental ranks, some children of the nobility, and military veterans; later, in the 19th century, the term was associated with the middle and lower-middle merchant and educated classes. Many members of the intelligentsia were considered *raznochintsy*.

cultural activity on a large scale. A shameful cabal of a sort had been cemented: the ruling class (internally falling apart itself) did much to provoke the revolutionary intelligentsia, while the revolutionary manifestations of the latter faction provoked a new, often reflexive and uncritical resistance from the government, which went on to impose an oppressive regime upon society and the people. Starting from the latter half of the 19th century, these extra-social processes were found to be in a particular and characteristic conjunction with the general imperialistic politics of Russia. With its typically Western principles and methods, Russian imperialism worked in direct concert with the social Europeanization of Russia; consequently, it possessed its own unique link with every trend that set as its task the neutralization of the spiritual-national principle essential to Russia by means of inculcating cultural elements of an alien nature; and, simultaneously, from the direction of these very same trends, Russian imperialism drew enraged incomprehension and internal hostility for the entire guise and impulse toward the expansion of Russian great-power statehood.

The circumstances were such that conscious and semi-conscious popular-public criticism of the state principles of that time could not lead to the desired transformation, and only led to the kind of power struggle and abuse of one's own power that became one of the most corrosive elements in the revolutionary ideology of the Western intelligentsia. Thanks to the absence of any clear way out of the situation, healthy opposition to foreign templates of governance easily morphed and were distorted into the typical psychology and tactics of revolution; however, because of its own Western roots, the revolutionary approach corresponded to the Westernizing conservatism of the reigning authority.

One must take lucid stock of the fact that it was precisely the authority of the Russian state which first threw down the gauntlet of burgeoning popular autonomous initiative and set an internally false dilemma before Russia concerning her development: should Russia become cultured Europe or barbaric Asia? In doing so, the state was not even conscious of the possibility of a third way – the development of a self-determining Russian culture.

If, in the epoch of Peter I, an inclination toward the West had provided Russia with truly new possibilities for the realization of her natural capacities as a great power, then in the latter tsarist reigns, this inclination had become strictly pestilential, for it had begun to distort the very style and internal sense of the Russian state. The reigns of Peter III, Catherine II, Pavel I, Alexander I, and Nikolai Pavlovich, despite their vastly different values, progressed nonetheless under one common sign – the state-driven Europeanization of Russia; in the course of this process, the supreme authority naturally disintegrated and lost its organic foundations, exchanging them for eclectic ideologies and theories of power; within these theories, memories of the Muscovian-Byzantine rule of orb and scepter were bizarrely combined, at different periods, with ideas first of French royalist absolutism, then of the Austro-Prussian police state and militarism. But perhaps the worst evil insinuated into the organic development of Russia was caused by those official ideas and governmental-international tactics which led to Russia's participation in the reactionary internationals which began at the end of the reign of Alexander I and the 1840s; this very well could be the place where one ought to seek the conception of our current revolutionary international. Fearing the French Revolution and the subsequent sociopolitical process that had taken place in Europe, Russian reaction began to build a barrier against these possibilities by setting the entire organic structure of Russian life in active opposition against revolutionary Europe; at that time, the organicity of Russian life was seen as the direct antithesis of all that had transpired in Europe; the reactionaries would realize this opposition by promoting an abstract, cosmopolitan doctrine of guardianship and by conducting a reactionary form of Europeanization in Russia, which primarily and naturally required that the Russian people be suppressed – that they be excluded from playing an active role in social life. The living subject of statehood was to be transformed into an object of idiosyncratic and frequently mercenary patronization and even exploitation; the inert continent of the people served as the basis for introducing into life the idea – bearing no relation to the national interests or requirements of Russia – of maintaining a pan-European order.[71] The significance of this entire system of ideas and politics to the general process of de-nationalizing the ruling class has yet to be sufficiently understood by the broad public; but it is precisely then, in the epoch of Nikolai Pavlovich, that we must seek the fruition of that malignant social metamorphosis which ultimately turned the majority of the ruling and civil class in Russia into typical representatives of faceless international dignity and classless bureaucracy. Now that we have seen the full expression of the process by which the *raznochintsy*-intelligentsia have fully fallen away from the sources of Russian culture, resulting in a naked contempt for all things Russian, we must understand and remember with a heightened sense of responsibility that such a process is comparable to the disintegration of the ruling elites; this latter phase may be considered the initiatory one. In these times, we cannot dispense with an understanding of the causality of these processes (more specifically, the two aspects of one and the same process – the Russian state-cultural collapse), because responsibility for the Revolution is all too easily placed

---

71 In the context of our day, it would be interesting to recall the exceedingly notable book by Nikolai Danilevsky *Russia and Europe* (first published in 1869), which impresses one with its quality of authentic genius. This book contains a particularly brilliant and biting critique of Russian politics in the 19th century. In the second chapter, "Affecting Europeanness – the Disease of Russian Life," Danilevsky writes: "Instead of bearing the banner of the Cross and of liberation for truly oppressed peoples, we have become the knights of legitimism, the paladins of conservatism, the keepers of the sacred oaths of Versaille's *bon-ton*, as this is what is accepted by students of French emigres." This "heartfelt loyalty to European legitimism and conservatism" indeed dislocated the center of political activity from the interior of Russia and into Europe, naturally serving the political aims of Klemens von Metternich first and foremost.

Ideas and Methods

on the "intelligentsia," while "reaction" is seen by many as the revival of a trampled "truth" belonging to the pre-revolutionary autocracy.

The revolutionary intelligentsia (the *Narodniks*) were partially correct in their appropriation of the people's discontent. Nonetheless, revolutionary psychology's inability to accept the constructive value principles of the people's worldview spoiled the revolutionaries' whole critical approach and transformed a necessary unmasking into a revolt against God and a hatred of Russia. As concerns the ruling elites, their unwillingness to understand and rely on those concrete circumstances and features of Russian statehood which alone were capable of serving as her foundation led to the emergence of doubts as to the truth of the fundamental principles of religion and statehood, aiding in the oncoming adoption of exhortations in favor of nihilism and heresy. In this manner, the substantial values of the Russian state idea were debased due to a lack of lively critique and reformational initiative. While the radical intelligentsia defamed the most sacred dogmas and canons of the people's faith and daily life, considering these to be nothing more than barbarity and obscurantism, the government saw, falsely and ignorantly, political revolution where there were merely excessive peasant revolts; these revolts attested to the fact that the masses were not able to get used to the existing cultural and state standards of life. On the one hand, no one had the right to criticize; on the other, there were not enough such rights to promote and defend the organic character of Russian life. However, the reason for the two modes of cultural blindness mentioned above lay in a single factor: in both cases, people had lost the capacity to holistically comprehend the primitive elements of the nation, in which its positive and negative principles were so equally crucial in importance that, without an even-handed perception of what the people believed and rejected – without the ability to love and hate in equal measure along with the people – a fruitful approach to the people was impossible, and what was least realizable was a fruitful governance of the people in the course of state life.[72] Neither the attitude of the revolutionary intelligentsia, nor that of the ruling class, were responsive to this situation; and, even today, neither the monstrous Bolshevik contempt for the people, nor the restorative schemes of the emigrated monarchists correspond to its realities.

III

In order to find a viable bastion for the Russian restoration, we must return anew to a creative assimilation of the primitive sources of Russian being. *This is, first and foremost, a problem of worldview,* for creative primitivism, in all spheres and manifestations of human living, is the projection and realization of an autochthonous cast of consciousness; in this new consciousness, the whole multiplicity of spiritual and psychological phenomena belonging to human life – the entirety of vital events and processes – rests upon and is constructed in accord with certain precise laws of religious world-comprehension, combining the primordial and foundational with the ephemeral and incidental, and subsequently bringing these into a singular form. Put differently, all that is real in life is derived from an all-encompassing metaphysical unity. And, vice versa, perception of the entire concrete multiplicity of phenomena is erected (as though returning) into an immediate and organically whole contact with the first principle. In this manner, it is as though each phenomenon is enveloped in a certain circle, the beginning and end of which are one's very perception of life. (This special cast of consciousness, bearing upon various spheres of human activity and creativity, yields multifarious and adequate forms of incarnation; in the sphere of God-consciousness, this attitude allows for an internal,

---

72 Naturally, we are outlining here only the most general schema of the distortion of the Russian state and culture which, given a detailed analysis spanning separate epochs of Russian history, would require partial alterations so as to make our interpretations applicable to each era individually; in doing so, the schema would become significantly more complex, but the general sense would remain the same.

Ideas and Methods

regulated, and creative comprehension of dogmatology and of the philosophemes branching therefrom; in the sphere of ecclesiastical art, it provides the basis for those internal laws of construction proper to it which determine the phenomenon of style; in the sphere of real life, the orientation toward creative primitivity produces *everyday life* – as a *style* of life – and determines one's ability to correctly and regularly qualify *events*, which furnish the basis for both personal and spiritually collective [*sobornoe*] being.)

The necessity of turning to the original structure of a worldview in order to derive therefrom a meaning and a will to real action is, at present, great and pressing. The Bolsheviks themselves, despite all their attempts to sever Russia's historical roots and traditions and to strangle her primitivity and auto-genesis, are resurrecting Russia's religio-historical image against their own will and with all their might. They force us once more to trace and understand every sequence and chain of historical events in Russia's past, and to be inspired by the original principles thereof.

Both appeals of the orientation toward creative primitivism – which, today on the strength of the very events of the Russian catastrophe, is the sole fruitful form which any worldview can take – must be expressed: both in the direction of our religious first ground, and in that of state constructivism. For the Revolution has given us two experiences: the living reflections of Russia's primordial endowments – the experience of rebellion against God [*bogoborchestvo*] and of divine sight [*bogovidenie*], as well as the experience of the elemental turmoil which, nonetheless, is of the greatest significance to our statehood. In rejecting at every turn the crudely calculating assault on the value of faith, we ought, however, to recognize that nature itself, quality, the sense and the meaning of events which we are now experiencing, make the intersection of practical plans of action and contemplative religiosity indispensable; modern, everyday phenomena have transcended the edifice of concepts belonging to formal politics and sociology.

There are epochs in which people perceive God, and there are epochs in which people are deaf to Him. In our time, the veils lying between the earthly and providential spheres have thinned, and one truly gets a sense of the world's dependence upon forces that are of an alien nature in relation to it. We may directly say that, in these days, religious experience is accessible to anyone, provided he is somewhat vigilant in his circumspection. And if the European West is no longer capable of precipitating a religious renaissance on the scale of a broad mass movement – if the very "striving for harmonious accord" has now apparently vanished there – then the task set before Russia of comprehending its exclusive spiritual experience, gained within the catastrophe of Revolution, and of finding the right words and appeals for the widespread activity of a new "epoch of faith", is made all the more urgent. First and foremost, this experience forces all who have more or less spiritually reinforced themselves to come out from their closed circle of personal, intimate perception of God and into the sphere of general religious action. Only the growth of primitive, religious elementality on the part of confessional forces, through which meta-history is built, being plastically incarnated in images and events, in which the miraculous and the blessed is inseparably connected to the simple and the real – only this can determine the concentration of will required to overcome the Revolution and to erase its evil.

Russian Orthodoxy has always gravitated toward external, substantial self-unfolding without, however, any sense of a conscious cultural sanction. To the contrary, the Russian enlightenment took every measure in struggling with an incriminating ritualistic faith and the ritualistic "excesses" of the Russian construction of daily life. But now, the full scope of the fatal danger posed by a faceless, amorphous, and petrified civilization has been defined with utter clarity, which inevitably leads to general disintegration, being a fundamental

Ideas and Methods

basis for religious soullessness and new iconoclasm. Therefore, the special task of uncovering the laws for a concrete realization of religious experience and, in conjunction with this, the justification of the so-called religious materialism of Russian Orthodoxy and the substantiation of its inner sense and social meaning (that of gracious pragmatism), stands before Russian theology and cultural philosophy (in the Russian spiritual type, both of these disciplines are particularly close to each other in original foundations), along with the efforts of the speculative theological intellect.

Standing in immediate connection with this task is the problem of Russian Orthodoxy's ecclesiastical style. In the creativity of the church, style is no mere proficiency or artful manner, often expressed through the multifarious lens of psychologism upon the soil of art, but turns out to be the criterion and sign of the deep, internal coherence of the true primordial foundations of worldview with their formally adequate realization. This rootedness of style within the very first-principle of the church also dictates a true and authentic ascent – the growth upward through this style toward a perception of the religious mystery, guaranteeing security from all external distortions and delightful illusions. In consequence, the true style of the church may become a universally applicable factor in purification, unification, and dispensation (which the monasteries have demonstrated in their time). In our age – that of the greatest socio-ecclesiastical fall – appeals to the stylistic regulations of religious creativity can and must become one of the forces for exhaustive self-evaluation and for a broad clarification of the essence of the church.

The Russian intelligentsia's orientation toward the values of Orthodoxy all the same bears the character of an unformulated religious awakening, often falling into the temptation either of religious pan-emotionalism and Latinophilia, or of neo-Schleiermacherism. Moreover, only an Orthodox confessional pragmatism, broadly and thoroughly understood, may become

Ideas and Methods

the disciplining and structuring principle of the Russian spiritual restoration. It was Gogol who called for Russia to be "our monastery," who urged Russia toward a harsh and heroic feat, nearly monastic for the "asceticism it entails." All the more does our current Russian reality, in which all of Gogol's phantoms have become waking life, demand even greater self-sacrifice and a severe bearing of the spirit and will!

Thus, too, must the tradition of Russian theology reinforce itself in our time of strife and the temptations of gnostic self-will, and must do so on the correct, confluent paths of spirituality, constitution, and benefit (Orthodox ecclesiastical pragmatism).[73]

IV

The fact that the spiritual-ideological auto-restoration of the intelligentsia would be impossible without a tenacious and disciplined adherence to the church, and that only this

---

73 One should here keep in mind that, until our current era, systematic theology figured only partially into a general conception of Russian God-consciousness [*bogosoznaniya*], whose primary and immediate organs and sources were the communal church liturgy, daily life, the wisdom of the elder clergy, and hagiographic literature. Of course, this phenomenon is not an accidental one, but rather one that deeply characterizes the Russian spiritual type and the very structure of Russian God-consciousness.

We may already find the elements of a systematic theology in the missives of the venerable Theodocia Pechersky, Iosif Volokolamsky, Filofei's coenobite, the monk Danil, Dmitry Rostovsky, and in the Kiev-Mogila school; but ancient "folk theology" is no less important, expressed for example in certain decrees voiced at the Stoglav Council, the Domostroi, the writings of Ivan the Terrible, and in many codifying monuments, in which the principles of *philokalia* occasionally carry within themselves a surprising structuredness and authentically living expressivity. Moreover, the whole tragic saga of the Russian schism and the Old Believers serves as a living picture of "folk theology," of real confessional torments, rooted in the depths of a specific religious experience and God-consciousness. In this respect, the chronicles relating to the schism are all remarkably interesting, from those of Archpriest Avvakum to those of the Denisov Brothers.

The foundation of systematic Russian theology was naturally laid by Khomiakov, who was rightly named by Yu. Samarin as the "teacher of the church," and it is toward his tradition that we must turn in our time in order to find an authentic path between the temptations of Latin "mystagogy" on one hand, and of the theological "methodology" of Protestantism on the other.

Ideas and Methods

adherence can save the current religious movement away from narrow self-foreclosure and set it on the path toward an authentic national movement is well attested in light of the total failure of the pre-revolutionary Russian "renaissance." Already after the 1905 Revolution, a widespread ideological switch had been observed in Russian social thought. "Nihilistic moralism" and militant materialism were condemned and, along with them, as expressed in the formulae found on the pages of *Vekhi*, came resounding calls for a "concrete idealism" and "religious humanism." And even before the formulations of *Vekhi*, the 1890s and early years of the 20th century progressed in Russia, as in the West, under the sign of religious languor and symbolist inclinations. This prefatory development of new socioeconomic ideals via a religious, romantic reaction against the "Men of the 1860s" (the prefatory development carried out by Vladimir Solovyov in *Vekhi*) was a highly indicative phenomenon in relation to Russian culture. However, no matter how radical this general change in inclinations may have seemed, it was actually incapable of influencing the broad course of developing events; and, despite claims of "renewed ideals," the second revolution broke out, now taking place under the fanatical leadership of those committed to the obsolete principles of militant materialism.

Pre-revolutionary Russia found itself in need of a widescale, socially constructive movement which would capture the entire girth of expired philistinism with its ideological content and objective directedness of will; and, at the same time, in leading the inflamed consciousness of the intelligentsia out of the circle of revolutionary idealization, it would manage to set before them the problems of the future in the aspect of creative national work and self-knowledge.

Unfortunately, however, the religious and ideological-social "renaissance" of the 1890s and first years of the 1900s was never transformed into widespread pan-national work. It had not become the task of the epoch and, instead, turned out to hold meaning for only a limited milieu within the intelligentsia,

Ideas and Methods

which was then undergoing its own internal crisis. The reasons for this lay primarily in the fact that the new tradition of Russian mysticism and romanticism, on the basis of its primordial substratum (Solovyovism), very quickly began to disintegrate and created in the subsequent generation a number of morbid and self-contradicting phenomena. And that epoch's general turmoil and dissolution made such phenomena inimical even to the values of the Russian church and state. It is sufficient merely to recall the blindness and tendentiousness of the way in which the intelligentsia evaluated the mystical *Khlysty* and other sects to recall the disfigured attempts made in that time to bring about a synthesis of religio-mystical surrogates with the militant politics of social-revolution – and to recall how easily and readily the public accepted mystagogical sermonizing, "mystical anarchism," aesthetic mysticism, and the inflamed mystalalia then being voiced as authentic religious enlightenment! Only by conclusively immersing oneself in the delirious mystifications of romanticism is it possible to explain the trembling assent with which a certain faction of the non-materialist intelligentsia received the falsely heroic pathos of Revolution. It is in this fact that the whole internal kinship between revolutionary romanticism and pseudo-religious, extra-ecclesiatical "God-seeking" – the identical essence of their fruitless, inflamed emotionality – was unveiled.[74]

When one considers this process of spiritual obfuscation on the part of the intelligentsia in light of the disintegration of the ruling elites, the whole environment in which the forces of Revolution found themselves, realizing that it would cost

---

74 A characteristic phenomenon of the obfuscated and morbid epoch of the 1900s was the brilliant personality of the now completely forgotten arch-monk Serapion Mashkin. Being an exalted mystic, ascetic, an active professor, and a creatively potent theologian, all while sermonizing on "societies of just laborers" and the "circle of the just," he referred to socialists as brothers all over the world and made open justifications for the idea of just terror, which he identified with the Red Terror. It is interesting that revolutionary Marxist circles, with benevolence (and not without justification), opposed the active "ascetic" mysticism of S. Mashkin to the "salon-and-drawing-room," "verbal" mysticism of Chulkov, V. Ivanov, Merezhkovskii, and other "modernist" mystics.

Ideas and Methods

them nothing to take advantage of the moment in order to turn Russia toward the ideological atavism of Mikhailovsky, Chernyshevsky, Dobrolyubov, et al, becomes comprehensible. It must be believed that, after all that has happened, the recent, yet to be defeated tradition of mysticism, along with the deviation toward "revolutionary idealism," will be forever rejected, and that contemporary generations will return to the societal pillars of Khomyakov, into the sphere of authentic God-consciousness, constructed and affirmed upon the axis of ecclesiastical, dogmatic realism.[75]

Only this attitude – removing the anti-religious attitude toward dogma, seen as a schematized scholastic fiction, and replacing it with an organic understanding of Christian dogmatology as simultaneously a universal method of human knowledge and the blessed limit and norm of that knowledge while revealing mysterious regularity of the world and its processes – can lead to the problem of authentically ideal pragmatism in its full scale and universal applicability. And it will do this as only a part of a larger whole – allowing for the construction of a system of formal sociology and for the discovery of paths and norms that establish a new system for the coming social life. In this case, it is the Russian revolutionary experience which requires us to denounce all pseudo-ethical and political prejudices and to arm ourselves with a strictly empiric method, thereby separating the realm of the material from that of psychological temptations in order to draw up universal laws for the spirit and the flesh.

---

75 At times, a perhaps blasphemous thought emerges that Christianity calls upon itself such terrible revolt as a result of the fact that too much has been given and unveiled within it, that the human psyche and consciousness, without a voluntary and consciously predisposed probation, is incapable of simply withstanding such a level of revelation with respect to transcendent reality. It is more difficult to believe in a real miracle than to believe in an abstractly rational schema or utopia. It is precisely for this reason that Christianity affords such great meaning to repentance and general spiritual predisposition, without which the laying bare of the Mystery becomes unbearable – a coarsening temptation. "God is light and tells us of His luminosity to those to whom he is united in accord with their level of purification" (the venerable Simeon, *The New Theology*, 25th Saying).

Ideas and Methods

The socioeconomic idealism found in the Russian renaissance of the 1900s, which emerged as a reaction to orthodox Marxism, did nothing in essence to associate itself with the religio-mystical ideas of its time, but instead based itself on the autonomous principles of idealist humanism. Because of this, the Slavophiles' attempt at synthetically formulating the religio-historiosophical and sociopolitical problem was partially perverted and, ultimately, forgotten.[76]

Recent events have now shown us to what extent the fragmented and autonomous arrangements of particular and private problems, uncoordinated with the fundamental routes of Russian being, are alien to Russian consciousness and historical reality. Russian Bolshevism is nationalistic insofar as it embodies (in an admittedly disfigured form) the Russian people's national demand that the problems of their being are posed with the utmost concision and in their all-encompassing entirety. Naturally, it is now useless to ponder what might have come to pass if there had been a closer mutual relationship and influence between the two fundamental tendencies of pre-revolutionary Russian consciousness, one having been determined by Vladimir Solovyov, and the other by Petr Struve. To suggest that conditions might have changed for the better can hardly be countenanced since, in the mystonomic conceptions of Vladimir Solovyov, at times having exhausted the pathos of his creativity in deliberate self-association with certain regular schemas rooted in an essence deeply alien to Orthodoxy, there was much for Russian national Orthodoxy to reject; this could be observed in the works of some of Solovyov's epigones. However, this in itself does not strip responsibility from the leaders of that day's novel socioeconomic tendencies; such leaders did not comprehend

---

76 In the current day, as we criticize the various socioeconomic conceptions of the Slavophiles with complete justification, we ought nonetheless to understand the full significance of their basic premise, which consisted in the development of a synthetic Russian worldview that would allow for the possibility of coordinating the whole practical and actual regime of the state and society with the ontologically primary being of the Russian faith.

Ideas and Methods

the necessity of promoting a formal critique of Marxism along with providing a system of first-principle values belonging to a national-organic worldview that could be opposed to the false ontology of socialism. In that case, patriotic pathos was by no means sufficient. The shadow of Vladimir Solovyov that had fallen across the newly reborn religious consciousness of the intelligentsia, and the fact of Petr Struve, around which the new pathos of social-patriotic feeling had concentrated with the greatest brilliance – as phenomena of Russian culture, summoned in the pre-Bolshevik decade to define the renovation of broad societal circles in Russia on the basis of a worldview – turned out to have been equally unlucky. And this lack of luck was symptomatic: in the sphere of Russian spiritual life, foreign ontological elements (which were undoubtedly present in the Latinizing philosophy of Vladimir Solovyov) always proved exclusively harmful, dismantling the surrounding cultural environment with the fundamental otherness of its own principle; and without an organic connection to the profound bases of Orthodox being and its historiosophy, neither the notion of Russian "Patriotica," nor that of "Great Russia" is thinkable.[77]

Now, after the Revolution, the restoration of a conception of an organic worldview that unites within itself both the

---

[77] In any attempt to determine the fundamental trends in the social life of pre-revolutionary Russia, one encounters the fact of the "Kadets." No matter how great its role between the first and second revolutions might have been, it would have been possible to characterize the actions of the Kadets internally as "political aestheticism." Being deprived of essential religious and organic roots, and not possessing a feeling for the true economic and national essence of Russia, the party of "Kadets" was totally defined by a political formalism and by tendencies toward Western-Enlightenment "decency" (Anglomania); given this fact, the Kadet party united around itself a large number of people whose qualifications came not from a force of internal gravitation, but from their demonstration of a certain, specified "good tone," which at the time was perfectly natural and, to a certain point, even lawfully ordained in light of the degeneration and the lack of style which characterized the then government. However, the "Kadet renaissance" in Russian social life and its style of political snobbery quickly evinced the full reality of its ghost-like, illusory nature, its detachment from the organism of Russia, and its essential miscomprehension of the laws of that organism's being. The Kadets' readiness to relinquish power was typical of them.

problematics of religion and culture and the idea of formal sociology is an urgent necessity. The real matters of the state must be welded into the chain of a broad cultural-ideological movement. Politics and economics must be associated in our times with religio-cultural symbolism and historiosophy; and this symbolism and historiosophy must, within the multidimensional expanse of events, create the required plastic forms and images. Moreover, the politics of both "rightists" and "leftists" are extraordinarily lacking in their comprehension of the tasks which stand before them. This is for no other reason than because the entirety of anti-Soviet politics expressed by those in emigration, moving along their own arbitrary paths, is steadily and progressively falling out of the stream of Russian culture; in their interpretation of events and their various prognoses, the true meaning, scale, and rhythm of that which is occurring vanishes. There is evidently some degree of confusion in spiritual vision, of psychological distortion, and of error in the very methods for discerning the truth which prevents the circles of Russian emigration, in their activities up to now, from finding an orientation toward the very historical essence of the Russian Revolution; and, without this, one cannot even begin to think of building a system of political action. In this sense, both "rightists" and "leftists" find themselves in an identical position, and this is quite significant.

Thus have events transpired; such have been the historical conditions of Russian life that the concepts of conservatism and liberalism have never been simple categories of formal application in Russia. To the contrary, in the face of governmental conservatism, fraught with its foolish, bureaucratic insensitivity to reality and by the pre-revolutionary bravado of the "Black Hundreds" – in the face of every sort of liberal tendency, in whose bosom, it goes without saying, the Russian Communist Party gradually formed – it is as though there were always two types of worldview at war with each other. Usually, these two worldviews are regarded as polar opposites, setting aside the

Ideas and Methods

fact that they are both no more than projections from different sides of one and the same essence – Russian nihilism. This nihilism, serving as the inner foundation for a terrible type of Russian spiritual underdevelopment and receiving expression on all levels of Russian society, long considering itself to be the principle of universal negation, was practically reduced and continues to be reduced to a blasphemous predation upon the hierarchical structure of an organic worldview; and this has led to an installation of arbitrary objects of self-deification. The violation of the hierarchical principle, which undoubtedly characterizes the activities of the Russian revolutionaries, was at times the grievous sin of those attempting to preserve the Empire as well. This was expressed with particular clarity during the pre-revolutionary period when the structures of authority were disintegrating. In opposition to revolutionary radicalism, which "perfected" its methods and ideological demagoguery with each passing generation, governmental conservatism was unflaggingly dismantled as time went on, and this was eventually disclosed in a number of its unnatural fusions and juxtapositions of different ideological and tactical elements, often incompatible and even hostile toward the state which mobilized them. This circumstance critically muddied the substrate which nourished and continues to nourish the religious, preservative consciousness of Russia. On the other hand, the supreme values of the Russian spirit and Russian culture – with which the fallen regime of the final era of imperial Russia only falsely identified itself for the sake of calculation and politics – were everywhere reviled in Russian society. In the actions of that regime's representatives who have survived to the present, such a false identification continues as an elementary basis for their tactics and propaganda. Today, the work of fracturing and deconstructing these unlawful fusions and of giving an exhaustive definition to the essence and composition of both "Russian liberalism" and "official Russian conservatism" stands before us. We cannot do without elucidating the mutual relations of these two camps, in both their historical-genetic and systematic aspects, nor without clarifying their relationship to the true religio-national essence of Russia. Perhaps then the usual signs which oppose these two types of worldview will be finally replaced with the sign of their coordination.

Until this is accomplished, the true order of things, both for the "right" and the "left," will remain essentially unintelligible; this will continue to be the case until those on the right finally break with their method of defaming supreme values and recognize the primacy of religion, the Church, and the national-historical will above the organizational principles of power and political order; this is to say that our state of affairs will persist until the right moves away from its reactionary nihilism and the left, on its part, perceives and accepts the utterly unchanging essence of the positive Russian worldview. Only in this reciprocal metamorphosis will it be possible to derive a basis for reconciliation between society and the authoritative party which is so necessary for the future of Russian statehood. But, so far, this solution is contradicted both by the stubbornness of socialist circles who consciously have no desire to disengage with the worldview rudiments of their formal sociological positions, and by the rigidity of right-wing tendencies which remain, as before, dominant in their restorational plans through a false semblance of preservation, a right-wing anti-hierarchical arrogance which leads to the total falling out of these tendencies from the structure of actual culture and which guarantees their hostility toward it.

The most recent circumstances underline with special clarity the unresolvable crisis of the former ruling class. Relying, at one end, on Orthodoxy – in trying to turn a forced religious movement into a spiritual bastion of reaction and thereafter depending on it as if on the primitive ground of Russian history – the restorational legitimism which splits off into a number of different interpretive camps simultaneously, in the sphere of politics, wishes in no way to return to the primitive ground of folk-state creativity; on the contrary,

Ideas and Methods

this faction is attempting as quickly as possible to set ready-made formal schemes in place where one should instead pose the problem of authority and state-building in its full scale and creative immediacy. The moment of legitimism, which may in itself be undebatable in the practical and ideological conception of monarchy, is nothing more than a dead, yet provocative formula in the conditions of contemporary Russia. The crisis of Russian monarchism is exceedingly profound; it is connected both with the clouding of the very idea of the monarchy among the folk masses, and with the personal and social disintegration of recent bearers of supreme power who have fallen from the sphere of Russian culture, , as well as the circles close to them who stood and informed the power of its external appearance and instilled the basic principles of governance. Now, the utter falseness and morbid degeneration of official style belonging to the pre-revolutionary epoch, and of all of its concepts, ideas, and presuppositions, stands forth especially sharply in memory and is becoming more obvious.

Besides this, one should always remember that the absolutization of the conditional and the finite leads invariably to the devaluation of whatever is of value within such things. In the common hierarchy of the people's spiritual-historical values, the principle and fact of power are, naturally, subordinate and intermediate values. To this fundamental situation, in the environment of contemporary Russian reality, is also compounded a whole series of real conditions and circumstances: the absolutization of dynastic legitimism is overthrown by the historical fact of Revolution, by which all the concrete conditions and the socio-juridical structure of the former power are annihilated, both in generations immediately affected by the catastrophe, and in the foundational positions on governance belonging to the past. For anyone who has faith in the monarchical strength of the Russian people and who, in this light, takes sober stock of the radical reconstruction of the contemporary social environment of Russia, the sole advisable undertaking may become, along with a total dissociation from the notion of restoration, the conscious formulation of those juridico-religious norms and the preparation of that spiritual, psychological organizational structure which, being place face-to-face with the monarchical will of the people, would have the power to decide the problem of Russian tsardom in its full breadth, renovation, and historical reality; in other words, this could be effected by means of raising and affirming the prerogative of a new dynasty, seen as a living focal point for all the creative achievements of the new epoch. The conscious act of selection would indeed impress a profound renewal of Russia's social and state organization and would redeem all traditions, associations, and styles of the pre-revolutionary monarchy, which was unable to establish itself in that which was necessary and imposed by duty, and which fell due to its acceptance of impotence and the diseases of its enemies. Moreover, such an act would open up the possibility of creating a new idea and a new visage of the Russian Tsar.

Speaking about the restoration of the leading supremacy of power, one must take the utmost care in relation to the idealization of that form of its restoration known as "Bonapartism." In essence, "Bonapartism" is not an overcoming of revolution, nor is it the negation thereof; it consciously continues to be a revolution, merely having transformed and adapted itself to the requirements of statehood. The Russian Revolution is primarily an auto-denunciation, a catastrophic unveiling of the very depths of the falsehood of the culture and state of Europeanized Russia. Therefore, the exit from Revolution must be found in a radical negation of everything which led to it. In itself, Revolution is evil and, besides this, a symptom of evil – an evil of that which is internal and of the past which gave birth to it, on the basis of which we are given the ability to make a diagnosis. And so, to overcome the Revolution, we must first of all remove its sources and the first causes which called such a symptom into being. "Selection," understood as the outcome of Revolution, containing within itself the entirety of the revolutionary experience, the creative

Ideas and Methods

forces of uprising, and an acknowledgement of the new socio-economic reconstruction, would at the same time be an exit from Revolution, a concrete symbol depicting our refusal of its spiritual-ideological bases, a real sign that the new times have commenced. In the arrogant auto-coronation of Bonapartism, there can be no question of exiting the sphere of Revolution, since it is only in its connection with the ideas, emotionality, and methods of Revolution that it acquires its stability. If we consider that "restoration" is just as connected to the psychology of pre-revolutionary decadence as "Bonapartism" is defined by the essence of Revolution then, with regard to the obvious indispensability of a radical refusal of both, "selection" arises alongside "legitimism" and "Bonapartism" as the third and perhaps only desirable principle of the supreme restoration of power, into which truly new and creative possibilities for the establishment of power could be incorporated...[78]

Since none of the "rightists" pose the problem of the Russian monarchy in this particular form, we can say that all monarchist movements, as well as social liberal ones, are only bad reminiscences, interfering with sermons that allow the free assimilation of the meaning of everything that happens. Of course, it is simpler and less spiritually tumultuous to give oneself up wholesale to the next self-induced belief and, unwilling to see the reality of the situation, to feed oneself from year to year with one or another manic hope and to console oneself with an illusory future. But a vision of the Russian historical perspective, to some degree unobscured, is decisively immune to such an arrogant anti-historical approach to events. If Russia has been allotted a great future, then this future consists first of all in a difficult and creative trial, in which Revolution must be organically overcome. The people belonging to the previous ruling class and circles of

---

[78] The internal differences between these three principles are interesting primarily from a methodological perspective. It is self-evident that real circumstances, if events were to turn Russia onto the path of monarchy, would allow for the combination and apparent transformation of the two latter principles [Bonapartism and selection] in the most unexpected manner.

the oppositional intelligentsia are incapable of such an act of overcoming, for they are historically bound by a protracted and absurd struggle for power and Revolution – and now they have been witheringly exposed. This burdensome state of mutual conditioning in the past and present prevents either group, lacking the convictions to understand their mistakes and to head from their respective directions toward a single goal, from restoring Russian statehood. Memories of the recent past are so torturous that no one in the next few generations will live them down; and it is truly inhuman and unwise, after all that has occurred, to inculcate the demand for Russia not only to forget and forgive this past, but even to find inspiration in it, and to restore once again the right of even a single figure bearing connection with it to govern.

It is plain to see that the future must be founded on new generations, new people that are not tied in such direct ways to the germ of Revolution and, therefore perhaps better able to understand the forms for overcoming and undoing it. However, one ought not lose sight of the fact that the "new" generations, both in Russia and in emigration, find themselves in a difficult crisis, either morbidly struggling against the poison of Revolution or ultimately succumbing to it. If, on the practical level, a sort of qualitative selection has taken place in Russia (via a circumscription of new socio-economic and administrative forces), then an analogous process of crystallization in the spiritual-ideological sphere has yet to be observed. It is this circumstance which calls us with all urgency to do everything possible in order to open the eyes of all the "new" Russian people who have come to stand apart and have emerged upon the surface of life, and to demonstrate to them that the concept of revolutionary renovation has its limits (and very narrow ones), beyond which a disastrous disintegration and national death begins. If, at the beginning of the Revolution, communist fanaticism was unconsciously perceived by the Russian masses as a means, as energy for the realization of a social-agrarian revolution, it should be understood that, at present, this

Ideas and Methods

fanaticism has become a monstrous end in itself – and this must be understood first and foremost by those to whom the Revolution has actually given something. Since elements of a newly selected ruling class have already appeared in Russia, even if in embryonic form, those participating in this process must and shall understand that the new position which they have come to occupy also obligates them to take responsibility for the historical fate of their people; they are obligated to comprehend, with renewed strength, all the historical dogmas of Russia which were forgotten and distorted by the previous leaders of social and state life.

The Revolution ultimately crushed (an already long destroyed) normal succession in the cycle of Russia's culture-leading generations. At present, culture is guided on one hand by ideological forefathers and, on the other, by the revolutionary youth. Only that generation whose consciousness and experience carries the memory of the pre-revolutionary past, a conscious experience of Revolution, and an orientation toward the future, is capable of laying a sturdy foundation for the establishment of a new cultural succession; such a generation must combine these three elements of their consciousness into a kind of necessary and precise composition, and must define them in an exclusively effective proportion.[79]

Ultimately, the entire success of overcoming the revolution depends on this same circumstance, and, if by a whim of circumstances, the post-Bolshevik social reaction would begin to be led by such generations, in whose consciousness the combination of these moments would not lead to the necessary synthesis (due to an extreme attachment to the past, or to a total detachment therefrom), then the organic convalescence and correction of the damages sustained by Russian life would be threatened by a new danger.

It was not weak or frightened Russian people who overthrew the Tatar yoke; the hunted Rus' which was undergoing its first

---

79 This, of course, does not negate selection, both from the midst of the above mentioned generation, and from those generations adjacent to it.

age of enslavement was too impotent to accomplish that which the spiritually strengthened and reinforced later generations were. The internal yoke of Revolution can, of course, be overthrown sooner than that imposed by a foreign oppressor. But in our time, as in the 14th and 15th centuries, Russia will be liberated only by new people, for whom the hypnosis of revolutionary fear will not exist; but this will come with the condition that their spiritual strength be like that of the great historical ages of the past.

The idea of historic Russian pioneering, coinciding in our time with Russia's orientation toward the East (for only in this about-face does the active dissociation from the spiritual and ethnographic desolation of Europe become achievable), must become the fundamental force of inspiration for the new post-revolutionary generations. In order to break the back of the Revolution, we need only enlighten the crucial minority of the Russian people. And, further into the future, their healing may become as deep-seated and elemental as their headlong dash into the abyss of Revolution. However, we ought not to delude ourselves with false conceptions: the collapse and depravity of the current Bolshevist generations is profound and malignant. Therefore, the future shall require a forced restoration of the defamed foundations of Russian life, a willful straightening of its battered spine. But such a compulsory mending of the Russian soul can be successful only under the condition that the new generations come to a precise understanding and true discovery of the fundamental historical gravitational pull of the new Russia; for, otherwise, the possibility of repeating the failures of the White movement is not excluded, nor is it impossible that the elemental flow of life could once again erroneously burst out of its set channel and dam and spill forth as a new devastating flood.

The initiative and task of the future Russian reaction is difficult precisely because it must combine in itself, flexibly and organically, the beginning of a new, unyielding self-preservation with the broad perspective of socialist-liberal

Ideas and Methods

pragmatism. This initiative, this composition, must be fastidiously posed before the people's consciousness, who in turn must faithfully take up and comprehend it; otherwise, the events of anti-Bolshevik reaction could overflow into anarchic oscillations and interruptions, and the desired governmental balance will arrive only after many chaotic years of new civil conflict, during which its forms may reveal themselves in the most unexpected and unacceptable ways.

On the basis of the new, culturally rich, and comprehensive complex of experiential data, ideas, and positions, we must then transcribe these complexities into something simple with the utmost responsibility, and produce a simple, succinct scheme of tactical worldview capable of organizing society on a broad scale, of serving as a selective and disciplinary principle. The ideological-volitional centralization of Bolshevism must be opposed by a resistance of equal concentration and resilience.

In the capacity of a practical opposition to the idea of the Third International which has been realized today in Russia, we must promote with all possible breadth and strength of will the idea of a Third Maximalism. Given the circumstances in which contemporary Russian ideological-political consciousness finds itself, in the sense of its various gravitations and searches for concentration, we may directly say *tertium datur*[80]: besides the maximalism of social-communism and the maximalism of restoration[81], a third system of ideas must be

---

80 [Trans.]: Latin: "A third option is given."

81 To consider the contemporary restorational trends of the emigration as forms of right-wing maximalism would of course mean wildly exaggerating their significance. To date, none of their multifarious positions have given us anything more than tepid, deeply provincial, and stunningly tasteless reminiscences. It is interesting to note that, in the interests of reconciling society with itself, they must conform to the order of "progressive self-development," and some of them even fall into the tone of "social liberalism." To this day, we can only speak of a maximalism of restorational activity in the form of a shameful parody of itself; this is because such activity has, until now, been guided by a fruitless demagoguery of pogrom sloganeering.

However, it is psychologically possible that political passions will move toward a more creative form of reaction and attempt to utilize the blind hatred of Bolshevism for the elementary and fruitless infringements of restoration.

found – and is already being developed – whose manifestation depends upon the distillation of a new volitional intentionality and the production of new generations and cadres who are devoted to the new idea. We call this system of maximalism *Eurasianism*. Without establishing any correlation with the third international, Eurasianism asserts the need for maximum spiritual-ideological tension and maximum concentration of volitional forces alien to the revolution. It is for this reason alone that Eurasianism affirms the formula: maximalism against maximalism.

In opposition to the two maximalisms of socialism and restorationism, corresponding to one another in parity and bound by the signs of the epoch and the generations which gave birth to them, the third maximalism must enter life as an independent world, dissociating itself from the other two maximalisms alike. Above all else, the third maximalism must be internally and to its very depths predicated on a consciousness and will toward the authentic renaissance of the Orthodox religious essence; it must actively strive for this, pushing to the extent it is able to realize the true canons of human benevolence, without masking any form of politicking or soulless juridical rigorism with an insincere appeal to supreme values. Such an appeal must also not bear the character of artificial archaicism; it must not be defined by the impotent (and at times selfishly calculating) notion of an elementary return to the "days of old." That which is primordial and unshakeable must be combined with the contemporary and the necessary. Unlike the hollow, obsolete forms of self-serving European chauvinism, we must provide the total fullness and richness of a new culturally creative and profoundly national Russian being, and we must understand that the culture of Russia is a tortuous, expansive, and synthetic phenomenon – yet, being a national culture, it is at the same time a piece of light.

The system of ideas proper to the third maximalism must become a method for gaining knowledge of Revolution,

Ideas and Methods

doing away with the blind and elementary struggle against it and, in its place, establishing before all else an exhaustive relationship with the current Russian reality, as with the means and conditions for creating a new, self-determining culture – a Eurasian culture. In connection with this, alongside a thorough, merciless, and systematic unmasking of the ideas and principles of Russian communism and its sources, we must indicate with total sobriety those sides of Russian modernity which, given a change in governing ideas, are most capable of becoming the foundation for new cultural-state structures of the future; for, despite the Revolution, the logic of the Russian historical process never ceases to find living strength for its manifestation in the national organism of the people.

To the very end, the sociocultural structure of the old Russia still contained many creative elements of self-governance, which came to be discredited only under conditions of a blind and decomposing statehood. This should be understood and provisionally adapted to the future Russian model, for, despite its spiritual and national fall, Bolshevik Russia has already evinced certain positive attitudes and transformations of social and state life which, in the conception of the future creative reaction, must be preserved while, of course, dispensing with all other fundamental ideological motifs.

The third maximalism must secure for itself a supreme perspective which will guarantee a good relativism in relation to the already obsolete laws of necessity and facts of actuality, to the concrete historical reality of yesterday and today. An acknowledgement of facts and even a "permissiveness" in the sphere of socio-political reconstruction must be balanced with a strengthening of unshakeable attitudes toward the dogmatic pillars of Russian historiosophy and its timeless values.

We must acquire both our lost vision and a clear comprehension of that truth which, as an expression of the Absolute itself – as the original source of all spirituality – is alone capable of renewing the decrepit norms and regularities of law and social morals, which have become pseudo-autonomous and arrogantly dogmatic.

In our times, "law" and "truth" have parted ways – not only in Russia – and this separation has had a pernicious influence on these very concepts, their connectedness and their mutual conditioning. In many cases, the law has become a formal and dogmatic defender of untruth, while all attempts to arrive at truth are beginning more and more to find expression in lawless and destructive forms, as a consequence of which these self-directed searches for truth are becoming the immediate facts of evil.

The ideological system of the third maximalism must, finally, affirm the obvious truth that the temptations of the Third International can only be overcome in a completely autonomous sphere, free from all correspondence with it; it is a methodological error to disseminate the already widespread notion in which many believe: that it is possible to find within the Third International the means and methods for defeating it. Russia cannot be saved by a White International or restorationist conspiracies, but only through a total ideological and tactical exit from the sphere of all correspondences, by uprooting everything which led to the Revolution, by redeeming the distorted truth within it.

We must think through the very depths of the task, meaning, and predetermination of Russia's fate in the general changing of the times and the sequence of historico-cultural cycles; we must divine, see, and set before ourselves the creative task of finding in this fate a new type of culture, new objects of reality, new protean forms of being for state power; we must find inspiration in new principles and methods of the social life of the people; and, most of all, we must express this in our discovery of organic forms which allow for the synthesis of spiritual, national, and economic freedom throughout the regions and lands of Russia-Eurasia, bearing the authoritative yoke of a common fate of statehood, holding and restraining everyone and everything within the single protean form of a great whole.[82]

If the Lord intended for Russia to become the field of experiment for the realization of the International's ideas, then perhaps he did so in order that Russia, in its very essence, should heroically annihilate the very first ground of all Revolution, burning it down without a trace. Therefore, for the creative generations of Russia, these penetrating words of Khomiakov's should be granted a special meaning in our time: "Ahead of the laborer who throws down his fruit-bearing seed goes the plow, splitting the soil, uprooting the weeds, and setting down the furrow... The labor of one age is the sowing of the future, and the work of sowing is not easy."

"The labor is ours, but the harvest shall be universal."

***

---

82 The contemporary atomization and particularism of Europe's petty-bourgeois milieu, along with the forced communization of life in today's Russia, are naturally phenomena of close kinship which easily pass into and out of one another, for if petty-bourgeois atomization leads to a communist unmasking and retribution, then communism is undoubtedly a factor of petty, autonomic individualism, under which thousands of human units, each in their blind and arrogant alienation, start seeing themselves each as the sole center of the universe.

WE AND THE OTHERS

Nikolai Trubetzkoy[83]

***

I

As an ideological movement, Eurasianism first explicitly declared its existence and began its process of crystallization in the conditions and context of the Russian emigration. The Russian emigration is a political phenomenon, an immediate consequence of political events. No matter how Russian emigres might strive to depart from politics, they are in no condition to do so without ceasing to be emigrants. The essence of a refugee is determined by the panic that sets in as a result of certain political events: as soon as the reasons that caused this panic cease to exist, the refugee, since he is only a refugee, can return to his homeland. The essence of emigration is defined by an irreconcilable difference, aggravated to the extreme, between the convictions of one sector of society and those of the ruling circles: until this difference in convictions is done away with, the emigrant will not be able to return to the Motherland, even if the causes of panic (terror, famine, etc.) have been changed for the better. And since returning to the motherland is everyone's cherished dream, refugees always inquisitively ask each other whether what made them panic has passed, and when to consider the danger to have passed; and the emigrants try one another with questions about the character of government which would allow them to begin seeing their differences in conviction as insubstantial. It is for

---

83 Originally published in *The Eurasian Annals*, book 4 (Berlin, 1925).

this reason that political questions escape not the mouths, nor leave the heads of Russian emigrants. It is for this reason that the emigrants, despite all desire to swear off politics, are incapable of doing so. And it is partially for this reason that all belonging to the emigration approach each ideological project from the perspective of its political content. It is naturally from the very same perspective that they approach Eurasianism.

They pose the following questions to the Eurasianists: "Who are you – rightists, leftists, or centrists? Monarchists or Republicans? Democrats or Aristocrats? Constitutionalists or Absolutists? Socialists or partisans of the Bourgeois order?" And when they fail to receive direct responses to such questions, they either suspect the deeply hidden presence of secret machinations, or they shrug their shoulders in contempt, declaring that this "movement" is of a purely literary character and nothing more than a simplistic attempt at novelty.

II

The reason for this misunderstanding, this inability to find a common language, consists in the fact that, in Eurasianism, the problem of relations between politics and culture has been posed in a manner entirely different from that to which the Russian intelligentsia is accustomed.

From the times of Peter the Great, two ideas or, more precisely, two complexes of ideas have lived in the consciousness of every member of the Russian intelligentsia (in the broadest sense of the word, understanding "intelligentsia" to refer to the educated class): "Russia as a Great European Power" and as a "European civilization." A person's "orientation" has to a great extent always been determined by his relationship to these two ideas. There are two dramatically opposed types. For one, Russia as a Great European Power has been more valuable than anything else; it is they who say, "No matter the cost, even if that cost should be the total enslavement of the people and of society, imbued with the rejection of the traditions of Enlightenment and humanism handed down from European civilization, give us a Russia that is a mighty, great European power." These were the representatives of governmental reaction. For the other type, most valuable of all are the "progressive" ideas of European civilization; they say: "No matter the cost, even if that cost should turn out to be the rejection of state might and Russia's status as a great power, let us see the manifestation of ideals from European civilization in Russia (i.e., in the opinion of some – democracy; in the opinion of others – socialism, etc.) and make Russia into a progressive European state." These were the representatives of the radical progressive section of society.

The tragedy lies in the fact that neither tendency was capable of fully responding to the conditions of Russian life. Each side drew attention to the inner contradiction and insubstantiality of the other, but could not see that it itself was tainted by the same shortcomings. The reactionaries were wonderfully aware that, by defending the freedom of Russian democracy, which is to say (from the European point of view) the semi-savage elemental force of the peasant masses, the progressivists would thereby deal an irremediable blow to the very existence of European civilization in Russia. On their end, the progressivists correctly pointed out that, for the sake of preserving Russia's place in the "concert of great European powers," she must reach in her internal politics the level of the other European states. But it goes without saying that neither the reactionaries nor the progressivists understood her utopianism and her internal inadequacy. Of course, there were also representatives of the "golden mean," "rational conservatism," and "moderate liberalism," who combined patriotism for a great power with the necessity of liberal internal politics. But, in the end, even this sector of the Russian educated class lived for the idea of a utopia. Both of the fundamental ideas which collaboratively created the varieties of Russian political tendencies in their different combinations – the idea of Russia as a Great Power, and that of manifesting on Russian soil the ideals of European civilization – were at their roots artificial. They were both born of the reforms of Peter the Great. Peter introduced his reforms by force, without asking for the consent of the Russian people. Neither Russia as a great European power nor the ideals of European progress spoke to the Russian people. Russia's status as a Great European Power, on the one hand, and the European enlightenment of the elites of the Russian nation on the other, might have lasted a long time on Russian soil, on the condition that the folk masses remained artificially silent and passive. But both the former and the latter tendency must unavoidably have created a chink in the armor of state and begun to collapse just as soon as the very masses of the people, making up the natural fundament of the entire Russian edifice, began to stir. The disagreement between the Russian "tendencies," which were in essence merely different combinations of the notion of Russia as a Great European Power and the ideals of European progress, were therefore fruitless and idle. Upon scaffolding which they themselves had not built, the engineers raised the walls of the edifice and then got to arguing over which roof would be the best to build, having utterly forgotten why and how the very scaffolding, over which the whole dispute was held, had been outfitted; the scaffolding turned out to be alive and shifted; the walls of the edifice cracked and collapsed, burying beneath themselves a number of engineers, and the argument over the roof lost all meaning.

It is perfectly natural that, as soon as this picture should fully reveal itself to consciousness, a complete change of approach to those political questions which to this day have troubled Russian society should prove indispensable. After all, these questions were previously discussed under a premise of known cultural-historical concepts which entered the minds of educated Russian society in the post-Petrine epoch, but which have remained organically alien to the Russian people. In realizing this, denying faith in the universality and incomparable value of European culture, and not recognizing the universal necessity of the "laws of world progress," we must first of all seek a new cultural-historical basis for political matters. And it is upon this that all the misunderstandings that arise in the minds of those representing the old Russian "tendencies" encountering Eurasianism are based. Eurasianism does not reject one or another political conviction held by proponents of the old movements, but rather that cultural-historical context with which such convictions are bound in their consciousness. Rightists, leftists, moderates, conservatives, revolutionaries, and liberals – they all exclusively circulate in the sphere of notions pertaining to post-Petrine Russia and European culture. Whenever they speak of one or another form of government, they think this governmental form precisely in the context of European culture, or of that developed in Europeanized, post-Petrine Russia; the changes and reforms which they consider necessary to their political structure or ideas affects strictly that structure or those ideas, but has nothing to do with the cultural context itself. For Eurasianism, what is of the greatest importance is nothing else than the alteration of culture; changes made to the political structure or to political ideas without a corresponding change of culture are swept away by Eurasianism as insubstantial and unfeasible.

III

The culture of any people who live out their daily lives under the state must by all means include among its elements political ideas or a political doctrine. Therefore, the call to create a new culture also implies a call for the development of new political ideologies. Detractors have accused Eurasianism of promoting political indifference, an aloofness toward political matters, and such accusations are based on a misunderstanding. But one of their more significant errors is their common tendency of identifying Eurasianism with any number of the old ideological or political trends.

Eurasianism rejects the non-appellational authority of European culture. And, since it is conventional to associate European culture with "progressiveness," it appears to many that Eurasianism is a reactionary trend. Eurasianism calls for a national culture and unambiguously declares that a Russian national culture would be unthinkable without Orthodoxy. In turn, based on the habitual association held by many, such a declaration evokes memories of the notorious formula, "Monarchy, Orthodoxy, the People," and even more strongly reinforces their conviction that Eurasianism is a new form of the old ideology propounded by the Russian reactionaries. It is not only the leftists who submit to this illusion, but also many rightists, who rush headlong to claim Eurasianism as "their own." This is a profound misunderstanding. In the mouths of Russian rightists, the formula "Monarchy, Orthodoxy, the People" has taken on a very specific meaning. Strictly speaking, this entire formula could be changed by the replacement of a single word: "Monarchy." It was Count Uvarov who defined an orientation toward "the People" as a unification of the monarchy with Orthodoxy. As concerns "Orthodoxy," the representatives of governmental reaction used this term (as they continue unconsciously to use it today) to mean a synodal, chief-prosecutorial Orthodoxy. The full extent of the "Russian spirit" contained by the Russian reactionaries goes no further than a counterfeit folk phraseology, a most haughty affirmation of *"du Russe* with cockerels," a sinister quasi-Russian lubok[84] of the nineteenth century, through which a tunic of Prussian cut and parade-ground drills can be seen; their "Orthodoxy" goes no further than a pontiff's solemn prayer service on a ceremonial day, during which the longevity of the most supreme persons is proclaimed. For the reactionaries, Orthodoxy and an orientation toward the

---

84 [Trans.]: The "lubok" is a form of traditional Russian art in which mythical or folk scenes are depicted in woodcut prints.

people are no more than a demonstrative accessory to the monarchy which has reached the status of tradition.[85] And only the monarchy is treated as an absolute value. In their search for an ideal in the Russian past, these reactionaries find it in the reigns of Alexander III or Nikolai I. It goes without saying that none of this has anything to do with Eurasianism, but is rather directly opposed to it. By proclaiming national Russian culture as its slogan, Eurasianism ideologically repulses everything belonging to the post-Petrine, Saint-Petersburgian, imperial, chief-prosecutorial era; and that profound religious Orthodox feeling which the whole of the people feel and which, with the strength of its burning, melted the Tatar yoke down into the power of the Orthodox Russian Tsar and transformed Batu Khan's domain into the Orthodox state of Muscovy, is the primary value of Russian history in the eyes of the Eurasianists. Eurasianism looks upon imperial monarchy as a degeneration of the authentic, national, pre-Petrine monarchy (speaking, of course, of this monarchy as a spiritual essence and not in relation to its external, political accomplishments, which were enormous in many respects): having severed itself from that "everyday confessionalism" which served as the ideological support of tsarist power in ancient Rus' and simultaneously, in the person of the Tsar, found its most fervent zealot, the imperial monarchy was naturally and inevitably obliged to rest on foundations of slavery and militarism. Eurasianism can find no reconciliation with Orthodoxy's transformation into a simple accessory of the monarchy, nor with the reduction of an "orientation toward the people" to a state-sanctioned declamation. We demand an authentic Orthodoxy, the "Orthodoxification" of everyday life, a true national culture which sits on a foundation of "everyday

---

85 That this is indeed the case is apparent, if only from the fact that, at this very moment in right-wing circles, people are often tempted by the current situation of the Russian Church, that cases of conversion to Catholicism have only grown more frequent and that there are voices resounding about the necessity of acquiring an ally for the monarchy in the guise of Catholicism at the price of various concessions.

confessionalism" and which recognizes as its own (its ideal) only such a monarchy which arises as an organic consequence of national culture.

IV

The unambiguously negative relationship of Eurasianism to imperial Russia, as well as our emphasis on the values of an authentic identity of the people, may give rise to yet another misunderstanding, namely the identification of Eurasianism with revolutionary populism [Narodnichestvo]. However, Eurasianism sharply distinguishes itself from such populism. No matter the case, Russian revolutionary populism has always been and remains a variant of socialism. And socialism is an offspring of Romano-Germanic culture, making it spiritually foreign to Eurasianism. If, in more moderate branches of populism, the socialist element appears in a weakened form, this does not change matters in principle. The populists' relationship to so-called "Russian identity" is radically distinct from that of Eurasianism. Populism has artificially selected only certain elements from the everyday life of the people, from the people's aspirations and ideologies: communal farming, village assemblies, the "principle of the labor team," the idea that "the land belongs to God," rational sectarianism, surreptitious hatred toward "landlords," bandit songs, etc. These elements of everyday life, worldview, and cast of mind have been stripped of their historical context, idealized, and declared to be of sole consequence and authentically of the people, while everything else is swept away. Naturally, such a selection has been carried out with an eye toward what is favorable to socialism. Anything in the everyday life and worldview of the people which was seen from this point of view, has been relegated as unfavorable to the realm of "backwardness" and "the ignorance of the peasant masses," and has been slated to be overcome by means of schooling and propaganda. Schooling and propaganda must also inculcate the people with those traits that they "lack," but which are characteristic of the "democracy of the leading countries of the West." The populists have envisioned the future Russia as a model democratic republic, complete with parliamentarism, an unprecedentedly broad form of suffrage that extends almost to adolescents of both sexes in equal proportion, separation of Church and State, the total secularization not only of governmental, but also familial life, and so on. In this idea, which is derived entirely from Romano-Germanic ideologues, the role of Russian identity is reduced to nothing more than the notion that the land is to be distributed based on the rights of labor use, in the course of which even this distribution, carried out on the scale of the entire state, is nothing but an abstract reminiscence of the Russian "village counsels." And so, for the populists, identity simply plays the role of a trampoline which would allow the people to jump into the embrace of a nullifying Europeanization. Ultimately, their "going to the people" is nothing more than a special tactic, a device for carrying out Europeanization and enshrining in Russia the well-known ideals of Romano-Germanic civilization. The paradoxical and internally contradictory combination of outer identitarianism with an inner, decidedly Westernizing content has always been the Achilles' heel of Russian revolutionary populism.

Precisely because of its socialist and Westernizing essence, revolutionary populism is utterly unacceptable to Eurasianism. Eurasianism approaches national Russian culture without any desire to replace it with Romano-Germanic forms of life (having either already become manifest in Europe or presenting themselves to the imagination of European publicists); on the contrary, Eurasianism approaches Russian culture with the desire to liberate it from Romano-Germanic influence and to set it on the path of authentic, self-sufficient national development. Of course, Eurasianism does not accept everything that is or was characteristic of the Russian people without a sense of selection; we also make our choice between that which is valuable and that which is either harmful or inconsequential. But, in making this choice, Eurasianism is guided not by the question as to whether a given phenomenon of Russian culture or the everyday life of the people is favorable to the manifestation of one or another ideal derived from the Europeans (socialism, democratic republicanism, etc.), but is driven exclusively by the internal value of that phenomenon in its general connection to Russian national culture. From this point of view, it is necessary to make a distinction between random, transitory phenomena and deep-seated phenomena with enduring meaning, and further between creative, constructive phenomena and destructive phenomena. In this sense, the communal farming on which the populists so singularly insist is a transient form of economy that arose historically and is doomed to disappear in the process of history: the destruction of the peasant commune and the transition to individual land holdings is a historically inevitable phenomenon which cannot be slowed by any artificial measures. And since communal land ownership is retarding the development of peasant agricultural productivity, it should even be recognized as a culturally harmful, destructive phenomenon; moreover, we ought to aid in the process of its replacement by other agricultural forms. In professing Russian identity, Eurasianism does not include communal farming among the substantial marks of such an identity. When observing the worldview of the people and its manifestations in folk creativity, to include their submission to the will of God, their idealization of tsarist power, their spiritual verse, their piety, and their ceremonial confessionalism, the populists either passed over these traits in silence or attributed them to the people's "darkness"; and, all the while, it was precisely these traits - endowing the people's fundament with resilience - which, from the perspective of national culture, were the most valuable. On the contrary, all manifestations of revolt, whether in temperament or in folk creativity - the people's hatred for the "masters," songs and legends idealizing bandits, folktales that mocked the "priests" - were of particular value to the populists, even though it is clear that these purely negative anti-cultural and anti-social manifestations contain no culturally creative potentials to speak of. What is more, within these negative elements of the people's psychology, the populists could find value only in what was most negative: hatred for the "masters" was valued to the extent that it was a "social" hatred, while it was precisely in this form that, in destroying national unity, such a hatred was undoubtedly harmful, and could perhaps only be seen as positive inasmuch as the "master" was regarded as a foreign person from a non-national culture.

But Eurasianism departs most fundamentally from populism on the basis of religion. Like the socialists, the populists are, by and large, atheists or, at the very least, abstract deists. Out of everything to be found in the religious life of the people, the populists have been able to "understand" and value only rationalist sectarianism. Eurasianism stands on the soil of Orthodoxy, propounding it as the sole authentic form of Christianity, and recognizes the fact that Orthodoxy, precisely in its capacity as the one true faith, could play the role of a creative stimulus in Russian history. As we stand on the soil of Orthodoxy, it is impossible not to see that Protestantism and rationalistic sectarianism are the fruit of religious folly, the degeneration of religious feeling, and are therefore fallen forms of religion. The existence and partial success of Stundism, Baptism, and other rationalistic sects among the people is a most deleterious consequence of two centuries of Europeanization, during which the heights and depths elites and the dregs of the nation were separated from one another by an abyss. Closing their eyes to the spiritual riches of Orthodoxy, the intelligentsia and quasi-intelligentsia looked upon it as a peasant faith and were infected by fallen forms of Western Christianity, while the government, having frozen and formalized the Russian Church, depriving it of all initiative and freedom of action, took no measures either to raise the level of the clergy or to disseminate an authentically Orthodox enlightenment. If, during these difficult centuries of Russian history, the Russian people often left the Church because of its lack of the authentically Orthodox spirit they unconsciously craved, and then relented to the temptations of cheap rationalism which had penetrated them by way of the intelligentsia and quasi-intelligentsia who had been knocked off of the true path, then we may observe in this sad phenomenon nothing more than a symptom of illness. Naturally, in battling this symptom (and by means of the police), the government acted unjustly, for they ought to have cured the very illness. But the populists, who discerned in these symptoms something vigorous and healthy, were in even greater error. From no point of view could rationalist sectarianism be considered a favorable phenomenon; from the religious position it is degeneration, and from that of national culture it is a microbe that disintegrates national unity and retards the nation's amicable collaboration on the sowing field of spiritual culture.

To a Christian, Christianity is not some element of a particular national culture, it is a ferment capable of entering various cultures and stimulating their development in a definite direction without casting away their identities or unique forms. To extract Christianity from Russian national consciousness, or to replace therein true Christianity (Orthodoxy) with a fallen, rationalist counterfeit, is to sterilize Russian culture and to set it on the path to disintegration. It is for this reason that the divergence of Eurasianism from populism on the grounds of the religious question precludes the possibility of any proximity between the two movements.

It should be emphasized that the essence of this divergence rests precisely in the religious sphere and in the resultant positive or negative evaluation of those elements of the national psyche on which a national culture must be constructed. Our political divergence from populism is less substantive. Revolutionary populism insists upon republicanism. If one imagines such an Orthodox Russian Republic in which each temporarily elected president ("head of state") would look upon himself as the responsible representative of the people before God and as the defender of Orthodoxy, and if the presidential and deputy elections in this republic did not depend on a manipulation of the people's passions and hatreds, then Eurasianism would have nothing against it; in any case, such a republic would be preferable to an "enlightened European" monarchy that would propagate Europeanization from the top down and hold the Church in bondage. But, independent of the question as to whether such a republic is even possible, we may doubt that it would satisfy the revolutionary populists.

V

Finally, we must illuminate yet another question: that of the mutual relationship between Eurasianism and Bolshevism. Lovers of dubiously "apt" quips sometimes attempt to characterize Eurasianism as an "Orthodox Bolshevism," or as the "fruit of lawless union between Slavophilism and Bolshevism." Even though the paradoxicality of such a *contradictio in adjecto* ("Orthodox Bolshevism" is tantamount to a "white blackness") should be clear to anyone who hears it, the questions concerning those points at which Eurasianism and Bolshevism either converge or diverge calls for a more careful analysis.

Eurasianism resembles Bolshevism in its rejection not only of certain political forms, but also of that entire culture which existed in Russia immediately prior to the Revolution, and which continues to exist in the countries of the Romano-Germanic West; moreover, both movements demand a radical reconstruction of this culture. Eurasianism is also like Bolshevism in its call for the liberation of the Asian and African peoples enslaved by the colonial powers.

But this likeness is merely of an external, formal character. The internal motivations of Bolshevism and Eurasianism are diametrically opposed. The Bolsheviks refer to that culture which is to be removed as "bourgeois," while the Eurasianists call it "Romano-Germanic"; and the Bolsheviks think of that culture which is to replace it as "proletarian," while the Eurasianists think of it as "national" (or, in relation to Russia, as "Eurasian"). The Bolsheviks begin from the Marxist assumption that culture is created by a particular class; the Eurasianists perceive culture to be the fruit of activity on the part of particular ethnic units, whether a nation or a group of nations. Therefore, for Eurasianists, the concepts of "bourgeois" and "proletarian" culture are completely illusory. In any socially differentiated nation, the culture of the elites is distinguished from that of the lower classes. In a normal, healthy national organism, this distinction is reduced to the degree of one or another culture. If, in this regard, the elites are referred to as the "bourgeoisie" and the lower classes as the "proletariat," then the replacement of bourgeois culture with proletarian culture amounts to a reduction in the level of culture, to its simplification, feralization; this could hardly be promoted as an ideal. In unhealthy nations, infected with the malady of Europeanization, the culture of the elites is distinguished from that of the lower classes not so much in a quantitative sense (by degrees), as in a qualitative one: i.e., the lower classes continue to live with the fragments and debris of a culture which had once served as the lowest degree and fundament of indigenous national culture, while the elites live with the highest degrees of another foreign, Romano-Germanic culture; in the interval between the lower classes and the elites we find a layer of people who lack any culture whatsoever, who have broken away from the lower classes, but who have yet to arrive at the elites, precisely on the strength of the qualitative heterogeneity of both cultures, which have been commingled in a given nation. When it comes to nations built on this latter model (which included the post-Petrine, pre-revolutionary Russia), one may speak of the desirability of replacing the culture of the elites with that of the lower classes – but, even then, only metaphorically. In this case, one ought to think not of how the elites can transition to the culture of the lower classes, which would inevitably be of an elementary nature, but rather of how the elites can create a new culture with the intention that, between it and the culture of the lower classes, the distinction would not be qualitative, but a matter of degree. Only given this condition can the philistinism found in the nation's middle layers be abolished while the national organism becomes culturally whole, healthy, and capable altogether of further development, both in its highest and lowest strata. It is precisely this which Eurasianism promotes. But, here, it is clear that we are speaking of a transformation not on the basis of class, but on the basis of the ethnic nature of culture.

Finding themselves entirely subject to the authority of Marxist schemes and approaching the problem of culture exclusively from the perspective of such schemes, the Bolsheviks naturally reveal themselves to be utterly incapable of fulfilling that which they have set out to accomplish, i.e., the creation of some new culture in place of the old one. Their "proletarian culture" is expressed either as a feralization or as some parody of the old, so-called "bourgeois" culture. In either case, we find that their activities are reduced to simple destruction without any creation to speak of. In no way does a new culture result from this – and this is the best evidence to prove that the very theoretical conceits of Bolshevism are false and that the very task of "proletarianizing culture" is impossible. The concept of "proletarian culture" is inevitably hollow, for the very concept of the proletariat, as something purely economic, is bereft of any other indication of concrete culture, save those of an economic nature. Things are entirely different with regard to the concept of national culture, for every nation – being either a practical or potential bearer and creator of a definite, concrete culture – contains in its very concept the concrete signs of elements and trends of cultural construction. Therefore, the creation of a new culture is only possible when it is the culture of a particular nation that hitherto has not possessed a self-sufficient culture or has found itself under the oppressive influence of a foreign culture. And this new culture can only be set in opposition to that of one or many other nations.

It follows from this argument that, if the common tasks of Bolshevism and Eurasianism are the rejection of the old culture and the creation of a new one, then Bolshevism is capable solely of the first among these two tasks, while the fulfillment of the second is impossible for it. And it need not be said that the fulfillment of the first task without a simultaneous act of creation cannot under any circumstances lead to desirable results. First of all, the destroyer, possessing either an unclear or a false understanding of that which must be erected in the place of that which is destroyed, will inevitably destroy (or attempt to destroy) that which ought to be preserved. Moreover, when the tempo of destruction exceeds that of creation, or when an authentic act of creation fails to follow upon the heels of an act of destruction, the nation finds itself in a state of prolonged philistinism which cannot fail to find its reflection in ruinous effects. Despite the fact that the destructive work of the Bolsheviks is often directed precisely toward those sides of European culture which have been insinuated in Russia, and which the Eurasianists too think should be uprooted, Eurasianism cannot welcome such destruction actions. As regards Bolshevik attempts at creativity, the Eurasianists regard them with the utmost contempt, as they are either saturated with Marxist utopianism or are directed toward the transplantation of even newer elements of Romano-Germanic civilization on Russian soil; and these are primarily those elements which are the least acceptable to Eurasianism and bear the obvious signs of degeneration and decadence found in Romano-Germanic culture.[86]

---

[86] The sole realm of creativity which is truly, vitally indispensable to the Bolsheviks as a party is that of governance. Since a false step in this sphere, precipitated by preconceived utopian theories, may constitute their fall from power, the Bolsheviks apply their theory least of all in their governance, instead striving to be strictly practical. Some of their inventions in such an applied governance are undoubtedly successful and have prospects for the future.

We and the Others

In light of all that has been said, it is apparent that, even on the question of Russia's relations with peoples not belonging to the Romano-Germanic world, the similarity between Bolshevism and Eurasianism is merely external. Eurasianism calls on all peoples of the world to liberate themselves from the influence of Romano-Germanic culture and to step once more onto the path by which they may develop their own national cultures. In this respect, Eurasianism recognizes that the influence of Romano-Germanic culture has been especially intensified thanks to the economic domination of the so-called "civilized" peoples over the "colonized" and, as a result, calls for a liberation struggle from this economic domination as well. But Eurasianism does not view this economic emancipation as a goal unto itself; rather, it is merely one of the necessary conditions of a greater liberation from Romano-Germanic culture – a liberation which would be unthinkable without the simultaneous fortification of the foundations of national culture and the indefinite, independent development thereof. In all of these questions, the Bolsheviks are pursuing aims directly opposite to ours. They only play upon the nationalist moods and vanities of the Asiatic peoples, viewing these feelings as nothing more than the means of raising a socialist revolution in Asia; and this revolution is intended not so much to eliminate the economic stranglehold of the "civilized" powers as to allow for the installation of a communist order with that specific "proletarian" culture which, in essence, is anti-national and is constructed on the very negative elements of the same European civilization, now taken to a caricatured extremity. Beneath the mask that flaunts an Asiatic nationalism, Bolshevism hides the same condescending, "civilizing" attitude of the European *Kulturträger*, and in an even more radical form than that seen from the Romano-Germanic colonial imperialists. The Bolsheviks wish to lead the peoples of Asia and Russia not toward the creation of an authentic national culture, connected by way of succession to the historical past, but rather toward national depersonalization and the destruction of all national foundations.

We and the Others

To summate, it may be said that Bolshevism is a destructive movement, while Eurasianism is a creative one. The two movements are polar opposites, and there can be no thought of their collaboration. This opposition between Bolshevism and Eurasianism is not arbitrary, as it is rooted in the profound essence of each. Bolshevism is the movement of theomachy; Eurasianism is a religious, God-affirming movement. There is a deep internal connection between the militant rejection of the Creator and impotence in relation to authentic and positive creativity, between the blasphemous negations of the divine Logos and a rationalist utopianism which contradicts the nature of life. But nature does not permit pure destruction. It imperiously demands creativity, and anything that is incapable of positive creativity is doomed, sooner or later, to perish. Bolshevism, like all species of the negating spirit, is deft in its ability to destroy, but has not been endowed with a wisdom for creativity. And it is for this reason that Bolshevism must perish and be replaced with the force that opposes it – a God-affirming and creative force. Whether this force will be Eurasianism – only the future will show. But, in any event, neither a restorational ideology which substitutes for creativity the mere repair and reinstatement of that which has been destroyed, restoring it to its old form, nor populism, as blind as Bolshevism to the positive tasks of cultural construction set by God and as infected by the fallen ideologies of a degenerated European civilization, possess the traits of an authentic, positive creativity.

The positive significance of Bolshevism is perhaps to be found in the fact that, having removed its mask and having shown Satan to the world without disguise, it has led many, in their certainty of Satan's reality, toward a faith in God. But besides this, with its senseless skewering of life (a consequence of its incapacity for creativity), Bolshevism has deeply furrowed Russia's virgin soil, has taken layers lying in the depths of the earth and has raised them to the surface, while driving the surface layers into the depths. And it may be that, when new people are required for the creation of a new national culture, such people will be found precisely in those strata which Bolshevism has accidentally raised to the surface of Russian life. In any event, the degree to which one is adequate to the matter of creating a national culture and is connected to the positive spiritual foundations stored up in the Russian past will serve as the sole index of these new people's selection. Those new people who have been created by Bolshevism, but who lack such indicators, will turn out to be unfit for life and will naturally perish along with the Bolshevism that birthed them; their demise will not come as the result of some intervention, but of the fact that nature not only refuses to tolerate a void, but also refuses to tolerate pure destruction and negation, instead requiring creation and creativity; and true, positive creativity is possible only through the affirmation of the national principle and a feeling for the religious link of man and the nation with the Creator of the universe.

***

THE TWO HEROIC FEATS OF ST. ALEXANDER NEVSKY

George Vernadsky[87]

***

During the time of Emperor Nikolai Pavlovich, a well-known book about Russia, "*La Russie en 1839,*" was published by the Marquis de Custine in Paris.[88] This book, written in the form of travel impressions, is a malevolent pamphlet aimed against Russia, the Russian Church, the Russian State, and the Russian People.

De Custine's book is one link in the grand chain of European Russophobia – one of the manifestations of Europe's hatred for and fear of Russia.[89]

De Custine does not limit himself to attacks on contemporary Imperial Russia; he strives at every opportunity to dethrone the Russian past as well, to undermine the historical foundations of Russian being. Among de Custine's attacks on the Russian past, one's attention is drawn to his ironic words on the memory of the holy, faithful prince Aleksandr Nevsky.

De Custine writes: "Alexander Nevsky is a model of caution; but he was a martyr neither for faith, nor for noble

---

87 Originally published in *The Eurasian Annals*, book 4 (Berlin, 1925).

88 [Trans.]: *La Russie en 1839*

89 If one were to trace the history of this hatred and fear, at least between the eighteenth and nineteenth centuries, such a piece of scholarship would serve as a handsome response to an interesting sociological task. I personally possess de Custine's book in its third revision (Paris 1846).

feelings. The national church canonized this sovereign as being more wise than heroic. He was a Ulysses among the saints."[90]

Thusly, in the 19th century, did this Western European Latinist and author strive to dethrone the holy Russian prince, whose every act was directed toward struggle with the West and its Latinism. The Europeans of the 13th century fell upon Alexander with the sword; the European of the 19th century has exchanged his sword for literary mockery; and even this "bloodless" weapon was, as it turned out, merely preparation for the sword's appearance (what should have come just a few years after de Custine's book but for the Crimean War and Sevastopol!).

The "wisdom" and "caution" of Alexander Nevsky at which de Custine jeers would appear not to be subject to mockery: these qualities were combined in the prince's person with the most authentic heroism and, at times, even a foolhardy bravery. Alexander demonstrated this quality in his struggle against the West. He carried out a feat of warfare on the banks of the Neva and on the ice of Chudovskoe Lake; with the sword, he imprinted the stamp of this feat upon the face of Birger Jarl. But, indeed, Alexander considered it necessary to present a peaceful face before the strength of the East. In the words of his chronicler, Alexander's wisdom was from God; his caution was, in fact, a feat of humility.

***

The 18th century proved to be a momentous epoch in Russian history. In the previous centuries, Russian culture developed and blossomed like a brilliant flower, as a unique combination and luxuriant upspringing of the rich saplings of Orthodox Byzantium, the steppe nomads of the East, and the Varangian-Viking North – all on Slavic soil.

---

90 *La Russie en 1839*, par le marquis de Custine, t. I (1846), p. 265.

The Two Heroic Feats of St. Alexander Nevsky

Kievan Rus[91] astounds with the glimmer and pomp of both its material and spiritual life, with the blossoming of its art, science, and poetry. Along with this came the solidification of a national self-awareness (it is all the same whether Bishop Hilarion and the chronicler Nikon the Great were a single person going under two names or two persons burning with identical passion and striving of thought and feeling).

By the 13th century, Rus stood before a number of terrible trials. Her very existence – her uniqueness and identity – hung in the balance. Having unfurled upon the great Eastern-European plain as a special cultural world located between Europe and Asia, 13th-century Rus fell into a vice grip, as it was subjected to woeful attacks from both directions – from Latin Europe and from Mongol Asia.

In 1206, in the heart of Asia, an event took place which would do much to define the future fate of history. In Deligun Bulak, at the head of the Orkhon River, a *kurultai* (a gathering of elders) of the Mongol peoples pronounced the local conqueror of the surrounding tribes, the warrior-prince Temüjin, their Autocrat (Genghis Khan). Then began the Mongol advance into China, Turkestan, Asia Minor, and Europe. Less than 20 years later, Genghis Khan's frontal cavalry detachments had already dealt a terrible blow to the Russian princes on the Kalka River.

Almost simultaneously – only two years prior to the Deligun-Bulak kurultai – a no less significant event occurred in Europe: in 1204, the Western-European crusaders took Constantinople [Tsargrad] in a sudden assault and viciously plundered it; the Byzantine Orthodox Church was overthrown; in its place, the Latin Empire was established.

After Byzantium, it appeared that Rus' turn had come. The attack began along the entire front line. Hungary and Poland descended upon Galicia and Volyn; the German crusaders

---

91 The term "Kievan" as it is applied here denotes not a territorial, but a cultural and chronological idea.

reinforced their position in Riga (the Livonian Order) and in Prussia (the Teutonic Order) in the early 13th century, from there waging attacks on Pskov and Novgorod; finally, the Swedes advanced on Rus via Finland; by fire and sword, the Germans and Swedes converted the pagan Lithuanians, Estonians, and Finns, as well as Orthodox Russians. The late 1230s and 1240s saw Rus imperiled on both sides, creating an atmosphere of the greatest possible strain. The first Tatar pogrom in Rus (primarily in the northeast) took place during the winter of 1237-38; in 1240, the Tatars took Kiev (6 December); in the same year, agitated by the Pope into a crusade against the "infidels," the Swedish ruler and military commander Birger Jarl landed on the shores of the Neva (July).

Caught between two fires, Rus might have perished in a heroic struggle; but she could neither withstand the pressure of two fronts, nor save Herself.

A choice had to be made between East and West. The two strongest Russian princes of that time made diverging decisions. Danil Galitsky chose the West and, with its help, attempted to wage battle against the East.

Alexander Nevsky chose the East and, under its protection, chose to repulse the West.

***

Danil Galitsky's politics were neither coherent nor straightforward. He maneuvered between the Roman Pope, the Ugrics (Hungary), the Czechs, Poland, Lithuania, the Tatars, his own boyars, and his brother princes. The first terrible blow to southwestern Rus was dealt by the Tatars toward the end of 1240 (the sacking of Kiev); all of Volyn and Galicia were desolate from that point onward; it was impossible to approach Brest due to the stench of rotting corpses; not a soul was left alive in Vladimir.

Danil made no attempt to put up a resistance. Before Kiev's sacking, he had departed to the Ugrics in search of aid from the

Hungarian king against the Tatars. Danil's trouble had been for naught. As is known, the Mongol wave descended upon all of Eastern and Central Europe – Hungary, Silesia, Moravia, Croatia, and the Balkans. The wave subsided (in 1241) not because the Mongols met serious military resistance, on the contrary, they won everywhere (at Legnica in Silesia; Solonaya River in Hungary) but due to internal complications in the depths of the Mongol state (the death of Great Khan Ogodai and attendant questions concerning accession to the throne and internal Mongol politics that had greatly worried Batu, the leader of the European Mongol horde).

Danil returned to Rus, where he was forced to wage a prolonged battle with the Galician boyars, the lord of Peremyshl, the former prince of Chernigov, Rostislav, the Ugrics, and the Poles. The battle was successful and concluded with Danil's decisive victory over the Polish and Ugric forces of Rostislav (near Yaroslav, 1249).

Meanwhile, in 1250, the Mongols once more took an interest in southwestern Rus. Batu sent the following message to Danil: "Give up Galich." Feeling incapable of further armed battle, Danil decided to submit and met with Batu personally. Against all expectations, Danil was received affectionately. Upon entering Batu's *vezha* (tent), Danil made a bow according to Mongol custom. Batu said to him, "Danilo, why has it been so long? Now that you have come, you are well met. Will you drink the black milk, our drink – the *kumys* of the mare?"

Danil: "I have not drunk it until now. But, if you order it, I will drink."

Batu: "You are now our Tatar – drink our drink."

Danil drank the beverage and bowed as was the custom.

Then Batu sent wine to Danil, saying, "You are not accustomed to drinking milk. Drink wine."

Danil stayed on with the horde for almost a month before achieving his aim: Batu granted him all of his lands. Gradually, the international significance of Danil's act became known: the West began to curry his favor; the Ugric king Bela IV sent emissaries to him with a bid for peace and a union of kinship. Danil's son Lev married the Ugric king's daughter.

Danil interceded on Bela's behalf in the issues and feuds of Central Europe to include the debate over the Austrian Duchy and matters concerning Czechia and Moravia. During the crusade of 1252, Danil's forces (undoubtedly the best among the regiments and guards) were armed and trained according to the Tatar ways. "The Germans marveled at such Tatar armament, for their horses wore shrouds and leather armor, while the soldiers were garbed in *yarytsy*, and His Lord's regiments were great..."

By submitting to Mongol influence, Danil partook of the worldwide power of Mongol expansion, thereby entering the stream of history.

Nearly immeasurable diplomatic possibilities opened up before Danil in Eastern and Central Europe. It was he himself who foreclosed on them with his inability to perceive the significance of that historical moment.

He had not fully and carefully considered his subordination to Mongol power; this had been no more than an accidentally deft act of political opportunism. Danil's political and cultural sympathies, habits, and tastes pushed him away from Mongol Asia.

Among his guard, fitted to the Tatar standard, in the aforementioned crusade of 1252, Danil remained in the Byzantine dress of the Russian princes. "Danil himself rode by the king (of Hungary) in the Russian fashion, for the horse on which he sat was wondrous; his saddle was woven from gold, his arrows and saber gilded and decorated with other fineries, such that they were amazing; his sheath was of Greek silk and sewn through flat golden lace, as were his boots of green leather; the Germans who beheld him were in awe."

The Two Heroic Feats of St. Alexander Nevsky

The gleaming, haughty prince must have enjoyed playing a role among the Western sovereigns and knights, evoking awe and astonishment in their midst. And, what's more, his dependence on what, from his perspective, were wild nomads and barbarians must have seemed humiliating. Batu's gracious attitude toward Danil was, therefore, insulting and difficult to bear. These sentiments were brilliantly portrayed by his chronicler[92]: "O, eviler than evil is the honor of the Tatars, paid as it was to Danil Romanovich, the formerly great prince who had once possessed the Russian lands, Kiev, Vladimir, and Galicia… Now he is on his knees and is called a lackey… O evil honor of the Tatars – [Danil's] father[93] was tsar in Russian lands, who defeated the Polovtsian realm and conquered many other countries."

Danil's offended vanity drove him to seek new paths toward liberation from Mongol dependency. The Byzantine kingdom had been overthrown: all that remained was the Latin West. If he wished to depend on help from the West – a new crusade – he would need to appeal to its formal head, the Pope. This is exactly what Danil did. He entered into talks with Pope Innocent IV concerning the unification of the Eastern and Western Churches.[94]

The Pope promised various benefits and charities; he would permit the Russian clergy to conduct services with leavened prosphora; the marriage between Danil's brother Vasilek and his close relative would be recognized; crusaders and spiritual figures would be forbidden from acquiring holdings in the Russian realm without permission from the great prince; the Pope promised the great prince himself that he would be endowed with a kingly title.

---

92 Here, as before, I refer to the Galician-Volynian chronicle found in the Ipatievski Catalogue (c. 1249-50).

93 The great prince Roman Mstislavich (of Volyn' and Galicia)

94 These talks were initiated before Danil's submission to Batu, and were mediated by the Italian Archbishop Giovanni da Pian del Carpine, sent by the Pope into the territory of the Golden Horde (1246-7).

The Two Heroic Feats of St. Alexander Nevsky

Finally, between 1253 and 1254, the Pope issued calls to the rulers of Central and Eastern Europe for a crusade against the Tatars in Danil's defense.

Counting on the West for aid, Danil began actively preparing for a battle with the Mongols: he accumulated soldiers and money, fortified cities, populated them[95], and did everything to magnify his power.

In 1255, in the city of Drogichin, Danil was coronated with a royal crown sent to him by the Pope.

However, Danil needed more than a crown. Above all else, he required military aid. Such aid never came: the Pope's calls to action went unanswered. As a result, Danil severed his ties with Rome.

Meanwhile, a storm was encroaching from the East. Danil saw that he would be impotent against it, unable to head off the desolation of his lands that had begun at the hands of the Tatars. He had no choice but to relent and to abandon his vision. In response to the demands of the Dnieper-area Tatar *baskak* Kuremsa, Danil halted his military preparations against the Tatars and demolished his fortifications around the cities of Volyn (1261).

A few years later, Danil died (1264). His "grand politics" had concluded in failure; he had been successful only in terms of his "minor politics", in his struggle against his immediate neighbors, the Lithuanians, whom neither the Mongols nor the Latin crusaders backed against him.

Danil squandered his efforts on everyday political trifles and let the main threads of historical events slip through his fingers.

He won some isolated battles, but he lost what was most important – Orthodox Russia.

---

95 The new inhabitants most often turned out to be Germans, Poles, and Jews; the consequences became apparent in the later development of these cities.

As a result of his politics, southwestern Rus was enslaved by the Latin West for long centuries to come.

Not even a hundred years had gone by after Danil's death before all of his inheritance – the lands of Galicia and Volyn' – had been captured by the neighboring Ugrics, Poles, and Lithuanians.

In certain areas of Rus, this Latin slavery has still yet to be overcome. Before the start of the world war of 1914 – and now, it appears – this slavery was renewed in the very same long-suffering lands of Volyn, its oppression as heavy or even heavier than before…

***

The actions of Alexander Yaroslavich were the total opposite of those carried out by Danil Romanovich.

With considerably less historical endowments, Alexander achieved far greater and incomparably more stable political results. The brilliant and tumultuous saga of Danil of Galicia had come to naught. But the profound and persistent political labors of Alexander Nevsky led to magnificent outcomes.

Danil had exclusively favorable historical and geographical forces at his disposal: an incomparable base of operations in the heart of central Europe. Had he but made use of the Mongol armies at his rear, he would have secured completely unforeseen and incredible results. He could have firmly solidified the positions of Rus and of Orthodoxy throughout Eastern and Central Europe.

On the contrary, Alexander took up his mantle under the worst imaginable historical and geographical conditions. The northwestern corner of European Russia presented him with limited international prospects. But if Alexander was in no position to acquire new lands, he was quite capable of losing some, if not all, of those which he already held. He stood to lose not only his "window to Europe," but also Novgorod and

Pskov; this was a question of the very existence of Rus, her culture and identity, and her central hearth. Alexander was tasked with upholding the living energy of Russian culture – Orthodoxy – and ensuring the security of what, already in that time, was the fundamental source of such energy – the motherland of Russian folkhood. If the Latin West had sacked Novgorod, Pskov, and Tver, northeastern Rus might have proved too weak to maintain her own independent life and may have dissolved altogether into the Tatar masses instead of incorporating the Tatar element within herself (as ultimately came to pass).

Alexander's historical task was of a dual nature: defending the borders of Rus from attacks launched by the Latin West and reinforcing national self-consciousness within these borders.

In order to resolve either task, he would need to gain a precise awareness and deep feeling – by way of instinct or by going with his gut, so to speak – of the historical significance of Russian culture's unique trait: Orthodoxy.

The salvation of the Orthodox faith was the foundation of Alexander's political system. For him, Orthodoxy was not something one spoke of in words, but was rather an actual, existing thing – the "pillar and affirmation of truth."

Once the foundation had proven itself to be dependable and unshakeable, Alexander had no fear of seeking whatever historical allies he might find in order to reinforce the foundation even further.

Given his profound and ingenious hereditary sense of history, Alexander understood that the primary danger posed to Orthodoxy and the uniqueness of Russian culture in his epoch came not from the East, but from the West – not from the Mongols, but from the Latin Catholics. The Mongols had subjected the body to slavery, but not the soul. The Latins, however, threatened to distort the soul itself.

The Two Heroic Feats of St. Alexander Nevsky

Catholicism was a militant religious system which strove to subjugate all, and to remake the Orthodox faith of the Russian people in its image.

Meanwhile, the Mongols had no religious system of which to speak, imposing a merely cultural-political one. They brought with them civil, political law (the "*yassa*" of Genghis Khan), but did not impinge upon religious or ecclesiastical matters.

We have grown accustomed to placing an equal sign between Tatars and Muslims. But the first Mongol wave into Rus was not Muslim. Only 40 years after the battle of the Kalka did Berke, Khan of the Golden Horde, accept Islam (c. 1260). But Berke himself had been no more than a regional lord – regional, not imperial. He was subject to the Great Mongol Khan Möngke (his cousin), after whose death he fell under the authority of Kublai Khan, whose wisdom and tolerance was so praised by Marco Polo.

The fundamental principle of the Great Mongol State was precisely a broad tolerance for all faiths or, perhaps even more, the protection of all religions. The first Mongol armies, having created a world Mongol empire by way of their incursions westward, consisted primarily of Buddhists and Christians (Nestorians). In the times of princes Danil and Alexander, the Mongol armies had dealt a terrible blow to Islam (the sacking of Baghdad in 1258).

It was precisely as a result of this circumstance that such a principally empathetic attitude toward all churches and religious organizations came to characterize Mongol politics, thereafter persisting to a significant degree even in the Islamic period of the Golden Horde.

The Russian Orthodox Church in particular maintained total freedom of action and enjoyed the full support of the Khanate, which was affirmed by special titles (letters of commendation) granted by the Khans.

The Two Heroic Feats of St. Alexander Nevsky

In light of this, Alexander Nevsky not only had nothing to fear from the Mongols, but could even count on their help. Therefore, his submission to the Mongols was not a purely mechanical act; it merely complied with necessity. In the Mongols, Alexander saw a force that was culturally friendly to the Russian people and which could aid him in preserving and affirming Russian cultural identity against the Latin West.

For this reason, Alexander's politics of compliance with the Mongol East was not an arbitrary political move like the decisions taken by Danil, but rather the manifestation of a deeply considered and profoundly intuited political system.

***

Alexander Yaroslavich – like Danil Romanovich – was a richly endowed personality, both physically and spiritually. *The Life of Alexander*[96] praises his qualities of mind and heart, his beauty and bravery: "Wisdom and wit, like those of King Solomon, were given to him by God." From a young age, "a fear of God had inhabited his heart, causing him to observe the Lord's commandments and to act in accordance with them in everything he did [...]. Throughout his youth, he remained humble with all his soul, abstaining and remaining vigilant, he stayed pure in both soul and body, obtained meekness, and turned away from vainglory [...]. The scripture of God was incessantly in his mouth, pleasing him more than honey." He read this scripture "with sincerity and attention, wishing to fulfill these verses with his actions."

Alexander's physical qualities corresponded to those of his soul. "He was very great in stature. The beauty of his face was like that of the magnificent Joseph; his strength was as though it had been derived from the strength of Samson; the sound of his voice was like a trumpet amongst the people; his bravery was like that of the Roman emperor Vespasian."

---

96   *The Book of Ranks of the Royal Genealogy* [*Stepennaya Kniga*], 8th Degree.

The Two Heroic Feats of St. Alexander Nevsky

Alexander Yaroslavich ascended to the princely throne just before the Mongol invasion. In 1236, Prince Yaroslav, having marched with his army from Novgorod to Kiev, installed his son as the prince of Novgorod. It was in Novgorod that Alexander ruled during the first Tatar incursion in the winter of 1237-38. As is well known, the Tatars did not manage to penetrate to Novgorod itself in this first attempt. "And some divine force forbade the filthy horde from reaching [the city]," as it says in the *Book of Ranks*, "and not only were they not allowed in the slightest to draw near to the borders of Great Novgorod, but they were also prevented from arriving to the place where they were to do battle with the opposed and inimical armies of Lithuania and the Germanic tribes."

Nonetheless, Novgorod was eventually subjugated to Tatar power along with the other Russian cities and lands. In 1236, Alexander's father Yaroslav was crowned Great Prince in the stead of his brother Yuri, who had perished in a battle with the Tatars. Yaroslav's political primacy was secured at the price of total subjugation to Mongol authority. In 1243, Yaroslav was personally summoned to the Golden Horde in order that he might express his loyalty and devotion. Batu Khan received him with "great honor" and said: "Yaroslav! May you grow older than all the princes in the Russian domain." Yaroslav sent his son Konstantin to Asia as collateral to be held by the Great Khan.[97]

Under the mantle of the Mongol world order in the East during those very same years, Yaroslav's second son, Alexander, repulsed all attacks from the West in magnificent form.

As we have already established, in July of 1240, the Swedish Jarl Birger, raised by the Pope to wage a crusade against the infidels (i.e., the Orthodox Christians), landed on the banks of the Neva. Having received news of this, in the words of the ancient biographical chronicle, Alexander "felt his heart combust into flame, went down to the Church of Holy Sophia

---

97 At the time, there was no Great Khan as such. Rather, the widow of Ogodei, Turakina, ruled the Empire.

The Two Heroic Feats of St. Alexander Nevsky

(in Novgorod), fell onto his knees before the altar, and began to pray with tears in his eyes [...]. And, having received the Psalm, he said: 'Lord, condemn those who offend me. Rebuke those who struggle with me. Accept my sword, my shield, and my host in exchange for your aid.' Having finished his prayer and risen to his feet, he bowed to the Archbishop Spiridon, who blessed him and sent him forth."

Alexander went on the attack "with his small company, not boasting a mighty force, but placing their hopes in the Holy Trinity."

At 6:00 in the morning on 15 June, the battle commenced ("a great bloodbath for the Romans"). Alexander's victory was total and decisive: "He vanquished an untold number of them" ("Romans," i.e., the Catholic Swedes). Upon the very face of Jarl Birger, Alexander "left a mark with the sharp blade of his sword."

This victory at the Neva took place under conditions of the greatest religious effort. It had been accompanied by a miracle: before the battle, a naval guard on the shoreline by the name of Pelgusy, being a former pagan who had been baptized an Orthodox Christian and named Filip, had a vision. Pelgusy stood "at the edge of the sea, he stood guard in both directions and passed the night in a heightened state of vigilance; just as the sun began to rise, having heard a terrible roar out over the sea, he watched as a single boat came sailing in; standing amid decks of the boat were the martyrs Boris and Gleb, wearing scarlet robes [...]. And Boris said: 'Brother Gleb! Let me row so that we might help our kinsman Alexander.'"

At the moment that Novgorod came under an attack by the Swedes, the Germans (the Livonian Knights) descended on Pskov and took it; the Germans, thereafter, proceeded to the Novgorod lands, where they attempted to reinforce themselves, building a fortress in Koporye.

In 1241, Alexander took Koporye with the entirety of its German garrison. In the beginning of 1242, Alexander occupied Pskov and immediately marched into the Chudskoe lands, which were in the hands of the Livonian Order. On 5 April, on the ice of Lake Chudskoe, a famous battle took place which would later be known as the "Slaughter on the Ice". The Germans and their Chuds formed into a "swine" (a wedge formation) and were able to break through the lines of the opposing Russian force but, just at the moment of their penetration, Alexander took a separate detachment and flanked them from the rear, thereby finishing the matter. The enemy's destruction was total. "And there was a mighty slaughter of the Germans and their Chuds," the *Life of Alexander* relates. "There was a great cracking of shattering spears and a terrible noise of swords rending flesh [...]. [One could not] see the ice, for it was covered all over in blood." One eyewitness reported having seen "the heavenly hosts of God in the air, coming to Alexander's aid."

Alexander's return to Pskov was triumphant: "A Candlemas was held in the brightly lit cathedral with venerated crosses and holy icons among the throngs of the people, lifting their praises to God and singing songs of thanks: the Lord, ever ready to lend his help to the meek David in his victory over foreign tribes, has also aided our great and faithful Alexander in his liberation of the Christian city of Pskov by means of the sword from the foul foreigners."

After a number of brilliant and glorious victories against the West, Alexander was forced to experience the strength of the East up close: he was summoned to Vladimir to bid his father Yaroslav farewell, the latter preparing for his journey to the Golden Horde of Batu Khan.

This obeisance in the East was followed yet again by victories in the West (including a number of victories over Lithuania in 1245 in the region of Toropets and Vitebsk). Also in 1245, Konstantin Yaroslavich returned from his captivity under the Great Khan in Asia. In August of 1246, Yaroslav participated in the kurultai, at which Güyük, son of Ogodei and Turakina, was crowned Great Khan. Soon afterward, Yaroslav fell ill and died (in the Khan's company).

After the death of his father, Alexander found himself in immediate proximity to the East; he had no choice but to make an independent decision regarding the East and the West. Both the East and the West were calling him to their sides.

In 1248, a Papal Bull was decreed in which the Pope promised Alexander the help of the Livonian knights against the Tatars[98] in exchange for the latter's recognition of the Roman throne.

From the other direction, Batu Khan sent the following message to Alexander: "Prince Alexander, the most illustrious among the Russian rulers, I know of your renown, and God has placed many people under my authority, and all submit to me. Do you alone, above all others, not please to submit to my power? Take care – if you think to maintain your lands unmolested, then hasten to me at once and see the honor and glory of my kingdom, into which you and your lands have been gainfully incorporated."

Alexander, along with his brother Andrei, set off for the realm of Batu Khan. From there, the brothers set off to see the Great Khan Güyük (the trek into Asia taking them two years). Vladimir was given to Andrei, while Alexander received Novgorod and Kiev. Their third brother, Yaroslav, was made prince of Tver. Being the eldest, Alexander demanded authority over his brothers. The aim of his politics was the unification of all the Russias under one Great Prince. Failing to find obedience in his brothers, Alexander was not averse to subduing them with the help of the Tatars. In 1252, the Tatar army of Nevryui drove Andrei from Vladimir; the great princely table was handed over to Alexander. In 1256, Alexander drove his other brother, Yaroslav (who, from Tver, had gone first to Pskov, and then to Novgorod), out of

---

98 This Bull was delivered to Aleksandr sometime around 1251, shortly after which Aleksandr gave his answer to the Pope that is documented in his biographical chronicle.

The Two Heroic Feats of St. Alexander Nevsky

Novgorod by force. Afterward, Alexander cruelly punished the Novgorodians who did not wish to pay tribute to the Tatars. In 1259, Alexander was personally present as the Tatars took this "tribute."

In 1262, Alexander fought against the West for the last time; he sent his son Dmitry and his brother Yaroslav (recently subjugated) to attack Yuryev-Livonsky. The Russians overpowered the Germans and burned down their settlement (however, they were unable to take the fortress).

Alexander himself was absent, as he had been called to the Golden Horde to propitiate the Khan, who was furious at the recent uprising: in many northern Russian cities in 1262, the people had beaten the Tatar tribute collectors, not realizing that behind each "*baskak*" stood the terrible power of the entire Mongol Empire. Alexander managed to turn the incident to his advantage: Khan Berke was pleased by his apologies and renewed pledges of loyalty.

Saving Russian lands from further devastation was Alexander's final political act. He spent nearly a year with the Golden Horde. On his journey home, he took ill (in Nizhny Novgorod) and died in Gorodets on the Volga (14 November 1263). Before dying, Alexander summoned "all of his princes and boyars, as well as the entirety of his staff down to the lowliest rank, and asked forgiveness of each and every one of them, forgiving them as well. They all cried bitterly at their parting with their master. It was terrible to see how, in the thick of the crowd, there was not a man to be found without tears in his eyes; but they all exclaimed: 'Woe to us, our dear lord! We shall no more see the beauty of your face, nor shall we relish in your sweet speeches! To whom shall we run? Who shall provide us with merciful charity? For no child has received such a blessing from his parent as we have received from you, our sweetest lord!"

Metropolitan Kirill was in Vladimir when news of Alexander's demise arrived. Coming out to address the people, he declared: "The sun of the Russian land has already set." Then, after a spell of silence during which tears welled up in his eyes, he said, "The great and faithful prince Alexander has passed away from this life."

"And, throughout all the people, there arose an inconsolable cry."

***

Alexander's reign was not exclusively and purely defined by political planning and calculation. His politics was intimately connected with his moral and religious views. It would be more accurate to say that what lay at the foundations of his politics were moral, religious principles. Alexander's political system was simultaneously a moral-religious system.

Alexander Yaroslavich was not simply a politician and a warrior: he was, above all, a man of profound faith and a learned theologian. When the Roman Pope sent him two cardinals with the intent of converting him to the Latin faith, Alexander – "having taken council with his advisors" – furnished a comprehensive refutation.

"He accounted for everything from Adam to the flood, from the flood to the confusion of tongues at the Tower of Babel and Abraham's emergence, from Abraham [...] to Caesar Augustus, from Caesar Augustus to Christ's Nativity and Passion and Resurrection, from Christ's Resurrection to his ascent to the heavens and the empire of Constantine the Great and the First Council of Nicaea held by the church fathers, and from the First to the Seventh Council. We know all of these things well; they are the essence within us. We virtuously observe these doctrines. They are professed throughout our lands, and their words reach to the ends of the universe as one of the holy apostles preached Christ's Gospel throughout the world, in accordance with the same traditions as those of the holy fathers of the Seventh Ecumenical Council. And we preserve this doctrine while rejecting those doctrines which come from you. We do not listen to your scripture."

Alexander Nevsky's religious, moral philosophy was simultaneously his political philosophy.

In the *Life of Alexander*, we find two main bases for his "journey to the Horde."

Alexander "thought to go to the Horde" (1) "imitating the noble jealousy of his honorable father" and (2) "for the sake of delivering Orthodox Christians."

We find an explanation of the second motivation in the words of Batu Khan: "If you think to maintain your lands unmolested, then hasten to me."

As regards the first motive, the biographical chronicle elucidates this by means of the following: "The great prince Alexander, wise in the ways of God, considered how his holy father Yaroslav had not troubled himself over his temporal kingdom. Alexander then went to the Golden Horde and, once there, lay down his life for honor and for all of his people, thereby guaranteeing himself the Kingdom of Heaven."

The willingness to lay down one's life for one's people is the same thing as what is expressed with the words "for the sake of delivering Orthodox Christians."

The willingness to set down one's life "for honor" fully reflects Alexander's stolid adherence to the Orthodox faith and his striving, come what may, to ensure the existence of the Orthodox Church.

The significance of the words "had not troubled himself over his temporal kingdom" is somewhat more complicated.

Similar phrases found in our chronicles usually express the ruler's preparedness to accept death and the martyr's crown in battle with the enemy, without fear or wavering, having exchanged his "temporal kingdom" for an "eternal" one.[99]

---

99 Cf. M.V. Shakhmatov's essay "The Feat of Power [*Podvig Vlasti*]" in volume III of *Eurasian Annals*.

But, in their application to the eastern politics of Yaroslav and Aleksandr – the politics not of armed struggle or uprising, but of submission and loyalty – these words must be read with a different meaning and implication.

We might once more juxtapose such words with those of Batu Khan: "Behold the honor and glory of my kingdom." That of which Batu Khan speaks – the glimmer of earthly glory (the "temporal kingdom") is precisely that with which Yaroslav did not trouble himself. On the other hand, Batu Khan did trouble himself with the temporal kingdom, as did Danil Galitsky.

Alexander, too, sacrificed such external shimmering and glorification of the earthly kingdom for the profundity of the foundations of imperial power which he understood so well: "for honor and for all of his people"; "for the sake of delivering Orthodox Christians."

For Danil and his conceits, "the honor of the Tatars was eviler than evil," while Alexander received this honor with humility.

It had been unacceptable for Danil to become the underling (the "bondsman") of the Tatar Khan: Alexander accepted this too with humility.

Alexander – "victorious everywhere and never defeated" – withstood temptation as Danil had done by arriving at a compromise with the Latin West in order to find allies against the East.

Alexander's submission to the Golden Horde cannot be interpreted in any other manner than as a feat of humility.

It is no coincidence that Pelgusy's vision showed none other than Boris and Gleb coming to Alexander's aid – the saints of humility *par excellence*.

It is not written in vain in the *Book of Ranks* that Alexander's "humble wisdom" was "greater than that found in all other men."

The Two Heroic Feats of St. Alexander Nevsky

The heroic Christian feat does not always take the form of external martyrdom. Sometimes, it is quite to the contrary – this martyrdom becomes internal. In this case, the martyr does not only suffer visible abuse, but also "invisible abuse"; he struggles with spiritual temptations and carries out an act of humility and self-discipline. And this heroic feat may characterize not only an individual person, but a ruler, as well.

The calling of the sovereign is a divine institution. But every sovereign encounters temptations and is attracted by his earthly environment – by outer luxury and vain ("temporal") majesty – toward power.

The feat of power may consist in valorously upholding one's external independence and the dignity of one's office – even to the point of death. But the feat of power may also consist, while fulfilling the fundamental obligations of that office – the defense of "honor and one's people" – in overcoming that which is external whenever it should be required for the fulfillment of a fundamental task, namely the worldly vanity of power.

As the venerable Theodore the Studite says in one of his pronouncements, "He who instructs and commands must observe a constant state of temperance and humility, for the Creator of nature has set him up as the most honorable and representative part of his body."

The feat carried out by Saint Alexander Nevsky with regard to the East was of precisely this kind. In relation to the West, this was not a difficult feat, but a simple one, a battle not only invisible, but also visible.

***

Alexander Nevsky's two heroic feats – that of decrying the West and of humbly submitting to the East – contributed to one and the same goal: the preservation of Orthodoxy as the moral, political strength of the Russian people.

This aim was achieved: the flourishing of the Russian Orthodox domain was realized on the soil which Alexander had prepared. And thus, it fell to Alexander's tribe to build up the Muscovian state.

When the times and intervals during which Rus accumulated its power were concluded, during which the Golden Horde underwent an inverse process of dwindling and weakening[100], Alexander's politics of submission to the Mongol yoke ceased to be necessary: The Orthodox Tsardom could then be openly and directly asserted. The Orthodox banner could be raised without caution.

It was at this juncture that the politics of Alexander Nevsky naturally transformed into the politics of Dmitry Donskoi.

The internal necessity of such a transformation was vividly emphasized in the *Saga of Miracles Surrounding the Repose of Blessed Alexander* – specifically in "The Miracle of the Donskoi Victory."

"In death, as in life," the *Saga* relates, "the marvelous autocrat Alexander neither forsakes nor forgets his pasture, but always provides and intercedes against enemies both visible and invisible [...]. In the famed city of Vladimir, in the monastery of the Holy Virgin and Mother of God and Her Sacred Nativity, by the sacred tomb of the great and blessed prince Alexander at one in the morning (8 September 1380), the sacristans who had been sleeping under the portico of the church awoke to find that the candles in the cathedral had lit themselves; and two venerable elders came down from the holy altar, drew near to the tomb of the blessed prince Alexander, and intoned: O, lord Alexander, rise up and hurry to the aid of your great-grandson, the great prince Dmitry, who is conquering the lands of foreign tribes. And at that hour, the

---

100 Fatal for the Turko-Mongols in this regard was their schism, as a result of which their western branch had converted to Islam.

The Two Heroic Feats of St. Alexander Nevsky

great, holy prince Alexander rose from his coffin and swiftly vanished before the eyes of the two elders."

And so, at the necessary moment, the conditions under which a feat of humility toward the Tatars was required were inverted so that humility became aggressive opposition.

This is, of course, precisely what occurred in history: Dmitry's army grew upon Alexander's humility. The Muscovian Tsardom was, to a significant extent, the fruit of Alexander's wise politics.

The *Book of Ranks*, which furnished this Tsardom with its spiritual-historical foundation, evinces a profound comprehension of history; among the founders of the Tsardom, the text affords Saint Alexander Nevsky a place of the highest significance within the "boundaries" of its narration.

***

Alexander Nevsky and Danil Galitsky represent the two primordial types of Russian and, more broadly, world history[101]: the "Western" type and the "Oriental" type.

Russian society in the 19th century was famously cleaved into the factions of the "Westernizers" and the "Slavophiles." These are simply variations of the two fundamental types mentioned above. The disagreement between Westernizers and Slavophiles in the middle of the 19th century found its primary manifestation in the context of literary criticism.

However, our recognition of the cultural contradiction between West and East must move beyond the bounds of literature – it must actively impinge on immediate reality.

We must renew our understanding and evaluation not only of literary criticism, but also of the deeds, heroic feats, and sentiments of the past.

---

101 Here we are speaking of the history of the Old World – of Eurasia.

The Two Heroic Feats of St. Alexander Nevsky

The figures of the two Russian princes – Danil Galitsky and Alexander Nevsky – gleam at us like the pendula of two world-senses.

The legacy of the magnificent but poorly considered feats of the one was the enslavement of southwestern Rus to the Latin West. The legacy of feats belonging to the other was the great Russian State.

***

ON THE TURANIAN ELEMENT IN RUSSIAN CULTURE

Nikolai Trubetzkoy[102]

***

I

The East Slavic tribes initially occupied only a small part of the vast territory occupied by modern Russia. The Slavs initially inhabited only a small western part of this territory, the river basins connecting the Baltic Sea with the Black Sea. The rest of it, the majority of the territory of modern Russia, was predominantly inhabited by the tribes often grouped under the name "Turanian" or "Ural-Altai". The Turanian tribes initially played a much more significant role than the East Slavic, Russian tribes in the history of this region. Even in the so-called pre-Mongol period, the Turanian states within European Russia (the kingdom of the Volga-Kama Bulgarians and the Khazar kingdom) were much more significant than the Varangian-Russians. The very unification of almost the entire territory of modern Russia under the rule of one state was first carried out not by the Russian Slavs, but by the Turanian-Mongols. The spread of Russians to the East was associated with the Russification of a number of Turanian tribes; the cohabitation of Russians and Turanians runs through Russian history like a red thread.

---

[102] Originally published in *The Eurasian Annals*, book 4 (Berlin, 1925).

On the Turanian Element in Russian Culture

If the fusion of the Eastern Slavs with the Turanian element is a basic fact of Russian history, if it is difficult to find a Great Russian in whose veins Turanian blood does not flow, and if the same Turanian blood (from the ancient steppe nomads) flows in the veins of the Little Russians (*Malorossy*), then it is absolutely clear that we Russians need to take into account the presence of the Turanian element in us for proper national self-knowledge, and therefore it is necessary to study our Turanian brothers. Until now, we have cared little about this: we have always been inclined to put forward our Slavic origin, hushing up the presence of the Turanian element in us, as if ashamed of this element. It is time to end this prejudice. Like any bias, it interferes with correct self-knowledge, and correct self-knowledge is not only the duty of every individual, but also an indispensable condition for the rational existence of any personality, including a nation understood as a kind of personality.

The name "Turanian" or "Ural-Altai" refers to the following five groups of peoples:

The Finno-Ugric peoples, who, based on linguistic kinship, are divided into Western Finns (Estonians, Karelians, Finns themselves and a number of small tribes), Lapps (in Sweden, Norway, Northern Finland and Russia on the Kola Peninsula), Mordovians, Cheremis, Permian Finns (Zyryans and Votyaks) and Ugrians (Magyars, or Hungarians, in Hungary and Transylvania and the "Ob Ugrians," i.e., Voguls and Ostyaks in Northwestern Siberia); the extinct (more precisely, completely Russified) ancient tribes also belonged to the same group of Finno-Ugric peoples - the Merya (in language related to the Cheremis), the Ves (in language a West Finnish tribe), the Muroma and the Meshchera, as mentioned in Russian chronicles.

The Samoyeds, divided into several tribes, are now almost extinct and survive only in small numbers in the Arkhangelsk province and North-Western Siberia.

On the Turanian Element in Russian Culture

The Turks, which include the Ottoman Turks, various Tatars (Crimean, Kazan, Azerbaijani, Tobolsk, etc.), Meshcheryaks, Teptyars, Balkars (Karachais, Urusbievs, etc.), Kumyks, Bashkirs, Kyrgyz-Kaisaks, Kara-Kirghiz, Turkmens, Sarts, Uzbeks, Altaians, Yakuts, the Chuvash and a number of ancient, disappeared peoples, of which the most famous are the Khazars, Bulgarians (Volga-Kama and "Asparukhovs"), Polovtsy (otherwise known as the Cumans or Kipchaks), Uyghurs and others.

The Mongols, to which Kalmyks and Buryats within Russia and beyond its borders belong, and the Mongols proper in Mongolia.

The Manchus, to whom, in addition to the Manchus themselves, also belong the Golds and Tungus (now almost entirely extinct or Russified).

Despite a number of common anthropological and linguistic features that are characteristic of all of the listed groups of peoples and allow them to be grouped under the common name Turanian, the question of their genetic relationship is controversial. Only the relationship of the Finno-Ugric group of languages with the Samoyedic can be considered proven, and both of these groups are sometimes combined under the common name of the "Uralic family of languages".[103] But still, even if the other three groups of Turanian languages and peoples are not genetically related to each other and to the "Uralians," the close mutual similarity of all Turanian languages and the psychological profile of all Turanian peoples is completely beyond doubt, and we have the right to speak of a single Turanian psychological type, completely abstracted from the question of whether this

---

103 The relationship between the Turkic, Mongolian, and Manchu languages (united in the general group of "Altaic languages"), which was considered very probable for a long time, has recently come into question as a result of more detailed study. The relationship between the "Uralic" languages and the rest of the Turanian languages is now resolutely denied by most linguists. And only recently have attempts been made again to scientifically prove this relationship.

commonality of psychological type is due to consanguinity or other historical reasons.

II

The Turanian mental profile is most clearly evident among the Turks, who, of all the Turanians, have played the most outstanding role in the history of Eurasia. Therefore, we will proceed from the characteristics of the Turks.

The mental profile of the Turks is clarified by examining their language and the products of their national creativity in the field of spiritual culture.

The Turkic languages are very close to each other, especially if we ignore the foreign words (Persian and Arabic) that have penetrated in large numbers into the languages of the Muslim Turks. When comparing individual Turkic languages with each other, a common type of language is easily identified, which is most clearly evident among the Altaians. This type is characterized by its extraordinary strictness. The sound composition of words is standardized by a number of laws, which do not tolerate exceptions in purely Turkic, non-borrowed words [...][104]

Summarizing everything that has been said about the Turkic language type, we come to the conclusion that this type is characterized by a schematic pattern, the consistent implementation of a small number of simple and clear, basic principles that weld speech into one whole. The comparative poverty and rudimentary nature of the speech material itself, on the one hand, and the subordination of all speech, both in sound and in formal terms, to schematic patterns on the other, are the main features of the Turkic language type.

After language, folk art is of the greatest importance for characterizing this national type.

---

104 [Editor: an extensive section on Turkic grammar has been left out here in order to maintain a focus on the central argument of the piece.]

On the Turanian Element in Russian Culture

In the field of music, the Turkic peoples represent much less of a unity than in the field of language: knowing the Ottoman-Turkish language, you can easily understand the Kazan or Bashkir text, but if you listen to an Ottoman-Turkish and then a Kazan-Tatar or Bashkir melody one after the other, you come to the conclusion that there is nothing in common between them. This is explained, of course, mainly by the difference in cultural influences. The music of the Ottoman Turks is overwhelmingly influenced by Arabic music on the one hand, and Greek on the other. The overwhelming influence of Arab-Persian music is also observed among the Crimean and Azerbaijani Tatars. When it comes to defining the truly Turkic musical type, Turkish, Crimean Tatar and Azerbaijani music, especially "urban" music, cannot be taken into account. If we turn to the music of other Turkic peoples, we will see that most of them are dominated by one specific musical type. This type, according to which the melodies of the Volga-Ural, Siberian, part of the Turkestan and Sino-Turkestan Turks are built, is characterized by the following features.

The melody is built on the so-called half-tone-five-tone (otherwise known as the Indo-Chinese) scale, i.e., as if on a major scale with the skipping of the fourth and seventh steps: for example, if the tones C and D are found in a melody, then only G and A can occur in it, but neither F, nor F-sharp, nor B, nor B-flat can occur. Moves of half steps are not allowed at all. Choral songs are sung in unison. On the rhythmic side, the melody is constructed strictly symmetrically, divided into parts with an equal number of measures, and usually the number of measures in each part of the melody is 2, 4, 8, etc. It is possible to establish a small number of basic melodic types, the most important of which are: 1) a type of melody built on a descending cadence, that is, based on the alternation of an upward movement and a downward movement, and each time the upper and lower limits of the movement are lowered, and the amplitude of the movement itself is reduced; 2) a type of melody based on the opposition of two parts, of which the first contains a small musical phrase repeated twice, and the second part contains two different phrases, rhythmically structured in approximately the same way and carrying out a short downward movement.

While there are some minor differences, both types are generally subject to the same laws: the harmonic law of the five-tone scale and the rhythmic law of symmetrical equality of parts and paired periodicity. Turkic songs composed according to this model are distinguished by their special harmonic and rhythmic clarity and transparency. Each such melody consists of one or two similar and very simple musical phrases, but these phrases can be repeated indefinitely, forming a long and monotonous song.

In other words, the same basic psychological features can be traced here that we noted above in the line of the Turkic languages: the comparative poverty and rudimentary nature of the material and complete submission to simple and schematic laws that weld the material into a single whole and give this whole a certain schematic clarity and transparency.

Regarding the oral poetry of the Turkic peoples, we must say the same thing that we said above about music: if we discard those forms of poetry of the Muslim Turks that are clearly inspired by the Arab and Persian models, then in the poetry of different Turkic peoples the features of one general type are outlined.

Since in most Turkic languages there is no distinction between long and short vowels, and the stress fixed on the last syllable of a word is not recognized by the speaker as a meaning-forming ("phonological") factor of the language, the Turkic poem is built on the number of syllables, i.e. is "syllabic": more precisely, versification is based on the correct repetition of "word divisions" (the boundaries between two adjacent words) at intervals filled with a certain number of syllables. The sound monotony of the beginning and end of Turkic words, caused by the sound laws consistently applied and regulating all Turkic speech, greatly facilitates the use of high-quality rhythm, i.e. adding to the main syllabic principle of versification a second, auxiliary principle in the form of repetition at the beginning or end of each metric segment of sounds of the same quality. Indeed, in the poetry of most Turkic peoples there are either alliterations or rhymes. At the same time, in accordance with the properties of the Turkic languages, which subordinate vowel words to the laws of harmony, vowels play a minor role in alliteration and rhyme: *Birinji* (the first) can rhyme with *Onunju* (the tenth). Along with external rhythm, the rhythm of sounds, there is also internal rhythm, the rhythm of meanings. Turkic poetry has a strong tendency towards parallelism. The poetic works of some Turkic tribes are built entirely on the principle of parallelism. All verses are grouped in pairs, with the second verse in each pair repeating the content of the first in different words; in those rare cases when the first and second verses are not identical in content, they are nevertheless constructed according to the same syntactic scheme, so that at least formal, syntactic parallelism remains. The matter in principle, of course, does not change when the verses are grouped not in twos, but in fours, and when parallelism exists not between two adjacent verses, but between the first and second halves of one quatrain.

With regard to poetic creativity, the individual Turkic peoples represent quite different types. Some (for example, the Kazan Tatars) are dominated by short quatrains with a rather weak semantic connection between the first and second parts (like Russian sung couplettes), but still with a clearly expressed tendency towards syntactic parallelism. Among other tribes we find couplets or symmetrically constructed quatrains with parallelism reaching the point of tautology. Finally, long, mostly epic songs are also known, but they are also constructed strophically, with each stanza subordinating the principle of parallelism, and often with the combination of several stanzas into one symmetrical-parallelistic figure.

There is an inextricable connection between the external and internal features of Turkic versification: rhyme and alliteration are inextricably linked with the principle of semantic and syntactic parallelism (for the most part, the same grammatical endings of parts of a sentence rhyme, falling due to syntactic parallelism in the same places in two adjacent verses); and at the same time, the same rhymes or alliteration, emphasizing the beginning or end of the verse, contribute to the clarity of syllabic division and strophic construction. If we add to all this that the number of meters used in Turkic poetry is very small (verses of 7, 8, 11 and 12 syllables), that the rhymes are mostly "grammatical", that parallelism mostly leans towards either complete semantic tautology, or towards exclusively syntactic analogy, while more complex figurative comparisons are relatively rare, then we will get a sufficient idea of the nature of Turkic poetic creativity. In this creative form we again see the same psychological features that we have already noted in language and music: the comparative poverty of means with a remarkably consistent pattern and schematic clarity of construction.

And so, consideration of the structure of Turkic languages, Turkic music and Turkic poetry has led us to the establishment of well-known features of Turkic psychology that appear in all of these manifestations of national creativity. In other areas of Turkic spiritual culture, the same psychological features are evident. When it comes to religious life, the Turks are not very active. Most of the Turkic tribes currently profess Islam; in ancient times there were Buddhists (Uyghurs) and Judaists (Khazars). The Turkic tribes that have preserved the national pagan faith are now few in number. Of these, the Altaians deserve special attention. The religion of these latter (since they still retain paganism) is imbued with the idea of dualism, and it is curious that this dualism is elevated to a consistent, pedantically symmetrical system. Here we again encounter that rudimentary schematism that we have already noted in language, in music and in poetry. In Yakut and Chuvash paganism we generally find the same dualistic tendency, but carried out less consistently and schematically than among the Altaians.

The specific features of Turkic psychology also find reflection in customary law, in particular in the tribal system, but in this area schematism is connected, so to speak, with the essence of the matter, and is also manifested in many other peoples, so this phenomenon is not typical. Nevertheless, it should be noted that Turkic customary law in general always turns out to be more developed and more systematically constructed than the customary law of other tribes of the same geographical zone (with the exception of the Mongols).

III

Thus, we will not be mistaken if we say that in all the spiritual creativity of the Turks one main mental feature dominates: a clear schematization of relatively poor and rudimentary material. From here it is possible to draw conclusions about Turkic psychology itself. A typical Turk does not like to go into subtleties and intricate details. He prefers to operate with basic, clearly perceived images and group these images into clear and simple schemes. However, one should beware of possible misinterpretations of these provisions. Thus, it would be a mistake to think that the Turkic mind would be especially prone to schematic abstraction. The specific ethnographic data from which we have extracted an indication of the nature of the Turkic mental type do not give us grounds for such a conclusion. After all, those schemes on which, as we have seen, Turkic spiritual creativity is built, are by no means a product of philosophical abstraction and do not even have the character of something deliberately thought out. On the contrary, they are subconscious and exist in the psyche as an unconscious cause of that mental inertia, thanks to which all the elements of mental material themselves fit in exactly this order and not in another: this is possible due to the special elementarity and simplicity of these schemes. On the other hand, it would be a mistake to think that the saddlery harnessing or schematic nature of Turkic psychology prevented the wide scope and flight of imagination. The content of the epic legends of the Turkic tribes strongly contradicts this idea. The Turkic imagination is not poor and not timid, it has a bold scope, but this scope is rudimentary: the power of imagination is directed not at detailed development, not at piling up various details, but, so to speak, at development in width and length; the picture painted by this imagination is not replete with a variety of colors and transitional tones, but is painted in basic colors, with broad, sometimes even colossally broad, strokes. This desire to expand in breadth, deeply characteristic of Turkic creativity, is internally determined by the same basic features of the Turkic psyche. We have seen that the longest Turkic word (for example, the Ottoman-Turkish *vuruşturamamışdınız* - "you did not force them to beat each other") is constructed according to the same phonetic and etymological laws as the shortest one; that the longest period is constructed according to the same syntactic rules as a short simple sentence; that in the longest song the same compositional rules prevail as in the short one; that long poems are built on the same rules as short couplets. Thanks to the elementary nature of the material and the distinct simplicity of the diagrams, the construction can easily be stretched to arbitrarily large sizes. And it is in this stretching that the imagination of the Turk finds satisfaction.

The described psychology of a typical Turk determines both the way of life and the worldview of the bearers of this psychology. The Turk loves symmetry, clarity and stable balance; but he loves that all this has already been given, so that this determines his thoughts, actions and way of life by inertia: searching for and creating those initial and basic schemes on which his life and worldview should be built is always painful for a Turk, for this search is always associated with an acute sense of lack of stability and clarity. That is why the Turks have always been so willing to take ready-made foreign plans and accept foreign beliefs. But, of course, not every foreign worldview is acceptable to a Turk. The worldview must certainly have clarity, simplicity, and most importantly, it must be a convenient scheme into which everything can be incorporated, the whole world in all its concreteness. Upon adopting a certain worldview, turning it into a subconscious law that determines all his behavior, a universal scheme, and thus achieving a state of stable equilibrium on a clear basis, the Turk relaxes and firmly holds on to this belief. Looking at the worldview precisely as the unshakable foundation of mental and everyday balance, the Turk shows inertia and stubborn conservatism in it. Faith that finds itself in a Turkic environment inevitably hardens and crystallizes as it is called upon to play the role of an unshakable center of gravity - the main condition for stable equilibrium.

A strange phenomenon results from this feature of Turkic psychology: the attraction between the Turkic and Semitic psyches. It is difficult to find two more different, directly opposite psyches. It can be shown, again on the basis of specific ethnographic data, language, music, poetry, and ornament, that the psychology of the Semite is strikingly opposite to the psychology of the Turk. And yet, it is no coincidence that the majority of the Turks are Mohammedans and that the Khazarian Turks were the only non-Semitic people in history who made Judaism their state religion. The Semite, who seeks out contradictions, who finds special pleasure in discovering contradictions and in overcoming them by way of casuistry, who loves to tinker with complexly intertwined and intricate subtleties, and the Turk, who most of all hates the disturbing feeling of internal contradiction and is helpless in overcoming it, are two natures that are not only similar, but also directly opposite to each other. But this opposition is also the reason for their attraction: the Semitic does for the Turk the work that the Turk himself is not capable of - he overcomes contradictions and presents the Turk with a solution (even a casuistic one), free from contradictions. And it is no wonder, therefore, that in looking for the necessary basis for a stable balance, the Turk constantly chooses the fruit of the creativity of the Semitic spirit as such a basis. But, borrowing this fruit of an alien spirit, the Turk immediately simplifies it, perceives it statically, in a ready-made form, and, turning it into the only unshakable foundation of his mental and external life, mummifies it once and for all, without taking any part in its internal development. Thus, the Turks did not give Islam a single major theologian, lawyer, or thinker: they accepted Islam as a complete given.

IV

The psychological characteristics of the Turkic tribe that we outlined above can be considered in general terms as a characteristic of all "Turanians" or "Ural-Altaians". Ethnopsychologically, the Mongols are one with the Turks. Everything that was said above about the typical features of Turkic languages, Turkic music, poetry, customary law, the orientation of the Turkic imagination, worldview and way of life, is equally applicable to the Mongols; only among the Mongols do these typical features appear even more sharply than among the Turks. There are no cases of attraction between Mongolian and Semitic psychology for historical reasons. Nevertheless, the Mongols, just like the Turks, borrow as the basis of their worldview and way of life the finished result of someone else's spiritual creativity; only the source of borrowing here is not Semitic Islam, like the Turks, but Indian Buddhism in the Sino-Tibetan transmission. If the Turks, as stated above, mummified and froze Islam and did not take any part in the internal development of Muslim thought, then even more can be said about the attitude of the Mongols to Buddhism.

If the Mongols, therefore, differ from the Turks in a more dramatic manifestation of all the typical features of Turanian psychology, then exactly the opposite should be said about the Finno-Ugric people. The features of Turanian psychology are also clearly manifested among Finno-Ugric people, but always to a weaker degree than among the Turkic languages; Finnic languages are generally built on the same basic principles as the Turkic ones, but these principles are applied less consistently.[105]

Irregularities and "exceptions" in every language inevitably occur due to unconscious mechanical changes that each language undergoes during its history and which are pertain to the very nature of the historical development of language: every more ancient stage of language development is always more "correct" than the newest stage. But the spirit of subordinating living speech to subconscious schematic laws in the Turkic languages is so strong that it completely neutralizes this destructive effect of historical processes. That is why the grammars of modern Turkic languages do not know (or almost do not know) "exceptions", and that is why individual modern Turkic languages are so similar to each other. In the Finno-Ugric languages, this restraining spirit of a clear pattern turned out to be much weaker; therefore, the grammars of some of these languages (for example, the language of Finnish proper - "*Suomi*") are full of exceptions, and individual Finno-Ugric languages differ significantly from each other.

Another difference between the Finno-Ugric psyche and the Turkic one is that Finnic creativity always has, so to

---

105 First of all, the linguistic material itself, the inventory of sounds and forms in the Finno-Ugric languages, is less rudimentary and more diverse than in the Turkic languages: there are Finnish languages with a rather rich sound system. All Finnish languages have quite a lot of cases, and many Finnish languages have quite complex conjugation systems: for example, they express not only the subject, but also the direct object of the verb with personal endings. On the other hand, the basic laws that determine the construction of words are carried out with incomplete consistency: the laws of vowel harmony and the use of consonants are not as clear, and most importantly, not as detailed as in the Turkic languages; there are a number of exceptions to the law on the unity of endings, that is, cases where two grammatical endings are combined; in some Finnish languages, prefixes are allowed on verbs in addition to suffixes.

speak, a smaller scope than the Turkic.[106] Finally, comparing the Finno-Ugric languages and manifestations of spiritual culture with the Turkic ones, one is convinced that the Finno-Ugric people are mentally and culturally much more passive than the Turks. In the dictionaries of Turkic languages, words borrowed from other languages are always available, but these words are mostly borrowed not from any neighbors with whom the Turks came into direct contact, but from peoples whose culture influenced the culture of a given Turkic tribe, so to speak, "from afar," in the order of foreign fashion: therefore, there are always many more such words in the literary language than in the folk language.

The Turkish vernacular language has quite a few Arabic and Persian words, but almost no Greek, Armenian, or Slavic words. But in the languages of all those peoples with whom the Turks came into contact, there is always a mass of Turkic words. The Finno-Ugric languages present a completely different picture in this regard: their dictionaries are positively replete with words borrowed at very different times, from ancient to modern, from all the peoples with which the Finno-Ugrics have ever come into contact. At the same time, the influence of the Finno-Ugric languages themselves on the dictionaries of the peoples who came into contact with them is strikingly weak: despite the centuries-old cohabitation of the Great Russians with the Finno-Ugrics, only a very small number of Finnish words can be found in the Great Russian

---

106 This position is clearly illustrated and symbolized by music. There are good reasons to assert that the main Finno-Ugric scale consists of the first five notes of the major scale: the songs of the Voguls and Ostyaks, the oldest songs of other Finno-Ugric peoples, and the most archaic gusle-like string instruments, such as among the Western Finns (*kantele*), and among the Voguls and Ostyaks (*sanguldap*), have five strings tuned in the same scale. If we recall what was said above about Turkic melodies, then the comparison of these melodies with Finno-Ugric melodies can be expressed as follows: in both of them, only five tones are involved, but while in Turkic melodies these five tones are located within at least an octave, typical Finno-Ugric melodies move within fifths. When perceived directly, typical Finno-Ugric melodies give the impression of constraint and, especially in comparison with Turkic ones, they are striking in their lack of scope.

language, and even then they usually do not go beyond the boundaries of some geographically limited regional vocabulary. The Magyar language had a somewhat greater influence on the neighboring Slavic languages, but mainly at a relatively later time, and, in any case, the number of Slavic words adopted by the Magyar language itself is much greater than the number of Magyar words included, for example, in the Serbo-Croatian language.[107] The same passivity, the same openness to foreign influence, is observed in all aspects of the spiritual culture of the Finno-Ugrics: let us note the Slavic influence, in particular Russian among the Volga-Kama and Trans-Ural Finno-Ugrics, the Turkic influence among the Western Finno-Ugrics, the influence of "Baltic" (Latvian-Lithuanian) and Germanic, and in more ancient eras all the Finno-Ugric peoples had Iranian and Caucasian influence.

When trying to isolate these foreign elements from the culture of one or another Finno-Ugric tribe and, thus, purify the purely Finno-Ugric core of this culture, the researcher is often left almost empty-handed. And yet, despite this continuous borrowing from everywhere, the culture of individual Finno-Ugric tribes has a unique character that is clearly distinct from the culture of those peoples from whom the borrowings were made. This originality depends primarily on the fact that, having once borrowed some element of culture from a given people, the Finno-Ugric peoples retain this element in a more ancient, archaic form than the form in which this element is preserved by its original bearer: thus, the Mordovians have preserved many cultural elements borrowed from the Great Russians, which among the Great Russians themselves either underwent complete annihilation or changed almost beyond recognition, the Slavic origin of which can only be concluded from the fact that they are still common among some other

---

107 Finno-Ugric influence only turned out to be significant on the vocabulary of the Samoyed languages, but at the same time the Finno-Ugric languages themselves (Zyryan, Vogul, Ostyak) were affected by Samoyed influence.

Slavs. Secondly, the originality also comes from the fact that the Finno-Ugric peoples synthesize elements borrowed from several heterogeneous cultures. Finally, if the motives and, so to speak, the material for constructing cultural values are borrowed, then the very methods of this construction and the psychological foundations of the forms of creativity among the Finno-Ugric peoples remain their own, Turanian. In general, we can say that the Finno-Ugric peoples retain all the typical features of the Turanian psyche, but in a somewhat softened form and with less mental activity than the Turks and Mongols.

Thus, despite the fact that the genetic relationship between individual families of the "Ural-Altaic" or "Turanian" languages is more than doubtful and that the individual Turanian peoples differ significantly from each other in many respects, we can nevertheless speak of a single Turanian ethno-psychological type, in relation to which the Turkic, Mongol, and Finno-Ugric ethno-psychological types are shades or variants.

V

To answer the question of how and in what way the Turanian psychological type might be reflected in the Russian national character and what significance the traits of the Turanian psyche had in Russian history, one must first clearly and specifically imagine the Turanian psychological type as applied to the life of a specific individual. This can be done based on the definition of the Turanian psychological type as given above.

A typical representative of the Turanian psyche in a normal state is characterized by mental clarity and calm. Not only his thinking, but also his entire perception of reality is fit into his simple and symmetrical schemes, his "subconscious philosophical system."[108] All his actions, behavior, and everyday

---

108 Fully aware of the paradoxical nature of this term, we have still decided to use it for lack of a better one.

On the Turanian Element in Russian Culture

life also fit into the schemes of the same subconscious system. Moreover, the "system" is no longer recognized as such, for it has gone into the subconscious and become the basis of all mental life.[109] As a result, there is no discord between thought and external reality, between dogma and everyday life. External impressions, thoughts, actions and everyday life merge into one monolithic, inseparable whole. Hence there is clarity, calmness and, so to speak, self-sufficiency. In practice, this state of stable equilibrium, subject to some reduced mental activity, can lead to complete immobility, to inertia. But this is by no means necessary, since the same features are completely compatible with mental activity. The stability and harmony of the system do not exclude further creativity, but, of course, this creativity is regulated and guided by the same subconscious foundations, and thanks to this, the products of such creativity themselves naturally enter into the same system of worldview and life without violating its overall harmony and integrity.

As for the social and cultural values of people of the Turanian psychological type, this aspect can only be acknowledged as positive. The Turanian psyche imparts to the nation cultural stability and strength, affirms cultural and

---

[109] It is important that the system becomes subconscious. In those cases where a system, within which everything (the external world, thoughts, behavior, everyday life) should fit into simple and clear schemes, is recognized as such and constantly remains in the field of consciousness, it turns into an "obsession" (an *idée fixe*), and the person obsessed with it turns into a fanatic maniac, devoid of all mental clarity and peace. This happens when the system is clumsy and bad, so that its being fits into it not on its own, but through violence against nature. Such a case is possible if a person of the Turanian type for some reason abandons that convenient system of worldview and life, developed by the gradual efforts of many generations, in which his other fellow tribesmen live, and tries to create a completely new system himself. Not being able to think fruitfully (and, consequently, to look for a new system) without the presence of a ready-made solid foundation in the subconscious, such a person for the most part creates a bad, inconvenient system, clumsily reworking and simplifying some alien one. Such cases, of course, are rare, and due to the inconvenience of the system that such people create, these systems usually do not succeed with other people of the Turanian type. With a particularly strong temperament and exceptional talent, the creators of such home-grown systems - *idée* fixes - manage to gather around themselves only a small sect of fanatics.

historical continuity, and creates conditions to economize those national forces that are conducive to any development.[110] The success of this development, of course, depends on the level of talent and mental activity of a given nation, and this level can differ, but there is no obligatory connection between the Turanian psychological type as a well-known form of mental life and any specific level of talent or activity. By asserting the social and cultural-historical value of the Turanian psychological type, we only assert that for each given degree of talent and mental activity, the Turanian psychological type creates certain favorable conditions for the development of the nation.

VI

The positive side of the Turanian psyche undoubtedly played a beneficial role in Russian history. Manifestations of precisely this typical aspect of the Turanian psyche cannot be overlooked in pre-Petrine Muscovite Rus'. The way of life in which faith and day-to-day existence were one ("everyday confession"), in which state ideologies, material culture, art, and religion were inseparable parts of a single system, a system that was not theoretically expressed and consciously formulated, but nevertheless, resided in the subconscious of everyone and determined the life of everyone and the existence of the national whole itself - all this, undoubtedly, bears the imprint of the Turanian mental type. This is precisely what

---

110 Of course, this only applies to the normal aspect of the Turanian psyche: people of the Turanian psychological type, but with a system that does not accommodate the outside world, thoughts, behavior, or everyday life without violence. In a word, those founders of the sects mentioned in the previous note are socially harmful. With their sectarianism they destroy rather than create national unity. Their creativity, based on a stubborn desire to reconcile the perception of reality, morality and everyday life with a biased and clumsily simplified scheme, introduces elements of very dubious value into culture. Thanks to their relentless fanaticism, fueled by an ever tightening obsession, they destroy far more than they create, and what they destroy or want to destroy is usually much more valuable than anything they can offer in return. It should not be forgotten that such people are rare exceptions among real Turanians.

old Rus' rested on, what gave it resilience and strength. If some superficial foreign observers did not notice anything in Ancient Rus' except the servility of the people before agents of power, and the servility of those same agents before the tsar, then their observations were undoubtedly incorrect. Unquestioning submission is the basis of Turanian statehood, but, like everything in Turanian thinking, it is follows through to the end and extends the idea to the supreme ruler himself, who is thought of as unquestioningly subordinate to some higher principle, which is at the same time the guiding principle in the life of every subject.

In Ancient Rus', such a governing principle was the Orthodox faith, understood as an organic combination of religious dogmas and rituals with a special Orthodox culture, a particular manifestation of which was the state system with its hierarchical ladder - and it is precisely this highest principle that was the same for each subject and for the tsar himself; it was not the principle of naked slavery that welded Rus' into one whole and governed it. The Orthodox faith in the ancient Russian understanding of this term was precisely the frame of consciousness into which everything naturally fit - private life, the political system, and the existence of the Universe. And in the fact that this frame of consciousness was not the subject of conscious theoretical thinking, but the subconscious basis of all mental life, one cannot help but see a well-known analogy with what was said above about the normative aspect of the Turanian psyche. Even if Orthodoxy itself was adopted by the Russians not from the Turanians, but from Byzantium, even if it was directly opposed in the Russian national consciousness to the Tatars - still, the very attitude of the Russian person to the Orthodox faith and the very role that this faith played in his life were in a certain way based in Turanian psychology. It was precisely because of the Turanian traits of his psyche that the ancient Russian man did not know how to separate his faith from his life, to consciously isolate non-essential elements from the manifestations of religion, and that is why

On the Turanian Element in Russian Culture

he turned out to be such a weak theologian when he met the Greeks. The psychological difference between the Russian and Greek approaches to faith and ritual, which was so clearly manifested in the era of the schism, was a consequence of the fact that Turanian ethno-psychological elements, completely alien to Byzantium, were deeply rooted in the ancient Russian national character.

The Muscovite state arose thanks to the Tatar yoke. The Muscovite tsars, far from having finished "gathering the Russian land," began to collect the lands of the western *ulus* of the Great Mongol Monarchy: Moscow became a powerful state only after the conquest of Kazan, Astrakhan, and Siberia.[111] The Russian Tsar was the heir of the Mongol Khan. The "overthrow of the Tatar yoke" came down to replacing the Tatar khan with an Orthodox tsar and moving the khan's headquarters to Moscow. A significant percentage of the boyars and other servants of the Moscow Tsar were representatives of the Tatar nobility. One of the origins of Russian statehood was the Tatar state, and those historians who turn a blind eye to this circumstance or try to downplay its significance can hardly be correct.[112] But if ignoring the Tatar source of Russian statehood turns out to be possible at all, it is because the internal content and ideological

---

111 The folk epic tradition traces the beginning of Moscow statehood right from this moment: "When Moscow rose, so did formidable Tsar Ivan Vasilyevich." Everything before Ivan the Terrible, who conquered Kazan, Astrakhan, and Siberia, is attributed by folk tradition to legendary epic antiquity, to the era of Grand Prince Vladimir. Even such an event as Ivan III's refusal to pay tribute to the Tatars ended up in the epic (about Vasily Kazimirovich), in which the traditional "capital city" is Kyiv, and the prince is Vladimir.

112 Being a linguist and ethnographer by profession, and not a historian, the writer of these lines does not dare to deviate into a scientific field alien to him. Still, I would like to note that terms like *denga* (money), *altyn*, (gold, later denoting a denomination of currency), *kazna* (treasury), *tamga* (from which the word *tamozhnya*, "customs", comes), and *yam* ("pit", "post", a village along a postal route, whence *yamskaya gon'ba*, "post rider service", *yamshchina*, the profession of "rider," *Yamskoi*, "postal horse/carriage," etc.) are of Tatar origin. This clearly indicates that in such important functions of the state as the organization of finance and postal communications, Tatar influence was decisive. When comparing the administrative features of the Moscow state with the ideas of Genghis Khan, which formed the basis for the organization of his state, analogies arise naturally. These questions deserve detailed development by specialist historians.

justification of Russian statehood clearly includes elements that do not find direct analogies in Tatar statehood, such as Orthodoxy and Byzantine traditions. The miracle of the transformation of Tatar into Russian statehood was realized thanks to the intense burning of religious feeling, thanks to the Orthodox religious upsurge that swept Russia during the era of the Tatar yoke. This religious fervor helped Ancient Rus' to ennoble Tatar statehood, to give it a new religious and ethical character and make it its own. The Russification and Orthodoxification of the Tatars took place, and the Moscow Tsar, who turned out to be the bearer of this new form of Tatar statehood, received such religious and ethical prestige that all the other khans of the western ulus faded in front of him and yielded to him. The massive conversion of the Tatar nobility to Orthodoxy and to the service of the Moscow Tsar was an external expression of this force of moral attraction.

But if statehood of Turanian origin and the state idea became Orthodox in Muscovite Rus', having received Christian religious sanctification and ideologically connection with Byzantine traditions, then the question arises: did not the opposite phenomenon also occur at the same time, i.e., a certain "Turanization" the Byzantine tradition itself and the penetration of the features of the Turanian psyche into the very Russian interpretation of Orthodoxy? Muscovite Rus', despite all the strength and intensity of religious fervor that determined not only its existence, but also its emergence, did not produce a single Orthodox theologian, just as the Turks did not produce a single outstanding Muslim theologian, although they were always more pious than the Arabs. The general features of religious psychology are evident here: in both cases, the dogma of faith is considered as a given, as the main background of spiritual life and external day-to-day being, and not as a subject of philosophical speculation; in both cases, religious thinking is characterized by a lack of flexibility, a disregard for abstractness, and a desire for concretization, for the embodiment of religious experiences and ideas in the forms of external life and culture. Instead of a consciously thought-out and finely detailed theological system in Ancient Rus', there was a certain unspoken "subconscious philosophical system" which was harmonious, despite its formal unconsciousness, and which found expression not in theological treatises, but in the entire everyday way of life resting on it. In this way, Russian religiosity differed from Greek, despite its dogmatic identity with the latter, and came closer to Turanian, with which there was and could not be any dogmatic similarity.

There is no doubt that the disdain for abstraction and lack of Orthodox theological creativity characteristic of ancient Russian piety was a disadvantage of this piety in comparison with the Greek. But at the same time, one cannot help but admit that "everyday confession", that permeation of culture and everyday life with religion, which was a consequence of the special properties of ancient Russian piety, was a plus, not a minus. Obviously, "this too should be done, and the same should not be abandoned." The well-known hypertrophy of Turanian psychological traits caused in Russian piety the inertia and sluggishness of theological thinking, and these shortcomings had to be dispensed with.[113] But this in no way diminishes the positive properties of ancient Russian piety that can be attributed to the Turanian mental traits. This was the case in the religious sphere, but it was no different in the state sphere: the inoculation of characteristic Turanian

---

113 It is all the easier to get rid of this deficiency because the very hypertrophy of those Turanian mental properties on which this deficiency is based affected not the entire Russian tribe, but only one part of it, namely the Great Russian part. The Little Russians, who were much less exposed to the Turanian influence than the Great Russians, have the positive properties of Turanian origin to a lesser extent (for example, they are much less capable of state building on a large scale than the Great Russians), but they show, perhaps, a greater ability for theological speculation and gave the Russian Orthodox Church a whole range of outstanding theologians, such as Dmitry Rostovsky, Simon Tadorsky, Sylvester Kanevsky - and the entire Mogila theological school, and the Russian theological-academic tradition that grew out of it. In the Church, as in many areas of everyday life, both main parts of the Russian tribe are called upon to mutually complement each other. By tearing away from each other, each of these parts would risk falling into one-sidedness.

traits into the Russian psyche made strong material for state building, allowing Muscovite Rus' to become one of the most expansive powers.

To sum up everything that has been said about the role of Turanian ethno-psychological traits in the Russian national image, we can say that in general they played a positive role.[114] Their disadvantage was the excessive sluggishness and inactivity of theoretical thinking. This shortcoming had to be dispensed with, but without sacrificing all those positive aspects of the Russian national type that were generated by the fusion of the Eastern Slavs with Turanism. To see only negative traits in Turanian influence is ungrateful and unconscionable. We have the right to be proud of our Turanian ancestors no less than our Slavic ancestors, and we owe gratitude to both. Awareness of one's belonging not only to the Aryan, but also to the Turanian psychological type is necessary for every Russian striving for personal and national self-knowledge.

VII

For every nation, a foreign yoke is not only a misfortune, but also a school. Coming into contact with foreign conquerors and oppressors, the nation borrows features of their psyche and elements of their national culture and ideology. If it manages to organically process and assimilate what it has borrowed and finally emerges from under that yoke, then the beneficial or

---

[114] Of course, we cannot close our eyes to the fact that people with the above-described properties of the anomalous aspect of the Turanian psyche also existed and exist in the Russian environment. These are Russian doctrinaire rebels, founders of sects, fanatical thinkers, many of whom, even in their appearance, represent the features of the Turanian anthropological type. As one might expect, the significance of such people in Russian history is mostly negative: they divide rather than build the nation, they destroy more values than they create. Due not to the purely Turanian, but the mixed character of the Russian nation, such people, exceptionally rare among real Turanians, are found somewhat more often among Russians. But, in general, among Russians they seem to be exceptions, and, of course, they are not the ones who should be primarily kept in mind when considering the role of the Turanian psyche in Russian history. In our considerations we must first of all keep in mind normal cases, and not exceptions.

harmful nature of the yoke as a school can be judged by the form in which the liberated nation appears.

The Mongol yoke lasted more than two centuries. Russia fell under it while still an agglomeration of appanage principalities, independent, scattered, almost devoid of concepts of national solidarity and statehood. The Tatars came, proceeded to oppress Russia, and at the same time, to teach it. More than two hundred years later, Russia emerged from under the yoke in the form of a perhaps "wrongly tailored", but nevertheless "strongly stitched" Orthodox state, welded together by internal spiritual discipline and the unity of "everyday confession", manifesting the power of external expansion. This was the result of the Tatar yoke, the fruit by which one can judge the harmfulness or benefit of the yoke in the destinies of the Russian people.

A little over two hundred years later, Peter the Great appeared and "cut a window to Europe." European ideas blew through this window. The Europeanization of the ruling class began with the increased attraction of foreigners to this class. That harmonious "subconscious philosophical system", which in Muscovite Rus' united religion, culture, everyday life, and the political system into one whole, and on which all of Russian life rested, began to be undermined and destroyed. As a result, the basis of statehood inevitably had to become the naked force of coercion. Military service and serfdom existed in pre-Petrine Rus', but Russia became a militaristic and serf-owning country *par excellence* only in the era of Europeanization. And if we remember that all this was at times accompanied by a fierce persecution of everything primordially Russian, the official recognition of national Russian culture as barbarism and the spiritual dominance of European ideas, then it is hardly an exaggeration to designate this period of Russian history as the era of the "European" or the "Romano-Germanic yoke." This yoke also lasted more than two hundred years. Now Russia has left it, but in a new form - the "USSR". Bolshevism is the same fruit of the two-hundred-year Romano-German yoke as Moscow statehood was the fruit of the Tatar yoke. Bolshevism shows what Russia has learned from Europe during this time, how it has understood the ideals of European civilization and what these ideals are like when they are carried out in reality. It is by this fruit that we must judge the beneficial or harmful nature of the Romano-Germanic yoke.

And when you compare these two "tests" with each other, that of the Tatar school and that of the Romano-Germanic school, you involuntarily come to the conclusion that the Tatar school was not so bad at all.

***

TO THE OPPONENTS OF EURASIANISM

Yakov Sadovsky[115]

***

(A Letter by Yakov D. Sadovsky to the Editor)

M.G.

Allow me to address you with the following.

I am a Eurasianist in soul and body. Therefore, attacks on the Eurasianists and Eurasianism trouble me, indeed, no less than they do the authors of *Exodus to the East*, *Pathways*, and *Russia and Latindom*. These attacks surprise me, as they are carried out in a unified manner by representatives of various camps, from the Third International to Russian national-monarchic circles. Undoubtedly, there is some latent misunderstanding in all this, and the slander leveled at the Eurasianists is unwarranted. It appears to me that the reasons for such a misunderstanding is to be found in the Eurasianists' inconsistency (across their numerous publications) and, more precisely, in the lack of clear and direct responses to many burning questions. I wonder, then, whether I might at least partially aid in the elucidation of this misunderstanding, having expressed a vindication of the average Eurasianist in the face of certain accusations thrown at his feet, which

---

[115] Originally published in *The Eurasian Annals*, book 3 (Berlin, 1923).

To the Opponents of Eurasianism

I have personally heard more than once. After all, such accusations – so frequent and vicious – may ultimately be reduced to a small number of conceits. Therefore, my response will perhaps serve as a general answer, from our point of view, to certain questions raised by our gentleman opponents. Of course, this response cannot pretend to be an exhaustive and precise exposition of the theses of Eurasianism. But the common world-sensation which serves as the linchpin of our minor brotherhood – that of the Eurasianists – will, I hope, serve to affirm the correspondence between the practical questions I have submitted for consideration and the spiritual foundations of Eurasianism (at least with regard to certain isolated issues, we have also had our disagreements among ourselves). If these considerations will have proved useful to some extent as a clarification of the positions of Eurasianism for our sympathizers, I will be satisfied.

***

The protests and accusations heaped upon the Eurasianists may be reduced to the following positions:

I. "The Eurasianists are passive God-seekers. They do not value worldly good, which now – in the midst of the grandiose task of restoring the Russian economy – is especially dangerous. The Eurasianists call for a departure to the *Thebaid*.[116]"

Such is the accusation cast by the opponents of the Eurasianists. But, in reality, there is no basis for calling us "God-seekers," for those who seek have either lost something or never had it; we do not seek either God or our faith, for we already have them. As a matter of principle, we do not

---

116 [Trans.]: The *Thebaid*, or "The Song of Thebes," is an epic poem that was produced by the Latin poet Statius in the first century AD. The text concerns a familial conflict between Eteocles and Polynices, sons of the former Theban king Oedipus, who war with each other over the contested throne.

promote passivity, nor do we evince it in practice. It would be more accurate to speak of the ideological activity of the Eurasianists – even in light of our current situation as emigres. As far as our "departure from God for the sake of the Horde" (in Moscow), the future will reveal who has been more active: the representatives of other trends or the Eurasianists. As for now, it is too early to say.

The Eurasianists do not reject material culture, nor do they de-emphasize its importance. They merely allot it a position that is secondary to spiritual culture; for, as it is said, "Man shall not live by bread alone."[117] Material culture must serve as a means for spiritual achievements and not an aim unto itself. The modern transformation of technology and material means into precisely such a self-sufficient aim is spiritually deleterious. The elemental, primordial forces of matter and animal drives are insufficient without a strong, immeasurably high-standing counterweight, for "what is a man profited, if he shall gain the whole world, and lose his own soul? or what shall a man give in exchange for his soul?" (Matthew 16:26). The Eurasianists set questions of faith and the Church in the immediate foreground. But this does not preclude the freedom of concrete resolutions. To take an example, it seems to me that it is possible, in practice, for the Eurasianists to call for a separation of the Church from the state; however, the implication of such a stance would be nothing other than the liberation of the Church from the wardship of the government, from the interference of secular power in ecclesiastical affairs, and from any attempt to instrumentalize the Church toward political ends. This would protect the Church from any possibility of becoming the government's servant. Our recognition of the possibility of separating Church and state, however, in no way implies a lax approach to such matters as the teaching of Divine Law in school (the general instruction of youth in matters of Church and religion!), the Sacred

---

117 [Trans.]: Matthew 4:4.

To the Opponents of Eurasianism

Coronation of the Kingdom, the government's recognition of religious holidays, and so on.

The Russian people are an Orthodox people. The entirety of their everyday lives is intimately connected with the Orthodox faith. If one strips the people of their prayers, which take the form of prayer services, memorials, baptisms, marriages, and consecrations of home, livestock, and crops, then a yawning emptiness opens up in their soul and in their day-to-day lives. The Russian people, along with their greatest creation – the Russian State – may be strong only when they are under the mantle of the Church and resting upon the rock of the Orthodox Faith. "Russian self-consciousness grows hollow and disfigured, having lost Orthodoxy..."; "Orthodoxy, too, begins to expire once it has abandoned the Russian nation in its titanic lunges toward creativity..." And we wish to resemble that wise husband who builds his home upon a foundation of stone so that the storm does not collapse it (Matthew 7:24-5). We are saddened by the absence of moral firmness and patriotism in the upper layer of our culture and society.

In our time, attempts on the part of the Catholic church to possess the spiritual Russian people, characteristically taking advantage of their times of troubles and misfortunes, have been unprecedentedly redoubled. We now observe a repetition of 1570, 1613, 1708-9, 1812, and all the black years of our history.[118] The Roman episcopacy has mobilized its Jesuits and its venerable "trappers" of human souls. And now a certain contingent of the Russian people, particularly representatives of the Petrograd nobility, having long been under foreign tutelage and only tenuously connected with the authentic, elemental essence of Russia, have given themselves up to the temptations of these Jesuits and have fallen to heresy, proclaiming their faith in the sinlessness of the Pope. In vain do those weak in spirit try to save themselves through apostasy.

---

118 The papal attempts at submitting the Orthodox Russian Church to the authority of Rome, as a constant accompaniment of each instance of Russian national-spiritual misfortune, almost to the point of serving as an emblem or even a "symbol" of such misfortune, have yet to receive a full and coherent illustration.

The Orthodox Church will mourn its stray sheep and will pray for the illumination of their minds and their return into the Church's bosom. We must enclose ourselves all the more steadfastly beneath her mantle in order to work toward the restoration of Russian culture and statehood.

II. "The Eurasianists call for a rejection of 'universally human' Western European culture. They call Russia to a cultural union with the 'barbarians' (to wit, Mongols, Kirghiz, etc.)."

We Eurasianists hear this accusation more often than any other. Undoubtedly, this question demonstrates the Eurasianists' radical departure from their opponents. Our departure profoundly concerns more than just an evaluation of European culture. The Eurasianists do not consider Western European culture to be something absolute and universal for all humanity. In the view of our opponents, Western European culture is tied to a definite place, time, and set of conditions. The Eurasianists believe that, for peoples who are not connected by blood to the Romano-Germanics, such a total assimilation is impossible. "Theories, like the conclusions derived from them through deduction, are true only in relation to the past, upon which – in addition to life – they depend; but the past is always nothing more than a corpse, discarded by the rapid flow of life – a corpse whose anatomy attains all things save the soul. Based on known data, the theory has produced known laws, and wishes by violent force to impose these logically correct laws on all unfolding data that are to follow" (Apollon Grigoryev). Everything which Grigoryev has said of life under theory may be applied wholesale to the question of the adoption (or assimilation) of Western European culture by other peoples. It is impossible to assimilate the soul of such a culture with such traditions, and so on. This position does not, however, imply that we reject the possibility and necessity of adopting certain partial, isolated features of the United States, Western Europe, or Japan. But we must also exercise caution with regard to the adoption of technological innovations; a consideration of our own conditions and data is indispensable. Let us recall what has happened to us. After all, our ideological servility to Western Europe has continued for around two hundred years. We appropriated their ideas, fashions, theories, and more. The authorities, along with the Russian cultural stratum, wished to see the Russian people transformed first into "Anglo-Hollanders," then into "Frenchmen," then into "Germans," and finally into nothing more than "manure for Western European culture" and its experiments (i.e., socialism). And then, whenever a question was posed by Russian reality, we developed the habit of seeking the ready-made answer in a theory developed by foreign thinking on the basis of the experience of an alien life. With its lack of circumspection, the movement of the Westernizers infected us with all the diseases of the West – rationalism, positivism, socialism, and any number of other "-isms." One result of this infection has been the current experiment of socialism carried out on Russia by the communists – the quintessence of Russian Westernization.

"Bolshevism is the realization of that socialism and that rule of the working class, concerning which they (the Western Europeans) have heard so many intelligent speeches, oracular divinations, and alluring promises... The idea of a seizure of power at the hands of the working class and of the forceful introduction of socialism is an idea of French origin" (P.B. Struve).

It is in this seduction of the "West" that we find the reason for why the average member of the intelligentsia – the civil servant, the landowner, the surveyor, the doctor (in a word, the average "lord") – upon coming into contact with the peasant masses, has evoked hostility, distrust, and smirking contempt. The speech of the "lord" was incomprehensible and comic in the eyes of the peasant man. Martians would undoubtedly find it easier to understand Saturnians than the intelligentsia the peasantry (and vice-versa). V.O. Klyuchevsky has been vindicated in his claim that "the Westernizers have lost all comprehension of living Russian reality." Let us recall, for clarity, that cult of Europe and that disdain for everything Russian, in which parents often raised their children, and which teachers of geography, history and other sciences almost constantly instilled in young people at school, regardless of their political views.

Now, when we are slandered for our rejection of the "idea of Russia's return into the family of European peoples," for our rejection of the idea of "Russia's new acclimation to European culture," we firmly respond that we, indeed, refuse to go by the old ways. The yawning abyss of these Black Troubles is a sufficient warning against going such a route. Of course, this may be unpleasant to hear for those of an advanced age, venerators of Western Europe who have been going on holiday to France, Italy, Spain, Germany, and Austria for decades and who are just dying of ennui in all the countries of the world, counting these countries alone as worthy of recognition and attention. In our midst, we find no small number of those who have tied themselves to Western Europe. To them we say: the global, spiritual, and politico-culturo-economic hegemony of Western Europe has ended along with the World War. No initiatives – no measures taken – will restore to Europe its former supremacy. We must recognize this fact, regardless of whether we find such a change agreeable. Europe cannot serve as a stable foundation for a powerful, future-oriented movement. Europe itself requires spiritual and material crutches. The geographical integrity of Eurasia, the economic possibilities of a future Russian State, in certain respects the kinship of Russian psychology with that of the Turko-Mongols and certain other "Eurasian" peoples, and our historical past – in a word, the full sum of our data and conditions, point to the fact that we are no appendage of France or Germany (nor Western Europe as a whole!). We can do nothing else than return to ourselves and begin to build a temple of Russian culture, consonant with Eurasian data which we are given by Divine Providence. The "Exodus to the East" is also our return to ourselves, but it is not a crusade to the "Mongols and Chinese" for more borrowings, as our Westernizing opponents try to quip. Clearly, these quippers have an exceedingly low opinion of our logicality. If we are not drawn in by the European uniform which is so alien to us, then why would we don the clothing of the Chinese Mandarin? Regardless of whether the "Europeanism" of our consciousness, the "Asianness" of our soul, or the "Asiaticism" of our character shall be overrepresented in our construction, or whether they all find a balance so that they are in harmonious conjunction – in any case, we must live and create without breaking away from our roots. What will unite us with our "Asiatic" neighbors is a unified Russian culture that has been organically cultivated within our conditions and, above all else, the first product of this culture will be Russian statehood.

III. "The Eurasianists disparage the imperial (Petersburg) period of Russian history and idealize the pre-Petrine period."

It seems to me that such a criticism of the Eurasianists is tantamount to projecting the ills of a diseased mind onto a healthy one. In our relationship to the past (as, I believe, with every Russian patriot), one must discern two distinct moments. Our souls mourn the errors of the authorities and society which occurred in the past, but "we understand our Tsars for their goodness, for their glorious actions..." We feel quite clearly that, even within the last few decades, amidst the ideological decline and spiritual decomposition of our circles of ruling elites and intelligentsia, great achievements in the realms of science, art, technology, and material culture have been realized in Russia. All of these things have been buried and half-buried by our "great" revolution; it would seem that they have given us – in the capacity of an epistemological, artistic, technological, and material basis – room to live proudly and peacefully, to work, and to develop. And it is not this basis, but precisely spiritual decomposition which is to blame for our self-humiliation; the upper classes of our society were so oblivious to reality that it was possible for fantastical, childish "plans for the radical restructuring of Russia based on rational principles" to emerge (the project of the "Witmerites"[119]). In our history, one could list an unending number of facts which might be chalked up as mere anecdotal occurrences if they had not, in turn, brought about our current tragedy. To take an example, let us consider the education of the youth. In the country of Tsars and Autocracy, under the noses of provincial custodians, according to textbooks approved at the highest levels, the youth were taught a profound respect and even love for Aristogiton, Demosthenes, Brutus, and others like them. To the extent that I am able, given my own sensation of reality, I shall reproduce some historical facts (I beg the reader's forgiveness for such a reproduction, fully cognizant of my modest historical knowledge): Aristogiton and his comrade stabbed their brother dictators in the back, thereby exchanging their country's peace, lawfulness, and order for anarchy. They committed these murders on the commission of a party. Demosthenes, an ambitious but myopic intrigant, fought with King Philipp of Macedon, who strove to unite the Greek lands, to give the Greeks peace and tranquility, and to bolster them in their battle with the East. Brutus murdered his mentor and patron, the great Imperator and Caesar, the latter having shown an unusual grandeur and nobility even in the hour of his death. Brutus rebelled against monocracy; he was a dull, unprescient politician who deprived his people of an ingenious ruler and cast them into the woeful thralls of internecine war. In our schoolhouses, these rebels and murderers were painted with the brush of heroism, having carried out the greatest feats in the history of Man. I now present a second, more striking example. Our schools openly

---

119 [Trans.]: The "Witmerites" were an academic, revolutionary group who were arrested on 9 December 1912 during a general assembly in the O.K. Witmer women's gymnasium. The participants, 34 in all, were quickly released, but were expelled from the gymnasium.

preached a cult of "the Great French Revolution"[120], while it is out of this revolution's bosom that all other revolutions have come. The French Revolution was generally depicted as a panacea against all evils. To wit, one could only create a new life by revolutionary means. To sink into a state of revolution, the nirvana of our times, was the shining dream of nearly all of our professors. The desire to live to see the revolution, to immerse oneself in it and to be happy, was pounded into the heads of fifteen- and sixteen-year-old boys and girls as an ideal. Of particular curiosity is the fact that the end of revolution was not foreseen (as Chernov has it, one must deepen, deepen, and deepen one's immersion in revolution). Such phenomena of our past as the romantic idealization of revolution (a truly ecstatic state of mind!) are no more than trifles. There were far more substantial errors made by society and the authorities at the time. These we cannot include as objects of our exultation. But, in criticizing the mistakes of the past, the Eurasianists strive to do so with care and circumspection, first remembering that he who does nothing makes no mistakes and, secondly, that one may harm the future with incompetent criticism. "We have too incautiously criticized and shamed our country in the eyes of foreigners. We have been less than adequately careful in our evaluation of her dignity and merits, her historical past" (P.B. Struve). It was this approach to our own history which led to the deeply rooted self-contempt of the Russian people and which cultivated in them a feeling of distrust regarding their own capabilities and strength. Despite their magnificent intellectual and spiritual endowments, the Russian people have suffered more misfortune, chaos, and catastrophe in their development than has any other people at any other time. One of the main reasons for all of our misfortune is our

---

[120] It is interesting that French historians have always shown the obverse side of the medal – the horrific atrocities of this tumultuous event. Only with this revolution's overcoming was it made fertile (the creativity of Napoleon). Historians of more recent times (Taine, Vandal, Sturm et al.) believe that the revolution was responsible for breaking the power of France, having introduced more negatives than positives. Our professors, meanwhile, have stayed mum regarding this shadowy side of the subject.

contempt for ourselves, our doubt of our own strength, and the impotence that comes with it.

As concerns the Eurasianists' idealization of the pre-Petrine period in our history, there is little to say. It is not to be doubted that the Russia of Tsar Aleksei Mikhailovich, Fyodor Alekseevich, and Sophia Alekseevna was a far healthier state and national organism than it was under the successors of Peter the Great (particularly after the moral schism between the upper and lower strata of the people), and that it was on a more normal course of development before Peter's reign than afterward. For the Eurasianists, these examples can at most be a kind of analogy and distant prototype for future construction, since the times and conditions are clearly incomparable.

IV. "The Eurasianists are National-Bolsheviks; the Eurasianists are anti-Semites."

We are nationalists, it is true – most sincere Russian nationalists. Of course, we are quite distant from the strange nationalism of those Russians who, to our great surprise, have passionately defended all national movements directed against Russian nationalism (P.N. Milyukov). We stand farther still from the institutors of the dozens of "republics" (up to and including a Jewish republic with its capital in Minsk) that have sprouted up on the territory of the Russian State, as well as from those whose work of uprooting takes Russian nationalism as its sole object. "Russia was ruined by the cosmopolitanism of the intelligentsia. This is the only time in world history that something like this has happened – the oblivious abandonment of the national idea by the brain of the nation" (P.B. Struve). The Eurasianists, as Russian nationalists, do not share those views according to which the masses of the people are seen as preservers of the national idea. The bearers of the national principle must be (and usually have been) the intelligentsia. A nationally strong and gifted professor or student, in some sense, is of equal value to a whole province. All abstract dreams and mystical reveries of the folk masses, as first mover and self-sufficient agent, must be headed off and curtailed by the Russian intelligentsia. We must fully comprehend the real flow of history; the masses as such are indifferent and passive; in order that they be otherwise, they must be given an impulse from numerous, but faithful and willful figures. Fervent, gifted patriots – always few by necessity – are the true "authors of history," the uncrowned captains of the nation in their capacity as bearers of the national idea. This claim in no way disregards the presence of a national instinct in the consciousness of the masses[121]; but this is precisely an "instinct," an idea and a feeling in its covert, minimal state. Much less do we reject the idea that the national instinct of the masses possesses a definite content; it is precisely for this reason that any idea bearing a "national character" is capable of becoming a "governing idea [*ideya-pravitel'nitsa*]" (see the essay "Allegiance to the Idea"[122]) – but we speak here only of that idea which alludes and responds to the content of the national instinct of the masses. Nonetheless, it is the spiritual activity of the intelligentsia which transforms this instinct into a "ruling idea," even if the members of this intelligentsia themselves, as has often occurred, emerge from the very thick of the people. In the massive, unencompassed span of Russia, nationalism is grasped and appropriated only with great difficulty. The Russian people consist of a mass of local, fervent patriots: residents of the Urals, the Caucasus, the Ukraine, the Don, and Siberia; within the masses of the people, Russian patriotism maintains a sluggish warmth and only rarely does it flare up. The steadfast pan-Russian patriots are no more than a handful of intelligentsia and civil servants – absolute in their significance, but relatively lost in the sea of the remaining population. And it is all the more tragic that, by the beginning

---

[121] It is only with this presence of instinct that we can explain the fact of the national visage's preservation at the hands of the masses under several years of rule or leadership by foreigners.

[122] Savitsky, Petr. "Allegiance to the Idea." Foundations of Eurasianism, II, PRAV, 2022, pp. 269–276.

To the Opponents of Eurasianism

of the 20th century, a considerable portion of this handful either lost or had never acquired a keen national feeling. As a result, the Third International has established itself "in the lands of Moscow." But even this cruel experience has failed to cure many of their delusions. Just recently in Prague, we heard the following words issuing from the mouth of P.N. Milyukov: "We wish to be national without nationalism... One can be national without the old trappings of *Signposts* [Vekhism[123]] or those of the more recent 'Eurasianism.'" We Eurasianists propose that only political corpses can do without "Signpost-ism" and "Eurasianism."

And so, we are nationalists. But wherein this resides our "National-Bolshevism" I am ashamed to say that I have no clue. As far as we can tell, the very term "National-Bolshevism" is a *contradictio in adjecto*. Of course, a national movement may employ internationalism toward tactical ends, but these two categories are principally incompatible. How one might combine Bolshevism (socialism, internationalism) with Russian nationalism is as much a mystery for us as it is for any other thinking Russian patriot.

At the other extreme, a question emerges as to the anti-Semitism of Eurasianism. With the same or even greater justification, one may call the Eurasianists anti-Roman, anti-German, anti-Anglo-Saxon, and any other conceivable "anti-." But even this would be somehow imprecise. The Eurasianists do not adhere to xenophobia as a principle. It is true that we do not nurture any particular inclination toward Europeans,

---

123 [Trans.]: *Signposts* [*Vekhi*] was an edited volume of essays, published in 1909, which was meant to consider questions such as the relationship between the intelligentsia and the Russian nation and the inadequacy of positivism, rationalism, materialism, secularism, etc. Important contributors to the volume include Nikolai Berdiaev (the premier contemporary philosopher of the "Russian Idea"), Sergei Bulgakov (Russian Orthodox theologian and one of the main promoters of Sophiology), Petr Struve, and Semion Frank. Pavel Miliukov, a liberal politician, minister of the Provisional Government after Tsar Nicholas II's abdication of the throne in 1917, and leader of the Kadets, was one of the publication's immediate opponents upon its appearance. The term "Signpost-ism" [*Vekhizm*], employed here by Miliukov, refers to the sweeping wave of public discourse caused by the book and the general anti-progressive movement it inspired.

but this is only because the Europeans themselves do not want us to love them. Both the governments and the societies of England, France, Italy, etc., are astonishing ignoramuses with regard to Russian life and history. The Russian State and the Russian people have been of interest to the Romano-Germanics only as sources of income and profit. Now, every emigrant who has spent time in the non-Slavic countries of Western and Central Europe is well acquainted with this contempt and ignorance. Moreover, many Romano-Germanic peoples have demonstrated an age-old and unfounded hostility toward the Russian people, which comes out all too easily at the first exacerbation of political relations between governments. Our flaming, all-conquering love for Western Europe has undoubtedly been a one-sided, unreciprocated passion. Our contempt for ourselves has done much to enable this state of affairs. One must hope that, now, members of the Russian intelligentsia will be cured of their zeal for all things non-Russian. As for us, we do not suffer from such zeal. But this is not to say that we are guilty of hatred for all things foreign. The same could be said for our "anti-Semitism." There is one respect in which we indeed differ from the majority of Jewish society. Our difference with them has to do with our evaluation of the ongoing troubles. For the majority of the Jewish people, and for all of the Jewish youth, the Russian Revolution is a "Great" one which has given them everything – even a dominant position among the existing authorities of revolutionary Russia (something which no Jew in the world could have seriously conceived of beforehand). The Jews accept this "Great" with all of the honors it bestows and act as its cement. This has been acknowledged by all the most far-seeing representatives of the Jewish intelligentsia in their admonishments to their people (Landau, Beakerman, Bruckus, Mandel). For us, the revolution is, above all else, none other than the Black Troubles – like a plague combined with the very worst natural disasters. If we recognize the "necessity" of the revolution, we do so only in a historical sense – the sense in which, given the conditions of society's historical source of authority, such a revolution could not but have occurred. And if we "accept" the revolution, then we do so as with every other historical fact which, once having taken place, cannot be reversed and must be taken into practical account. But, in and of itself, the process of revolution is both evil and destructive. It follows clearly then, that we are in no position to heap our trusting affections on any of the foreign precipitators and exacerbators of the Russian Troubles, nor on those who have accepted it as a "great nirvana" (to include the Jews). But there is another side to our views on Jewry. Every faithful Christian remembers just how significant the history of the Hebrew people is. In the case of the Russian Revolution, too – setting aside the empirical relationship between the Russian and Jewish people – there is a different aspect altogether, terrible and mysterious, involving attractions and repulsions which have woven both peoples into a tight tangle today. Our comprehension of the complexity of questions arising from this relationship (how does one unwind such a tangle?) is what, more trustily than anything else, insures us against any reduction of understanding to the level of vulgar anti-Semitism. Even less are we the enemies of all foreigners. On the contrary, we propose that a logically comprehended nationalism of the minor peoples does not preclude, but rather demands their participation in a broader Great Russian Statehood. Russian statehood guarantees more successful development for minor peoples such as Georgians, Estonians, Latvians, etc. By permitting the various regions – in the very broadest boundaries – to govern in matters local to the area, we will reinforce their attachment to the Russian State. But we are strangers to the views of those who declare themselves proponents of a "federative union based on the principle of voluntary (???) inclusion (sic!) of separate nationalities within the composition of Russia." And what if the Azeri Tatars should wish to see Baku become autonomous and isolated from Russia in its policies and import customs? What if the Estonians should "voluntarily agree to become a 'dominion of the United Kingdom' and turn Revel into an English naval base? What then? From our Russian point of view, this "voluntary" union – never before seen in the history of the world – is a harmful fantasy. Alas, one cannot avoid coercion in this world of ours. But this coercion must not be of a petty, narcissistic, artificial, or unfounded sort; rather, it must be organic, imposed by a great politico-economic whole in relation to its parts; the parts must then bear their allotted functions in order to support the life and development both of themselves and of the entire whole.

We believe that an authentically national Russian authority must govern with Russian interests in mind and that it is not obligated to consider whether the Tatars assent to Baku's oil flowing into Russia, or whether the Estonians assent to Revel serving as a Russian port. But this is in no way to suggest that we threaten the minor peoples with oppression; far from it – precisely because Russia possesses all that is necessary to be strong can she ensure the minor peoples the greatest degree of freedom, all the while guaranteeing herself the vital prerequisites of her own being as an economy and state, with the least necessary encumbrances and burdens upon the state. The national order of the Russian State proposed by the Eurasianists is the order of freedom on the basis of might.

V. "The Eurasianists weaken the potency of the Russian national spirit by exchanging the word 'Russian' for the strange, suspicious word 'Eurasian.'"

Many find the words "Eurasia" and "Eurasianism" aggravating. On the part of those inveterate Westernizers of a certain advanced age who stand upon habitual principle, such outrage is perfectly understandable. They sense a kind of threat in the word "Eurasia." Neither the "minor" nor the "major" troubles have dissuaded them of their hopeless Westernizing. Their interest cannot be piqued by anything – not by the air or charms of the Caucasus, Turkestan, the Russian "Rivieras,"

To the Opponents of Eurasianism

or other pearls of the Russian State; much less can they be interested by the coal of Kuznetsk, the ores of the Urals, the oil of Ukhta, or the other unutilized riches of Eurasia. They will die Westernizers, having ingloriously concluded their period of uncritical Westernizing and foreign adaptation; one must hope that they will then make way for the creative reaction of the youth. But, I must say, I am surprised by a certain irritation and dissatisfaction at Eurasianism that has been expressed by people of a national orientation who think in terms of the state. The Eurasianists do not promote some special "Eurasian" nationalism, nor do they seek to replace Mother Russia, the Russian name, or Russian nationalism. They reject internationalism in all of its forms and, therefore, cannot possibly employ the term "Eurasian" with any conceivably international (or national) meaning or tone. "Eurasianism" is but a slogan drawing Russia, by new paths, toward a "new life" with the "old might." "Eurasia" signifies the following: *Russia must live on its own, must prevail on its own, and must become its own light.*

We can and must be economically stronger than we were preceding the war. We must cease to be an appendage to the economic systems of the Germans, or of any other people's foreign economy. The current conditions could be favorable for our economic revival and flourishing. Of great significance in this respect are the entire host of conditions currently defining the global economy. Firstly, the United States is gradually bolstering the barrier to Western-European immigration; secondly, the United States is in possession of unfettered industrial capital; thirdly, Western Europe has large cadres of workers at its disposal who are prepared to emigrate – large cadres of highly qualified "specialists" in all categories – and, no less importantly, has an enterprising class of entrepreneurs, industrialists, and merchants who are currently seeking applications for their energies and means; fourthly, Russia controls vast reserves of natural resources which are either unutilized or under-utilized, as well as lands ripe for colonization. In the technical sense of this set of circumstances, the "Americanization" of Russia is both possible and desirable, but requires conscious activity aimed in a certain direction. However, we must defend ourselves from a "psychological Americanization," as a result of which technological and material comforts would gain the ascendancy over everything else, and the race for wealth would become the sole movement spring of both private and social life. The technological Americanization of Russia, carried out using the technological knowledge, means and power of foreign societies, is desirable only given the condition that the ruling circles of Russia are simultaneously saturated with an authentic nationalism and have a firmly religious emphasis. If the new Russian intelligentsia should turn out just as sycophantically Westernizing and non-Orthodox as before, this "Americanization" will pose a grave threat to the nation. The culturo-economic binding of the North and South, East and West of the Russian State, the weaving of economic knots which no sword can ever cut – this is the dream for which Eurasianism is so tirelessly working. Petrograd, as the capital of Russia, is unfit for this task. This city played its grand role in the past, but finished up shamefully and ingloriously. Now, Petrograd must take on a different, more modest mission in the economic and political life of the Russian State. It will be the premier Russian port on the Baltic Sea and the Northern – superbly refined! – center of Russian culture. Such a role for Petrograd is not to the taste of our Westernizers and White internationalists. They dream of the resurrection of "Petersburg" (precisely "Petersburg" and not Petrograd!) in its capacity as the governing center of Russia – the first capital. We think that this is both impossible and undesirable.

For the Eurasianists, Petrograd, as Russia's capital (to say nothing of "Petersburg"...), is the symbol of a former fascination with Europe, its interests, its thoughts, its rationalism, socialism, and other diseases. It is the symbol of disgust at one's native country and a refusal to know it. The "Window to Europe," hacked out by the Great "Father of the Fatherland," has been turned by his pitiful successors into the collapse of the entire wall. It is impossible to successfully govern the Russian State from Petrograd and bind its edifice, which has been built upon the vast, unique Eurasian space and is inhabited by a population of many tribes. However, the Eurasianists have firm knowledge and memory: they remember that Russian statehood came together not on the shores of the Black Irtysh or the Ob, and they believe that Moscow is undoubtedly the sole possible governing center of all of Russia. This is even more the case since we must now resurrect our sacred Muscovian traditions concerning the "gathering of the lands." As a counter to foreign intrigues, for the binding of the Russian State and the reinforcement of Russian state sentiment in the South, we must declare the "mother of Russian cities" – Kiev – as our second capital. All other considerations aside, the appointment of the second Russian capital and the most important cultural center in Kiev will secure a firm control and utilization of all the natural endowments of the South, which will cause a natural divergence from previous searches carried out by the cranes from overseas that were so habitual and characteristic for "Petersburg." This "exodus" to the South and "pivot to the East" does not imply a rejection of the "window to Europe." But this window will be used precisely as a window, and not as a breach, into which any sort of scum can come rushing whenever it should please. Our doors to the East and the South are broad. For the sake of our future, we must strengthen our political, economic, and cultural positions in the near, middle, and far East. Without studying our frontiers and without cultural exchange with the Turkic-Mongol world, as well as others, especially given the enamored fascination with the charms of the West, the Eurasianists are deeply convinced that no such task can be carried out.

To the Opponents of Eurasianism

VI. "The Eurasianists are reactionaries."

Not so long ago, such an accusation of "reaction" would have been both murderous and compelling. Now, while it might seem cosmetically frightening, it contains nothing substantially terrifying. This is explained by the fact that, at present, the concept of "reaction" is completely obsolete, as democratism, universal suffrage, parliamentarism, and socialism have been strongly discredited and are undergoing not only a crisis, but something more. The life of society is everywhere seeking some new path beyond official democratism and socialism (in Italy, this is a fascism that has emerged from below; in Spain, it is a fascism imposed from above), and the "conservatives" or "reactionaries" – which is to say, people who wish to secure a natural path of development for their nations and the emergence of a new epoch – are no longer opponents, but are rather proponents of official democratism and socialism. We do not count ourselves among conservatives and obscurantists of this sort, for we are naturally free from any deliberate adherence to "direct governance by the people" or socialism. This is not the place to elucidate a definite political program for which the time has not yet ripened and which is difficult and even impossible to realize as long as its promoters remain outside of their native element. But I would nonetheless like to express a few thoughts on matters both political and otherwise.

To make a disclaimer, the Eurasianists find favorable adaptations not only in the realm of technology, but also in the realm of motive forces – ideas – to be neither a mortal, nor a common sin. It is of no consequence whether it is a social, political, or economic idea which has been adopted, or whether the adopters are conservatives or radicals, or whether our very own ideas coincide with those of a milieu alien to us, so long as this idea is not opposed to God and is deleterious neither to the soul, nor the life of the people. The Eurasianists are no partisans of prejudice. Therefore, anyone who accuses us strictly of adopting things from elsewhere is neither to the point, nor to be taken seriously. We shall allow ourselves to touch upon the question of proportional representation and of a certain other "asset" of patent democracy. The Eurasianists hold that the anonymous representation of "all the people" can, with great benefit to every government, be replaced by a corporate representation of real, distinct interests. Life itself is driving toward such an arrangement: at every turn, we find the practical displacement of the "representation of the people" in favor of party representation, through which the parties (in a manner so far disfigured, but nonetheless transparent) are coming to manifest the interests of definite professions and classes while only nominally preserving the pretense and character of "the people." On one hand, this is borne out with the attachment of mandates to the parties, and not to individual persons by means of proportional representation; on the other hand, it is confirmed by the contemporary fracturing of parties on economic grounds. As concerns the governmental order of the Russian State, we believe that its foundations must generally hold in organic connection with our conditions; otherwise, we will not have a strong, sturdy state order. Our brains are not digesting the "democratic" theory of "direct governance by the people"; we do not operate with the logic of this idea's defenders. Therefore, if, in the words of these defenders, "the fragile mechanism of parliamentary monarchy is not suitable for Russia," we believe that the "republican democratic" order (P.N. Milyukov), which they propose, is even less suitable. In Russia, this European confection would bear monstrously deformed fruit. It is no great secret that the Eurasianists call into doubt everything that bears the mark of patent democracy. We believe that the masses of the people, as such, are incapable of creativity, creation, or self-governance. When a man daily and hourly solves the majority of the problems which life produces from the position of personal benefit, it is difficult to concede that he could denounce such a position when deciding questions of state. The intelligentsia may gradually come to

To the Opponents of Eurasianism

the conclusion that "benefit to the state will be the highest law," but the masses of the people never will. Therefore, "direct governance by the people" and "democracy," understood in this sense, are for the Eurasianists the bitterest of evils, leading ultimately to disintegration, collapse, and general decline. The cultural, conscientious, and ideological minority is not only qualified, but obligated to govern. When it comes to the matter of governance, a special inclination, giftedness, and tradition is required – specific habits, a frequent presence in a certain atmosphere saturated with questions concerning the good of the state. Otherwise, a curiosity will result: the stableman must possess the requisite knowledge and experience, but nothing is demanded of those who pretend to the governance of the country besides membership in a party. In such a situation, any shabby lawyer from Penza or Odessa can be elected as representative of the Vologda peasants (direct governance of the people...) and afterward occupy the post of, let's say, the Minister of War. And this is the least of the possible evils. Given a more strict adherence to "direct governance by the people," we face the threat of all extant academies and universities being closed due to their superfluity. Examples of contemporary "democracy" affirm our thesis. In practice, even in democratic parties, the ringleaders are never elected, and the structure of any democratic party is a living negation of its principles and slogans. The fact that the high level of cultural life has proven compatible with the official declamation of democratic slogans (whether things will proceed this way for long is a different matter) is explained to a significant degree by a similar "negation in deed." It is said that "democracy" is today experiencing its "twilight" (the precursor to night). It should be said that, besides all of the abovementioned, there are other reasons for the encroachment of this "twilight" upon "democracy." They are to be found in the fact that, for specific "democrats", in actuality, the ideas of Motherland and nation have been replaced by the notion of party-mindedness. For this reason, there are people deeply democratic to their very core, and yet are "hot" (as opposed to lukewarm) when it comes to questions of the nation, and who vehemently dissociate themselves from patent democracy; some Russian examples of this type are Kerensky and Chernov.[124] We do not think that the governmental structure of Russia could be "democratic" in the sense of patent democracy; but God forbid that any structure should be as disengaged from life, from the psychology and demands of the masses, as the old order in the final years of its existence. We would propose the following: without being "democratic" (i.e., governed by the people), the state structure of Russia must be "demotic" (i.e., people-oriented) in the sense that the authorities must simply "know their public," must be in constant contact with the moods of the popular masses, must broadly and consistently meet their demands, and must rest upon the people's moral support. All state aims, including the aims of common prosperity, are technically many times more solvable and may only be solved given conditions in which a cultural, conscientious, and ideological minority is in power. Here we encounter the question whether there exists a certain stratum of the population which could be the preserver of the ideas of nation and state, from which a ruling circle could be replenished. To its great misfortune, the Russia which preceded the Revolution suffered from a dearth of people who could replenish the upper and middle ranks of the administration. Following the Revolution, this question remains and shall remain of unprecedented concern, and the well-being of the Russian State depends on its solution. We cannot do without a stratum of the population which is neither soft-bodied nor without will, which does not suffer from a penchant for fantasy or a susceptibility to quick disillusionment; these people must be strict, hard, egotistically national, and with a strong taste for power. It is this layer of society that will be the bearer of the state idea and a strong national will.

---

124 [Trans.]: Alexander Kerensky was the leader of the failed Provisional Government, which eventually succumbed to the Bolsheviks in October/November 1917. Viktor Chernov was a founder of the Social Revolutionary party; while in favor of restructuring Russia into a federative socialist republic, he opposed the Bolshevik seizure of power and eventually fled the country.

To the Opponents of Eurasianism

The present is a period in which the roots and foundations of our ideology are being generally reevaluated. Much of what I am saying here has already been weighed, calculated, and has become a truth tried by fire. However, not all of it is accepted, nor is it being assimilated wholesale. It would seem that logic is impotent in matters of faith, and only morals and sentiments can compel people toward one or another decision. These sentiments of ours must not end up as an ephemeral spasm, but rather must become a supreme effort which will crush everything in its path and redouble its strength against all impediments. This effort will be equally applied in our economic and cultural activities, first abroad, and then at home, once we have cleared our native soil for widespread action. The foundation of our national life must be economic self-sufficiency, an authentic, broad calling of the "people," the masses, and the man in the street as opposed to the far rarer and more difficult (as we have said above!) call to ideological and historic self-sufficiency. The presence of economic freedom, the foundation of all other freedoms, is an indispensable condition for the efflorescence of our national economy. The yoke of state economic wardship must be abolished. This, however, in no way cancels the right and obligation of the state to interfere, in specific cases, in economic relations (the preservation of labor, customs protectionism). One might think that by changing the political conditions (the banishment of communists and socialists from power altogether), the economic restoration of Russia will occur without delay. To tell the truth, the mortal sin of struggle against material culture can be attributed most of all to the economic and non-economic literature of pre-revolutionary Russia. This literature one-sidedly hailed physical labor, "labor" yields, and so on. Private enterprise and economic creativity were shamed as "exploitation" and "*kulachestvo.*"[125] The reason for this antipathy toward economic

---

125 [Trans.]: The noun "*kulachestvo*" refers to the array of negative traits and stereotypical actions attributed to the class of petty landowners in the provinces, known in pre-revolutionary Russian parlance as "kulaks" (literally, greedy individuals who had their wealth clenched tightly in their fists).

creativity was to be found in a general feeling of repulsion toward "capital"; but without capital, a modern, even "labor-based" economy is unthinkable. "Capital" was a kind of terrible bugbear, and those who represented it could not only not count on an honorable place in society, but generally never encountered any empathy in their initiatives and were caught up in a hostile atmosphere. Such a formulation of the issue was responsible for embedding a pessimism and eternal anxiety in the minds of the workers, depriving them of a joyful outlook on life. Indeed, for the workers, the situation was illustrated in the most terrifying colors imaginable: they were always at the disposal of their enemy, their exploiters. The workers lost faith in their strength and capabilities; they were deprived of the ideal of an improvement of life (might they, themselves, not become the "exploiter"?); they sought salvation in the logic of the herd and its physical strength. A similar cast of mind has impeded and continues to impede successes in material culture; it is undermining the foundations of spiritual culture and, instead of filling it with a spirit of love, comradeship, and trust, they are injecting it with a spirit of envy, hatred, and unceasing malevolence. One hopes that what has occurred will open the eyes of Russia to the true meaning of private economic creativity and initiative and will dispose of the view of all authentically successful economic activity as something "sinful." A strong stimulus toward economic restoration is to be found in, among other things, the ability to compare the past and the present – the conditions of what came before the war versus the contemporary situation. For us, this comparative ability will not disappear in the course of decades. New cities, new railroads, and new factories will be constructed. But "we Russians must not build new cities upon the old ones; we must rather carry an even greater, more difficult act: we must recreate the ruined temple of the people's spirit, resurrect the prostrated and accursed image of the Motherland, as worn out as it has become in the souls of countless generations of Russia's honorable, faithful sons" (P.B. Struve). This is a most difficult task. Russia's history as a Great Power has not known encroachments on Russian national values and particularities for an entire century. This fact, combined with a fascination with the "West," has weakened the national consciousness of the majority of the Russian intelligentsia, decomposed its soul, and defaced its type. The masses of the people have been without an ideological, national, cultural leadership for all this time and have remained no more than raw material. The prolonged authority of the internationalists threatens to place impediments before the restoration of the undermined spirit of the people, impediments that will be overcome with only the greatest difficulty. Every day that the socialists remain in power, the putrefaction of the younger generations worsens. Unfortunately, in the world of the spirit, we do not have the same stimulus as we have in the realm of material culture (i.e., the ability to compare the past with the present). There are too few traditions of a healthy, creative nationalism in our cultural stratum, and the ones we do have are weak; the connections between our stratum and the masses of the people are weak and unauthoritative. All that binds us with the people and which has preserved the people is the Orthodox Faith. We believe that, without the Orthodox Faith, any restoration of the Russian people's spirit is impossible. Russia without Orthodoxy is unthinkable. Only from Orthodoxy can we draw the creative spirit: for "thou hidest thy face, they are troubled: Thou takest away their breath, they die, and return to their dust. Thou sendest forth thy spirit, they are created: And thou renewest the face of the earth. The glory of the LORD shall endure for ever."[126]

Yakov Sadovsky
Roztoky by Prague
20 September 1923

***

---

126 [Trans.]: Psalm 104:29-31

MASTER AND DOMAIN

Petr Savitsky[127]

***

The master, the master's will, and the master's eye

There is a word in the Russian language that is remarkable for the richness and generality of its content, a word that has a future in the study of economics and land management. At present, this word is only occasionally found in Russian books on economic-managerial issues and, as if by chance, without being fixed into systematic categories. This word will come to the fore as soon as the hour strikes for the creation of an independent Russian doctrine of "housekeeping" as "sovereign economics."

This word is *"khozyain"*: "master". Concisely and clearly - and at the same time in the most concrete and in the most general form - it expresses, both in everyday usage and folk language, the personal principle in the economic management of housekeeping. The "master" is at the same time the master of a household, the rural master, and the industrial master. "Master, allow me to spend the night" - this is how the master of a house is addressed. "Master, show me how to do it" - this can equally be said in the field or the factory.

It is necessary to distinguish between the "master in production" and the "master in consumption." In a large number of cases these are two sides or two functions of the same person.

---

[127] Originally published in *The Eurasian Annals*, book 4 (Berlin, 1925).

In both of these functions, the basic flow of the productive or consumption process respectively is determined by the master's will and takes place under the supervision of the master's eye. The entire sphere of decisions and actions, which, according to popular expression, is "the master's business," represents the domain of the expression of the "master's will." The master's eye performs control functions of management. "Managerial economics [*khozyaistvovanie*] is the quantitative control over the use of labor and materials in technical processes; domain management, or "housekeeping" [*khozyaistvo*] is the activity of measuring as well as organizing and purposefully directing means and ends" (Hermann). Here, first of all, there is no need to limit oneself to indicating "quantitative" control. Housekeeping (*khozyaistvo*) undoubtedly also carries out quality control of various types of products and goods. In addition, reference to the control, measuring, arranging, and coordinating functions of housekeeping should be supplemented by an understanding of their function as the source of the initial movement, giving technical processes impetus and determining their direction.

According to the basic distribution of managerial responsibilities established in modern societies, the above-named functions in the field of the consumer economy are entrusted to and are primarily the lot not of the master, but of the "*khozyaika*": the "hostess" or "housewife". Within the household, she controls, measures, arranges, coordinates, gives impetus and directs. The first two functions primarily go back to her "master's eye", the last four to her "master's will". And if the first two are expressions of the beginning of accounting in the management of her domain, the last four concentrate in themselves the principles of creativity and power in that domain, in this case, the household. We can safely say that in many cases, namely among "good housewives," genuine functions of creativity and power are also carried out in the sphere of the household. But the effect of the master's will as the beginning of creativity and power in the household is not limited to the boundaries of the home. The environment for the primary manifestation of the master's will, the sphere of significant application of the creative and power principles of the economy, is the area of the relations of production.

Modern economic doctrine does not know the "master of production"; it knows the "entrepreneur", and thus has overlooked the central figure in the sphere of housekeeping. There is a significant difference between the "masterful" relationship to business and the "entrepreneurial". It is necessary to distinguish between entrepreneurship as a certain empirical managerial-economic function and as a special spiritual-economic entity. The master is only a spiritual-economic entity. Since economic doctrine in its modern development has so far managed without the word "master", there is no need for it to designate any special function (the exception is the term "field master", which can remain as it was). It is all the more convenient to concentrate the entire meaning of the word "master" in its generalized essence on the spiritual and economic side of the issue. Not every landowner is a "master", nor is every master of an industrial enterprise. An entrepreneur can be a master, but not every entrepreneur is a master. The entrepreneur as a spiritual entity is only and in the first instance *homo economicus*, "capitalist man." He has only one attitude towards the "production unit", the system of people and goods he manages: obtaining the greatest net revenue. But is such an attitude toward business the only one possible in housekeeping? To think any other type of relationship would instead belong to altruism, aesthetics, or something similarly alien to the sphere of management excludes the logic of our language, which has been forged over centuries; but by the very nature of things the master's relationship to business is precisely something "masterful". In addition to the purely economic impulse to generate income, the master's relationship to management is determined by the desire to preserve, strengthen, and expand the full functioning and full development of that living and tangible whole, that spiritual system of people and things that the master perceives in managing his domain; the master considers generating more income to be just one manifestation of a more complete vision of his domain's functioning and development.

The concept of the master ultimately strives toward full revelation in the idea of the "Good Master" (we will accept this last designation as a "technical" term; in modern everyday language, the "Good Master" is called virtuous, thrifty, "real"). "The Good Master," with the above (and no other) relation to the management of a domain, is not only not a myth, not only not a figment of sentimental imagination or aesthetic invention, but is also a widespread economic phenomenon central to housekeeping. Examples of this image, through the most diverse technical conditions of economy and various forms of "production relations," come in thousands, millions, even hundreds of millions - from the Gospel the "Good Master" (as a living figure, in its direct meaning) and its distant prototypes to many, many "Good Masters" of our time in agriculture, industry, etc. The category of "Good Master" should be accepted without binding it to any particular legal forms. The right of "property" as such may or may not exist, or it may extend to a larger or smaller range of phenomena (it used to be possible to consider a person another's "property"), and the right of ownership may be subject to greater or lesser restrictions - nevertheless, control, power, and creative functions will, to some degree, remain the deed of the "master" and will be carried out by him. One may specifically examine what the positions and capabilities of the master are in various legal structures: in some structures, the category of the "Good Master" receives a special legal designation in certain aspects - recall the concept of *vir bonus pater familias* in Roman law. But it would be wrong to see the category of the "Good Master" as an economic category exclusive to the legal situation established by Roman law. The category of the master as such is by no means associated with any particular legal system.

What should a "Good Master" be like in relation to the people in his domain? Before answering this question, we would like to note: since we think of this relationship as a system, we are building an "ideal type." This in no way contradicts the above statement about the prevalence of the "Good Master" type in life: we collect individual features of reality, even if they are very common, into a value whose character is more consistent than actually occurs in the phenomena of life. Whether the master's domain is small or large, whether it is the farm of a peasant family or a factory with tens of thousands of workers, the "Good Master" is equally inherent in the conviction that the basis of this domain is the people who work in it. A Good Master's goal is to provide the material foundations of life for these people and, if possible, to ensure that they are satisfied with their lot; if he is unable to realize this goal, then his domain is, as it were, no dominion at all. For the sake of this goal, he is ready to make sacrifices at the expense of his revenue. At critical moments, he is ready to support the people integrated into his domain from his own capital to avoid severing the deep connection. The Good Master believes that no "fullness of functioning and completeness of development" is possible without the presence of a cadre of people devoted to the domain, and that ultimately, over years and decades, economic success and sustainable income generation are functions of creating such cadres. A large-scale entrepreneur who is a Good Master invests the majority of his wealth in the selection of employees and workers on his domain, just as a peasant master sees his main wealth in the human forces working on the farm. The master's attitude towards his people, the participants in his domain, is primarily expressed in their material provisions, which should be sufficient to create contentment. But it cannot be said that the master's attitude towards the people comes down solely to the adequacy of their financial situation. It is justified and evidenced by their situation, but not limited to it. In a master's managerial attitude towards his people, in addition to the material and rational elements, there is also an immaterial, irrational side. A Good Master attracts people to himself on the basis of human relationships with them, that is, in a sphere that is essentially irrational. He makes people respect and love him through the respect and care he shows for someone else's personhood. And thanks to this irrational side, the strength and firmness of that rational unity, which is (and should be) a "productive unity", the domain succeeds. In a large domain, where hundreds and even thousands of people work, the establishment of personal relationships between the master and each worker is virtually impossible. But in the domain of a Good Master, two circumstances contribute to this factual impossibility: (1) if the master lays down the management of the domain on the above foundations, a legend is created around his name, which sees his participation and his care in a much wider range of phenomena than those he is actually engaged with; the legend surrounds the "Good Master" in the same way as it surrounds an outstanding commander or an outstanding ruler, only in each of these cases the content of the legend is, of course, its own, special; the legend comes from below; (2) from above comes workers' participation in the master's functions; a Good Master of a large domain surrounds himself with people who are capable of acting in accordance with his will and spirit, acting in his stead where he cannot due to the limitations of human strength.

The attitude of the master is also manifest in his relationship with the things of his domain. A horse, a cart, a car, a building, or the land can be treated "in the master's way" or otherwise. The master's attitude towards all of the material (or natural) things of his domain signifies something special: we must take into account that in relation to a person, the earth is a continuously existing being, a building is a long-term being, a car, a horse and a cart are all shorter-lasting beings, in decreasing order. But no matter how the master's relationship changes depending on the differences in the nature of individual things, this relationship is based on some common features: the desire to improve their quality and tireless care. A Good Master strives to have the best horse, cart, car, building and land - within the limits of economic rationality (beyond a certain limit he cannot deviate from economic rationality, since there is no economy outside of rationality; and no matter how great the independent master's interest may be in the quality of a thing, this quality does not exist in itself, but in relation to economic rationality; see below for more on this). The master strives to ensure the greatest possible durability of the horse, cart, car and building, and to keep them in the best possible condition at any given moment. At the end of each production cycle, the master strives to leave the land (and in forestry, its growth) in a condition not worse, but, if possible, better (from an economic point of view) than the one in which it entered the cycle.

In short, the master's attitude is not based on the idea of activity aimed exclusively at obtaining the greatest revenue, at "squeezing" it not only from his workers, but also from every horse, cart, car, building, land - the master's attitude is instead based on an idea that, alongside the goal of generating revenue, he has set the independent goal of preserving and expanding the satisfaction of the people working in his domain as well as the maintenance and improvement of the order and quality of livestock and the various other things used in the operation and maintenance of the domain. One can, of course, say that such preservation and expansion, maintenance and promotion correspond to the correctly understood "interest" of the "entrepreneur". In judgments on this issue, everything depends on what is meant by "correctly understood interest." If the latter is interpreted broadly, including not only economic interest itself, but also a more general one, up to, for example, interest in maintaining the well-being of one's neighbor and even cosmic harmony, then, of course, such a statement would be correct. It is essential to note here that in the goal-setting of the "master", economic goals themselves appear in an expanded and transformed sense.

Between "relative" and "absolute"

The economic goal itself is a type of desire to achieve the greatest results with the least means, in particular, to obtain the greatest revenue - income - with the least cost (the economic principle). The "master" does not and cannot let such a goal out of his sight. Pursuing it, he moves in the sphere of economic categories proper. Here we come to the question: what exactly is the economic field proper?

In answering this question, we will not take the problem in its entire breadth, which would constitute a worthy subject for a special study. We will indicate only those features that will be needed in the future to characterize the master's attitude towards his domain. The economic world is a special world of existence in the human sphere. The beings of this world are marked by a number of long-established characteristics: they are capable of serving the satisfaction of human needs; at the same time, their number is limited in relation to these needs: they are subject to the principle of "scarcity". However, these characteristics are not enough. Economic goods are not the only things required to satisfy human needs, and they are not the only things limited "in quantity" - this characteristic, for example, could also be applied to a concept like "friendship": friendship serves to satisfy a need, and this need remains unsatisfied for many. Still, it would be wrong to consider friendship as such an economic good. The specific feature of the economic field is not in the nature of beings or its components, but rather in a special approach to them - from the side of the so-called objective "exchange" value, in the aspect of paid exchange, the saleability and purchasability of these beings. Everything that is exchanged, everything that is for sale and buyable - insofar as something is in reality or at least in conceptual interpretation exchangeable, sellable and buyable - constitutes the economic domain. Thus, what distinguishes the latter is the aspect of actual or conceivable exchangeability, saleability, purchasability. Since in such a delimitation we are forced to turn not only to actually completed exchange transactions, but also to some conceivable exchangeability, we affirm our definition not only in terms of the so-called "objective" exchange value, but also turn to the sphere of subjective assessments. We will proceed to adhere to this dual reference, simultaneously to the sphere of exchange, i.e., what has received a certain social "designation", and to the field of subjective values related to the personal mental sphere, for only with such an orientation can we cover the world of human values as well as the place in which we must establish economic values.

In the perspective of this dual reference, the aspect of actual or conceivable compensated exchange, venality and purchasability can be disclosed in terms of two concepts specifically applied to it. The first of these is the concept of specific substitutability. A Rembrandt painting, for example, is materially (naturally) irreplaceable, but because it is sold, it becomes "specifically fungible" with a certain amount of currency. The second concept is fundamental correlation. In order for this or that being to serve as an object of exchange, it must be thought of in a special way: in the status of a special lack of assertion in itself, a specific "mobility", in a rotation of relationship with other beings of the same world, ina constant transition into them, or as their conceivable replacement (moreover, the rate of such "transition" or "replacement" can be expressed in quantitative terms); this status of value in the social sphere is fixed in the "transition" and "replacement" of the real ones, in the fact of exchange. The concept of fundamental correlation thus captures those premises of value, that "status" of it, without which exchange is impossible. We will define the status of fundamental correlation wherever there is exchange, but it can also be found where exchange as a social phenomenon does not exist at all.

Let us imagine a borrower living on a subsistence farm somewhere in the wilds of Siberia. He has a certain amount of grain, which he can either sow on a suitable area, or feed to a pig to be converted into lard. In deciding what to do with the grain, the borrower will, of course, take into account what amounts of labor are needed for processing and harvesting the site and for fattening the pig and other factors of production respectively. In adjusting for these factors, the borrower will "balance" the amount of grain he expects to receive from the plot and the amount of lard the pig will produce. Depending on how the "correlation" develops in the area of his subjective assessments, things will turn in one direction or another. The fundamental "correlation" and "specific fungibility" of economic goods will remain in force in his assessments. The economic sphere is marked by the same feature in the conditions of both barter and subsistence economies.

Where there is no exchange, psychological premises and analogues delimit the economic sphere. It is much more difficult to imagine that the same borrower, if he is not a pathological type, would begin to "correlate" in his mind the value of the life of, say, his daughter and wife. Each of us can easily answer the famous Ricardian question: if a thief broke into your apartment, and you have a coat and three hats, given the opportunity to choose, what would you choose to lose - the coat or the three hats? But everyone would consider it blasphemous and ridiculous to ask which of the two people closest to him he would "prefer" to lose.

The economic world is primarily made up of that which is fundamentally "relative." Other, "non-economic" worlds contrast the economic as worlds of "absoluteness" of being, their affirmation in themselves, their non-exchangeability, non-saleability, non-buyability, specific irreplaceability, their fundamental irrelevance. The economic sphere is closely connected with these worlds of the "absoluteness" of being, for everything "economic" is auxiliary in relation to one or another absolute being. The purchase of food serves to maintain life (absolute existence), while the purchase of books serves to satisfy "spiritual needs."

Translating the above provisions into the language of value categories, we can say this: the economic world and non-economic worlds are opposed to each other as worlds of "relative" and "absolute" values respectively in the above sense of designation...[128]

From the point of view of the basic distinction between the "economic" and the non-economic, it is possible to distinguish two types of values in the human world, namely: "dual-aspect" values and "single-aspect" values. By the former we understand those beings that are simultaneously affirmed in human consciousness as "absolute" values and can be interpreted as "relative" or "correlated" (specifically "economic") values. Such, for example, is any work aimed at producing "absolute" values (for example, the work of a scientist, artist, etc.); as such, it constitutes an "absolute" value; at the same time, it can and does receive a monetary (generally economic) appraisal, i.e.,

---

[128] In order to avoid misunderstandings, it is necessary to emphasize in every way that the special "fundamental correlation" on which the distinction is built must be distinguished both from hierarchical correlation and from factual correlation. In relation to each of these two conceivable types of "relativity" the question is posed in a special way. The location of a value on one or another hierarchical ladder does not in any way "make it relative in principle", although this value is hierarchically related, of course, to what is above and what is below it; here there is no special lack of self-affirmation, no specific "mobility", no constant transition to other beings of the same world and their conceivable replacement, i.e., all those features in which the concept of "fundamental relativity" is alone affirmed. On the contrary, in the hierarchy of absolute values, each of them, although hierarchically "relative" to the others, is nevertheless affirmed in itself, specifically immobile, irreplaceable. Concerning the non-transitional, factual "relativity" it is necessary to note the following: the area of the factual-psychologically "relative" is wider than the area of the fundamentally relative. During a shipwreck, having the opportunity to save only one of two perishing loved ones, it is sometimes necessary, in a brief moment, to factually-psychologically "correlate" the value of the life of one and the other - and to choose. And when two of your friends cannot reconcile with each other to such an extent that there is no possibility of continuing communication with either one, you have to "correlate" the value of the two friendships - and choose with which of them you will continue communication and with which you will break things off. But behind these phenomena of choice (precisely choice, and not replacement - for no one and nothing can replace a lost loved one, a friend) there is no "fundamental correlation" - on the contrary, the "correlation" itself is produced here as if "with a strain", contrary to the fundamental attitude. That is why it can be asserted that the sign of "factual" correlation in itself does not constitute a difference that determines the economic character of the phenomenon.

it becomes "relative." But there are values that have only one of these two aspects - such as, for example, belief or love; the concepts of "venal conviction" or "venal love" are nonsense, and in those cases where they are spoken of, the absence of conviction and love is affirmed in essence to the point that we are talking only about some external actions usually associated with them; conviction and love are single-aspect, "absolute" values.[129]

> "I remove the icon case from the wall,
> to turn into sawdust.
> Everything is for sale, but hereupon
> Memory is not."
>
> -Marina Tsvetaeva

How does the matter stand, from the point of view of value categories, with such values as, for example, a work horse or car? It is absolutely clear that they are relative (i.e. economic) values - but are they also "absolute" values?

---

[129] It is necessary to put such "single-aspect" emphasis on the values of existence. In economic literature it is sometimes argued that, upon receiving a price, everything can become an economic good and thereby an object of economic activity; that "the economic stigma of price can be attached to absolutely everything. For everything can get a price, in other words, it can become 'saleable'. We see this in prostitution" (P.B. Struve). It seems obvious to us that in prostitution some manifestations of sexual relations are sold, and by no means, for example, "love"; and only such manifestations can be called, in our terminology, "dual-aspect" values; "love," having become "venal," thereby ceases to exist. Having become corrupt, belief as such ceases to exist. Revealing (professing) a belief is "dual-aspected"; but there is value in the belief that it is "single-aspected" in essence. In other words, you can not quite attach an economic price tag to everything. There are values that are fundamentally excluded from such branding. Even limited to just the examples we have given, there is enough evidence to state that this category is by no means a small one; it is worth remembering how diverse the possible types of conviction and love are; religious and scientific conviction, romantic love and friendship equally cannot be branded with the economic stamp of price, they cannot be transferred into the sphere of even a conceivable social "relativity". Feelings, like beliefs, are not comparable, not commensurate, fundamentally not "relative" - even in the sphere of ideas. Consequently, everything that can be assigned the "economic stamp of price" is just a set of externally, socially designated phenomena of the human world. Many values - internal, mental, "subjective" - do not lend themselves to economic stigmatization and have nothing to do with the phenomenon of price.

In some cases, a workhorse or a machine can, perhaps, be admired from an aesthetic point of view (that is, from a non-economic, and in a conventional sense, "absolute" view); in the history of art, horses, including work horses, and machines have been and are found and appreciated by artistic connoisseurs (images of horses constitute special genres of sculpture and painting, the beauty of machines were appreciated by Bosch and are valued by the "constructivists"). And yet, there are many horses and cars in relation to which the possibility of artistic admiration or another "absolute" approach has so little significance for their existential qualification that this possibility can and should be neglected. Even the last piece of bread a person has, which seems to have only absolute value for him, is, however, fundamentally "relative" to any other piece of bread or other good, in exchange for which this person could completely preserve or increase the amount of nutrients at his disposal. The same is true of the vast majority of food products, items of clothing, furnishings, and means of communication and production relative to other goods in the order of "objective" exchange and "subjective" appraisal. The inclusion of any "absolute" motives in the assessment of these goods, such as artistic appraisal or an approach from the point of view of personal memories, is a relatively rare exception. This great variety of values constitutes a world of "single-aspect", relative values. Single-aspect values of this kind constitute the economic sphere proper; they are primarily part of the vast and independent economic sphere. The area of "dual-aspect" values forms, as it were, a borderline sphere between the world of the "absolute" and the "relative", economic world.

Our scheme has not yet covered or placed in one group or another one of the most important types of values, namely human labor or human "labor power" (the name in this case does not matter), aimed at the production of "relative" or "economic" values. We mentioned labor and "labor power" aimed at producing "absolute" (scientific, artistic, etc.) values, characterizing it as a "two-dimensional" value. In what category should human labor be classified if its object does not relate to "absolute" beings? This work is one of the main phenomena of the economic world itself. Alongside the material "means of production," it is, as is known, the main element of any production process. Modern human consciousness does not at all see the beginnings of prostitution in selling one's labor and directing it towards purely economic goals. It is fundamentally acceptable for everyone to "correlate" so many hours of such and such work with such and such possible earnings or other positive results. Economic labor, from this point of view, is a "relative" good; taking into account its seemingly essential belonging to the economic ("non-absolute") world itself, it would seem possible to attribute it to the number of "single-aspect" values from the relative side. But here the most important circumstance appears: regardless of the emotions that accompany it, human labor, no matter what it is aimed at, is an expenditure of the human personality. The human personality, both for the person himself and in general in modern human consciousness, has absolute value. Therefore, the value of all human labor, including all labor aimed at strictly economic goals, is related to absolute estimates. However, it would hardly be correct to classify economic labor as a "two-dimensional" value. Such an attribution would conceal the originality and significance of this value phenomenon. Moreover, in this case, labor aimed at both the production of "absolute" and the production of essentially "relative" values would fall into the category of dual-aspect values. Meanwhile, these two types of labor, while agreeing that they are both a waste of the human personality, are different in their objects. In the scheme of value categories that we are constructing, from the point of view of the basic distinction between "economic" and "non-economic," labor aimed at the production of essentially "relative" values is subject to a special definition. Trying to capture the entire sum of its characteristics, we would designate it as a "single-aspect/dual-aspect" value. This definition consistently captures the main aspects of the value of economic labor noted above. However, this value does not exist in its dual, "relative-absolute" nature everywhere, nor in all phenomena of economic empiricism. Human labor, like other values that are addressed to the "absolute" and at the same time socially designated values, is subject to profanation. In economic reality, it can and does encounter an attitude toward and assessment of itself as an exclusively "relative" value - without any element of the "absolute". A reflection of this value order in the field of economic phenomena is the fact for which the concept of "exploitation" was coined in the history of economic teachings. The refutation, negation, and elimination of this value order is that system of values, which, in fact, is the subject of these remarks and on which we now focus our attention - the master's appraisal of his domain.

The master's appraisal of his domain

The master's appraisal of his domain is a bridge, a connection, and a bond between the worlds of "relative" and "absolute". Valuing his domain as a source of "relative" values, as a source of "net income," the "Good Master" at the same time values the domain "absolutely" - as a tangible unity, as a spiritualized system. Our previous comments about the nature of the master's goal-setting and attitude towards the economy were made precisely to state the principles of such "absolute" value.

The master's appraisal is oriented in two main directions.

On the one hand, it affirms the "absolute" value of human "economic" labor placed in the master's domain; since the master's will translates this assessment into activity, the master's appraisal reveals in the phenomena of reality the dual "relative-absolute" value nature of such labor. The master's appraisal protects labor from profanation, from interpretation in the sphere of pure "co-relativity." Outside of the subjective assessments of the worker, labor exists as a "single-aspect/

dual-aspect" value precisely in the master's appraisal. And just as the master's appraisal of human labor is a refutation of the purely "relative" point of view on the latter, his placement of human labor in production is the opposite of "exploitation." And if this were not so, if, along with "exploitation," the master's place of labor did not exist in economic reality, then economic life would be impossible: there would be no positive constructive principles in it whatsoever.

The master's appraisal is also addressed to single-aspect values, that is, the relative side, to the economic world itself. The economic sphere is a "service" sphere. Economic goods as such are not affirmed in themselves - they are "deceptive", "specifically replaceable", "fundamentally relative". Meanwhile, as we have seen, the multitude of beings of the human world are attributed to this sphere and as single-aspect values of the "relative" side, are found in it entirely and do not leave it. And so, the beings of this world become involved in other spheres of values, are revealed and affirmed in themselves, in only one way - through the master's appraisal of his domain. The master's appraisal, as it were, saturates this world with value. The area of the "economic" itself, this massive human-existential sphere, would not be complete, would not be revealed to higher horizons, without the master's appraisal. The master's appraisal is, as it were, the introduction of "relative" values into the environment of "absolute" assessments or, more precisely, makes an evaluative turn to the latter.

In the functions we depict, the economic value of the domain acquires, in the field of phenomena under consideration, the significance of an independent principle, and in the branch of knowledge addressed to these phenomena, it grows into a special category. More broadly and fundamentally than the group of "dual-aspect" values outlined above, it connects the "relative" with the "absolute", the "economic" with the "non-economic". In this respect, its place is symmetrical to the place of the value of "single-aspect/dual-aspect", human "economic" labor, which also contains the same principles. And, as we have seen, the master's appraisal is also directed toward this value and protects it from profanation in the field of "relative" assessments.

It is by no means possible to deduce from the foregoing an idyllic and embellished attitude toward economic reality. "The master's appraisal of his domain" has a spiritual and economic essence, but is by no means an immanent identity of any particular group of people, especially of any economic "class." The master and entrepreneur may have been or are "Good Masters," but they equally well may not be; and thousands, millions, hundreds of millions of such "Good Masters" who have lived and are living in human societies today can be contrasted with thousands, millions and hundreds of millions of masters and entrepreneurs in whom there was not and is not any "masterful appraisal." Any "charity" as such is excluded from the concept of the master's relationship to the economy. Everything that is first saved from revenue and then deliberately "transferred" for "good purposes" or "good deeds" already belongs to the field of charity, and not to the field of economy. What the master disposes of pertains to those benefits that have not yet emerged in the form of "income" from the production cycle of the economy. The master's appraisal is an essentially economic category only as a principle for disposing of such goods. In characterizing it as such, it is necessary to strongly emphasize the circumstance to which there are hints in the previous presentation: the master's appraisal is an independent economic category insofar as it is conceived in conjunction with strict adherence to the economic principle on the part of the master. An "absolute" appraisal would degenerate into wastefulness or be expressed in economic irrationality, and thus would undermine the very foundations of the existence of the "absolutely" appraised domain and lead to mismanagement incompatible with the concept of a "Good Master." And when the logic of language and popular wisdom asserts that there is no domain without a master's dominion, they fully regard the master as the one who implements economic principles. The master's will and the master's eye are steadily aimed at maintaining and strengthening the economic viability of his domain, at achieving the greatest results with the least means, and at maintaining frugality. But this desire is complicated by the appraisal of the existence and flourishing of the domain as such. In other words, adherence to the economic principle and the master's appraisal are two subordinate principles, and the master's appraisal is, in a certain way, a secondary principle - in the sense that, taking it beyond the limits of the economic principle requires following the latter as a prerequisite. From all that has been said, it is clear that the master constantly distinguishes between his desire to obtain the greatest income and his "absolute" appraisal of his domain; and in this regard, his activity is the implementation of the principle of a measure. And the most economical attitude towards a domain can be defined as being saturated with a sense of measure of the proprietary-entrepreneurial impulse to obtain the greatest income, a sense of the limitation of this impulse for the sake of the satisfaction of the people in a given domain and the organizing of the quality of the things within it.[130] The master's appraisal, as an "absolute" value, is not primarily directed toward the importance of money or to one or another abstract substitute for it. Fully taking into account the importance of money, in compliance with the economic principle, the master in his appraisal limits the extraction of monetary as well as

---

130 We cannot close our eyes to the fact that the question arises not only about the demarcation between the master's appraisal and the "economic principle" (the proprietary-entrepreneurial impulse), but also about the demarcation within the master's appraisal itself between the goals of pleasing people and the principle of qualitatively ordering things. There have been and there are conceivable cases where the interests of people working in a domain have been sacrificed to the "absolutely" valued ordering and qualification of things. There have also been opposite cases of the managerially-destructive neglect of things for the people's pleasure. In the master's appraisal as such, as an "ideal type," we also find that the principles of pleasing people and ordering things, that is making them qualitative, are associated and delimited in accordance with a principle of measure.

other means from the economy in order to achieve completeness and saturation of the natural-managerial process.[131] "Absolute" value refers specifically to the latter, and not to money as an economic entity. The absolute value of money is not only not affirmed, but is directly excluded by the "absolute" value of the domain as a tangible unity and spiritualized system. It is on money, despite all its economic importance or, perhaps, thanks to it, that the stamp of relativity is pressed most firmly, and the absolute value of money is possible only by creating a golden calf for oneself, even if it is made of paper rather than gold - an omen. The master's appraisal contradicts the creation of such a golden calf. It bases the well-being of the domain on the humane treatment of people, mercy on livestock, and care for the things of God's world.

This combination of elements creates a phenomenon that is strong in life and housekeeping.

The unlimited impulse to obtain the greatest income is fraught with its own very significant dangers; it borders on and degenerates into an underestimation of the importance of the future, into ignoring long-term interests of masterful management for the sake of quickly obtaining the greatest revenue. It raises the risk of "overpressuring" the people and

---

131 Without going into any philological or historical analysis of the words "economic" [*ekonomicheskii*], "managerial" [*khozyaistvennyi*], "economy" [*ekonomika*], "housekeeping" or "economy" [*khozyaistvo*], one can, however, note the following: a special meaning is sometimes attached to each of these words in ordinary usage. This is the case with the interpretation of "economics" [*ekonomiki*] (or "economy" [*ekonomika*]) of agriculture. It is absolutely clear that by "economics" [*ekonomikoi*] or "economy" [*ekonomiei*] here we mean the abstract-acquisitive, so to speak, speculative-calculating side of the matter, while by agriculture and housekeeping [*khozyaistvo*] we mean the natural production process. Similar shades are noticeable in, for example, the formulation of the tasks of agricultural zoning: "it is necessary... to outline a number of agricultural [*sel'skokhozyaistvennykh*] regions or, more precisely, agricultural-economic [*sel'skokhozyaistvenno-ekonomicheskikh*] regions" (A.I. Skvortsov). The "economic" [*ekonomicheskii*] is primarily related to the abstract existence of a given type of relationship, to the sphere of abstract monetary assessments, relative with value to abstract "speculation". The managerial [*khozyaistvennyi*] substrate is the natural flesh of housekeeping [*khozyaistvo*]; it is not an abstract speculative scheme, but a system of people and goods in all their concreteness.

thereby creating comprehensively destructive disruptions to the order of the domain. On the contrary, the master's appraisal ensures the stability of this mode, strengthening it in human souls; it thereby protects the future and justifies the well-being of not only the present, but also future generations. In the successive connection of all things, which by no means makes different things identical, but subordinates all different commodities to similar necessities, similar provisions apply to things. Also, in relation to things, "overexertion" is possible, and in connection with this, destructive failures or catastrophes are possible. No matter how wide the insurance network is deployed (up to, for example, crop insurance), it cannot completely eliminate the risk of loss; only the master's attention and care for things provides an additional guarantee against losses possible under human conditions. There is also a positive side to this issue: the master's attention and care provide things with a better condition and better functioning than would be the case without the "master's eye," than would even be possible for those who are not truly masters.

The master's appraisal of his domain easily lends itself to religious justification and, indeed, has often grown and continues to grow from a religious root. It is in the image and fact of the master that the connection between the religious and managerial spheres is established. It is through the personality of the master as the embodiment of a personal principle in the economy that religious and religious-moral principles enter the managerial sphere. At the same time as religious impulses educate a person into a "Good Master," they multilaterally increase his economic suitability, thanks to the above-mentioned vital-managerial power of the combination of elements that we find here. Throughout history, intensity of religious feeling has often determined economic success, making its bearers "Good Masters." With different forms of management and goal-setting within the Russian world, the success of economic undertakings can be traced back to these roots: on the one hand, ascetic monks, on the other, the Old Believers and their communities.

The compatibility of the principle of the "Good Master" with religious principles is explained by the fact that the master's appraisal, while establishing his domain as an "absolute" value, by its very nature supplies it with and subordinates it to a certain hierarchy of absolute values. The master's appraisal is justified morally and artistically. Being itself a reflection and consolidation of "housekeeping" in the realm of the absolute, it nevertheless follows from and, therefore, is subordinated to other values - religious, moral, or artistic, which are fundamentally placed above it. In other words, the master's appraisal, while transforming and elevating his domain, does not assert that the ultimate values are to be found in its holdings alone. Therefore, it is consistent with the principles of "subordinated domain-mastership" and "subordinated economy". Militant economism does not grow in line with the master's appraisal, by no means in the order of the latter's combination of the "relative" with the "absolute": militant economism grows on the basis of the mental reduction of everything existing to one "relative".

On the contrary, the master's appraisal is imbued with a powerful impulse towards the Absolute. There have been and are masters who effectively, to the best of their ability, sought to become like the Supreme Master of the world, whom, in His Being and in His master's appraisal of the world, their searching gaze looked towards. And no matter how imperfect these masters were in their achievements and deeds in comparison with Him, the Supreme Master, God, these aspirations indicated to everyone who is a "Good Master" by the nature of the image and likeness of God. The sphere of domain appraisal is the environ of the mediastinum, penetrating all horizons of human existence - from the lowest to the highest, connecting the ugliest and bleakest (an "impersonal" economic commodity) with that Image and Likeness in which we find both the beginning and end of existence.

We are not giving a religious justification for housekeeping here. We only want to point out the extent to which the problem of such justification addresses the idea of the "master". Anyone who even briefly familiarizes himself with the conditions of economic life in any of its branches will feel the empirical significance of this image. Anyone who ponders the universal essence of housekeeping will understand that the coupling of the sphere of the fundamentally "relative" and "economic" with the environment of "absolute" values is possible only through personal appraisals, through the personal principle in the economy, and will thereby confirm the philosophical significance of the idea of the "master."

Domain Sovereignty

The essence of socialism in all its forms can be reduced to the fact that socialism denies that the "Real Master" (the "Good Master" in the preceding exposition) can be a master-as-personality, and asserts that such a master can only be a master-as-society. The master-personality and the master-society are the two unities to which human thought, in its empirical appeal, can link the master's appraisal (and the master-society should be thought of here as an "ideal" super-personal bearer of the master's appraisal, and not a "legal entity" of civil law). Translated into the language of the categories established here, socialism's claims assert that the main functions of the master's appraisal depicted above —the protection of human economic labor from profanation in the field of "relative" assessments and the highest quality, i.e., the ordering of things in the economic world — are feasible precisely and only in a master-society. The demands of "socialization, nationalization, municipalization, association" (Fourier) and others. are equally traceable back to this premise. According to the theories under consideration, only the "state", only the community (municipal), or only the association can be a "Good Master". Therefore, according to these theories, only the state, only the community, only the association should be the master in production. It should be noted: the positive socio-economic goals of not only those mentioned above, but also of a large number of other socio-political theories, whatever their individual shades, can be formulated with the help of the concepts being introduced here - in all these theories, one can sense the desire to imbue and define economic life with the principles of masterful-managerial appraisal. In this sense, we will express the idea of socialism through the language of "master" categories (referring to the master's attitude, the master's appraisal of his domain, and related terminology): in the latter, a certain common spiritual and economic essence is imprinted. Establishing such expressibility requires limitation; in this regard, the categories established above are not applicable in their entirety; in particular, in relation to many socialist theories, the question of the religious justification of the master's appraisal disappears. One should also not artificially simplify the formulas that give this expression, and those into which the premises of individual socialist constructions fit. Not to mention the fact that in other cases the concept of the master in consumption is split off from the concept of the master in production, and the first quality is retained by the master-personality; in other projects, the latter is deprived of all "freedom of choice of economic goods", and all his discretion in this regard is replaced by a public "dacha". As for the quality of the "master in production", sometimes in this area the socialist construction does not include the denial of the master-personality as such, but only asserts the need to ensure (which is entrusted to the master-society) that the master and entrepreneur are personalities capable of being "Good Masters". This, in general, is the goal of the abolition of hereditary property (transfer of industrial property by inheritance) and the establishment of a "universal banking system", which Saint-Simonianism once projected. Other systems replace the individual master with the master-society in the production process itself, concentrating in the latter proprietary and entrepreneurial functions — rights; but they still recognize the auxiliary significance of the master-personality, although they degrade him from an independent master into an official, an implementer of public commands (Rodbertus). Still others completely overshadow the master-personality with the master-society and see the master-personality as the enemy of the economic-social cause (Marx). Let us not multiply examples, for they could fill many pages. Let us move on to consider the issue on its merits: how are the master-society and the master-personality related? What is the reality and basic characteristic of each? Can one completely replace the other?

The peculiarity of human ideas about the master-society is that the concept of such a "master" is much easier to manipulate arbitrarily than the concept of the master-personality. The existence of personalities, masters and entrepreneurs who are not "masters" (real or "Good") is beyond doubt. Generally speaking, the physical personality, including the personality as the master, is an immediate given, which is not simple or easy to change or even influence. Due to the obviousness of this circumstance, it is also difficult to deal with a master-personality in the field of projects and reforms. As a master-society, each projector and reformer can think in his own way, put any content into this concept, draw any image. That is why reformers and projectors, in approaching the problem that we call the master's appraisal, turn primarily and willingly to the idea of the master-society. Indeed, the master's appraisal of the economy can be necessarily assigned to the master-society, and the same appraisal might not necessarily be "assigned" to the master-personality. The master-society, in the precise sense, does not have a mental sphere. And the master's appraisal associated with it is resultant of the formation of social forces. The master-personality, like any physical person, has its own mental sphere - one can assign a specific external action to it - but it is precisely "appraisal," as we know, that cannot be the subject of a mechanically performed task. To the master-society, the very concept of appraisal is applicable, as we see, only in the order of some kind of turn of phrase. But in this way, one can formulate that the master-society lends itself to having the master's appraisal formally "assigned" to him; the master-personality does not lend itself to this. From the point of view of the above-mentioned goals of permeating and defining all economic life with the master's appraisal, the possibility of "formally predetermined" appraisal is the "advantage" of the master-society.

But is it possible, in a precise sense, to attribute the master's will and the master's eye to the master-society? Since we think of the master-society as a collective, we must definitively answer: No. The will of the "master-society" is objectified in some legislative or administrative act. In fact, this is carried out by an individual or a group of individuals. The existence of the master-society and these individuals are separate. Therefore, in this case, the will that actually acts is fundamentally not the master's will. Some individuals perform the functions of the master's eye for the master-society, but they are not the masters, and therefore, in the domain of the master-society, everything is observed and watched by eyes that are fundamentally not of a master. We are forced to give just such an explanation of this issue by the popular use of the word "master", which with complete consistency and realism applies this concept only to the physical person. And it is necessary to reveal a certain illusory nature of the "master-society" in order not to accept an abstract concept as a real existence, which in this case and in the scientific sense would be disastrous. But to say that in the domain of the master-society the master's will is not carried out by the master's will and control, that it is not the master's eye that functions, is saying quite a lot. This means noting that in the domain of the master-society the exercise of the basic power-creative functions is dulled and weakened. The master-society, in a certain sense, is an incomplete, weakened, damaged master.

Here we need to point out one more important circumstance. In the strict sense, the concept of personal responsibility is not applicable to the master-society. Individuals who perform the functions of his "will" and "eye" for the master-society bear, of course, certain criminal and civil legal liability for their actions; but it is precisely in legal responsibility that they are free from specific economic responsibility. The specific economic responsibility that we are talking about here is expressed in the incurrence of waste, damages, and losses arising from inappropriate (and in this sense "erroneous") actions, carelessness, or even the simple inattention of a person with managerial tasks. A managerial "official" can allow such inexpediency, inefficiency and inattention and yet, without deterioration, and sometimes with the favor of his superiors, and with an improvement in his personal position, remain in his place. True, he may suffer the disfavor of his superiors and the need to "leave", but such a necessity, by the will of his superiors, can befall a managerial "official" who otherwise exhibits full expediency, prudence and attentiveness in his actions, i.e., under such conditions in which, in the absence of *force majeure*, he would have, being an independent master, economic success. Replacing specific economic responsibility with responsibility to superiors means, at the very least, a weakening of this kind of responsibility.

Thus, the possibility of a "formal predetermination" of the master's appraisal and at the same time the weakening of the power-creative functions of the master and personal economic responsibility - these are the signs of the master-society. The impossibility of formally predetermining the master's appraisal and at the same time the full power of the master's power-creative functions and personal economic responsibility distinguish the master as an individual. When the physical person is the "master," he, as such, is stronger than the master-society. Although the master's appraisal is not predetermined by anyone except God, it is actually still given to him as a task, and the master's performance of his functions is more concentrated, more flexible, and more complete than that carried out by the master-society. But, on the other hand, when a physical person is unfit by the very qualities of his nature to be a master, the goals that are set in masterful appraisal can only be carried out through the intervention of a master-society.

Who, then, will more accurately nurture and determine economic life by masterful appraisal: the master-society or the master-personality? From the preceding it follows: in itself, neither one nor the other; a combination of both is necessary, a conjugation in quantities commensurate with each other of the personal-master and sovereign (as a symbol of the "social") principles.

In ensuring the business of the master, in some industries the master-personality is stronger, and in others, the master-society. Where protection is required and development is not, a master-society is possible. Where creativity and development are needed, the master-personality merges to the fore. The domain of the master-personality is ultimately also more perfect than the domain of the master-society in terms of creating the best possible environment for human labor. But identifying "Good Masters" is not possible or feasible everywhere. Different sectors of economic life contribute to or "resist" such separation to varying degrees.

The more tangible, the more distinct the economic-natural process in a given industry, the more specifically designated, the less covered in the veil of abstract "speculation" its economic-natural flesh, the easier it is to identify "Good Masters": the master's appraisal is affirmed in economic "naturalness" and specificity.

It is in the fields of agriculture, industry, credit, and, among them, most "naturally" and specifically in agriculture, that the distinction of "Good Master" is most often applied; it is in these that the master-personality should have the greatest and the master-society the least place. One possible exception is forestry. Forestry is largely amenable to rationalization, calculating - speculating - for decades to come. In addition, in it, the principle of conservation prevails over the principle of development. Forestry is therefore a possible sphere of the master-society.

Industry occupies an intermediate position. Human and material concreteness comes to the fore here, but there is no direct contact with biological processes. Production, to a greater extent than in agriculture, fits into the accounting-speculative scheme. In established, mature industries as well as in established enterprises, the action of the master-society is possible. All other areas of the industrial environment, everything that is not the "rear", is the lot of the master-personality. It is the complete master, not a weakened or damaged one, who fills and is the only one who can fill the main spaces of the industrial sphere with movement and life.

In the field of credit, the field of large credit institutions, the image of the master-personality loses its concreteness, and instead gets blurred and lost in the network of seemingly self-sufficient abstract schemes. Not only is there no relation to biological processes, there is also no direct connection to things. Hidden by anonymity, the master-personality turns into a ghost. Capturing the commanding heights of national economic life with the power of abstract capital, it turns the entire national economic whole into a ghost economy. In the field of credit, the image of the master-society, in comparison with the image of the master-personality, is perhaps no less specific. In relation to the basic relationship between the master-personality and the master-society, the principle of the nationalization of credit has a different and greater meaning than, say, the principle of "nationalization" of industry. But again, distinctions are needed here. Any advancement of the master-society in the sphere that underlies credit, the sphere of direct accumulation, must from the points of view developed here be recognized as absurdity: accumulation requires an unimpaired, not weakened, fully developed activity of the master's will and eye. We must be aware that any general reduction in the sphere of action of the master-personality inevitably reduces accumulation.

Understanding domain mastership from the point of view of managerial categories implies a certain attitude towards the specific historical and economic phenomenon of "capitalism". The term "capitalism" has, as is known, several meanings. Insofar as "capitalism" means an economic system that supplies human labor to an environment of qualitative means of production, providing labor with the opportunity to act with the help of these means and connecting it with them, the principle of "capitalism" is a positive technical-economic principle. But besides "capitalism" as a certain system that places the production process within the framework of certain external (material) preconditions, there is a "capitalist spirit", a spiritual principle that determines the existence of the concrete historical phenomenon before us. Three circumstances are predominantly distinctive of the established "capitalist spirit": (1) the real (not just methodological) positioning of the "pure" economic principle (the greatest revenue with the least cost) as the main and only principle of any action in the field of domain economics; (2) the immensity of its acquisitive striving, its internal mental limitlessness by anything other than forced-external circumstances in connection with this; (3) the disconnection of the economic field from the absolute and the transformation of economic impulses into a certain striving for a "non-absolute" and, in this sense, bad infinity.

It seems unnecessary to expand on what attitude towards the "capitalist spirit", in this indicated composition, follows from the affirmation of the "housekeeping" categories of a domain. The master's appraisal of his domain goes beyond the limits of the "pure" economic principle, its complication and transformation; the master's appraisal is the introduction of measure into any acquisitive immensity, it is the establishment of connections between the domain and the area of absolute values, the denial of any striving for the sake of bad (non-absolute) infinity. The master's appraisal is the elimination of the "capitalist spirit." At the same time, this appraising, by virtue of its bearer, the living human personality, refutes socialism and communism, which supply the master-society instead of the master-personality, where the replacement of the master-personality with the master-society is a substitution of reality with a ghost.

The phenomenon of capitalism corresponds to classical political economy with all its newer continuations in the field of real phenomena. Socialist political economy - from its distant predecessors to Saint-Simonianism, Marxism, syndicalism, and Leninism - provides, in projection onto reality, the image of a "socialist domain". The housekeeping categories of the domain will in concrete reality correspond to the system of "domain sovereignty".

Domain sovereignty should be the name for a system of ideological views and socio-political actions that will put the image of the "master" in the field of view and make its first (though not the only) task the saturation of economic reality with the master-personality principle (this principle, in its content and meaning, is significantly different, as we have seen, from the personal-economic principle of "capitalism"). The ideological views of each century to a certain extent shape the people of that century. The system of domain sovereignty, forcing the economic idea of domain into the social environment, can and will educate "Good Masters." Moreover, the principle of the "Good Master" was originally inlaid in human nature, and the master categories are only a conscious affirmation of what has long been unconscious but which to some extent still exists today, even in capitalist reality, despite the hostility of capitalist principles to the idea of a "Good Master." But human nature is imperfect: not everyone is capable of being the subject of the master's appraisal; therefore, all masters and entrepreneurs must feel the sovereign yoke in the system of domain sovereignty.

Domain sovereignty can and must accept and apply in life the elements of the socio-organizational applied science of recent European decades. Where the formal predetermination of the master's appraisal, from the point of view of the latter's goals, is more important than the reality of personal will and eye, the master-society in the system of economic power will take the place of the master-personality. But it is precisely the reality of the master-personality's will and eye that must ensure in this system the preservation of the level of technical and quantitative-economic achievements of capitalism, i.e., ensure the preservation of what is essentially unattainable in any socialist system. Precisely because socialism, as we have seen, replaces the concreteness of the master-personality with the illusory nature of the master-society on the most important fronts, the socialist system is in reality and essentially a system of economic decline.

Emphasis on the meaning and image of the master-personality can and should protect the system of domain sovereignty from the same fate. As a system of views, domain sovereignty marks the addition and partial modification of the main categories of the doctrine of housekeeping - first of all, the introduction of a logically outlined and vitally felt image of the master-personality. No matter how often political economy has approached the reality of domain phenomena, it has not yet captured them in systematic categories. And the reality of "capitalism" in many, many ways contributed to the dissolution of the specific master-individual into a faceless "subject of housekeeping" and "consumption"; and, despite the entire breadth of private economic autonomy inherent in the capitalist system, this reality in the specifically capitalist phenomena of "anonymous societies", credit, banks and the stock exchange, covered the master-personality with a shroud of illusion and scheming.[132] Domain sovereignty affirms personality. Domain sovereignty is the vision of the master-personality as a concretely defined personality. Neither capitalism nor socialism establishes a specific, living personality in a domain. In capitalism, a personality becomes "anonymous", loses contact with the absolute, while a nameless and "absoluteless" personality, strictly speaking, is no longer a person. Socialism fetters the activity of the master-personality, subordinating and replacing it with the master-society. We need a third solution. To establish a personality in the economy, one who is not nameless, but named, one who has not lost, but has accepted his connection with the absolute, and is not constrained, but active - this is the difficulty, but at the same time, the beauty of the problem of domain sovereignty. Capitalist and socialist principles can and should be contrasted with the principles of "housekeeping". The problem of domain sovereignty in its revelation establishes, in contrast to capitalism and socialism, the connection of the master-personality with God, affirms a God-confessing, and not a godless, personality. The connection with the Absolute defines the personality of domain sovereignty not as an atomistic, but as a "conciliar"

---

132 Here it is appropriate to characterize, from the point of view of the established categories, the third possible "master", namely the master-legal entity. By this we mean a legal entity of civil law, and as such, like the master-personality, is not subject to the "formal predetermination" of the master's appraisal. At the same time, it is precisely in the modern capitalist domain management that there is a tendency for the actual executor of the functions of the master's will and the master's eye of a legal entity to be the master, i.e., in everyday language, the tendency for the "managing director" of the enterprise to at least be one of its owners. In these two senses, the "master-legal entity" is only a special expression of the master-personality, even if the first one is called a joint-stock company or another a "society". But the housekeeping of a legal entity has a greater possibility of "bureaucratization" than the housekeeping of an individual. In addition, and this is extremely important, in the form of joint stock companies the master-personality itself becomes anonymous.

[*sobornoe*] principle (thus essentially different from the "capitalist" principle of personality). The totality of premises and requirements contained in the problem of domain sovereignty can be defined as a system of a special kind of domain-*sobornost*. *Sobornost'*, in contrast to collectivism, does not oppress, but affirms the individual and through it reveals some common (social) principle. This latter in the formula of domain sovereignty is represented by the principle of the sovereign, the reality of the sovereign yoke, the affiliation and feeling of the master-society over the master-personality; however, in the system of domain sovereignty, this feeling does not degenerate into fetishism (as often happens in socialism), but is associated with an understanding of the real possibilities and real limits of the master-society.

It can even be said that domain sovereignty does not deny the ultimate goals of socialism and communism, since these goals come down to placing, along with and above the atomistic, a certain social principle; but in the system of domain sovereignty, this goal is conceived in the forms of domain-*sobornost'*, and not economic (communist-socialist) collectivism.

Let us dwell on the issue of the relationship of domain sovereignty to personality. Domain sovereignty does not deny the possibility and importance of purely external measures to the organization of society, but it does not imagine the implementation of these measures without a personality. The same is true in terms of social reality: nothing is possible outside of a definite, concrete, human personality. The economic world is one of the areas of human values; any principles can be established in the economic field only by introducing them into the circle of personal values oriented towards economic phenomena. However, any system in general, including a system that denies the ontological principle of personality, in fact strives to act through the latter. The implementation of any socialism-communism is addressed to the socialist (communist) "conscious" personality. Research carried out in recent decades has shown that the development of "capitalism" as a historical phenomenon in the life of the European world is associated with the emergence and vital self-affirmation of a special type of personality, which can be called "capitalist man". And just as capitalism is turned to the "capitalist man", and socialism to the socialist-conscious personality, so is domain sovereignty turned to the personality of the master as the personal bearer of the master's appraisal...

Not every person can become a "capitalist" person, and not every individual, including a proletarian, can become a "conscious" socialist (communist). In the same way, not everyone can become a master. But we need to be clear about how widespread the principles of master's appraisal can be, and how widespread they actually are.

Limiting the scope of our attention to the management of the production (acquisition) economy, we must note: a stable domain is impossible without the participation of many people in the master's appraisal. It is possible to construct a special doctrine of participation in the master's appraisal along with the head of the "production unit," i.e., the master par excellence, as well as "employees" and "workers." Each type of social status corresponds to a type of participation in the master's appraisal. Let us also not forget that the master's appraisal, associated with the master-society, can and is created only in the order of some social "conciliar" [*sobornoe*] matter and that in this sense, the master's appraisal is potentially established in everyone who resides within the society.

The master's appraisal can be considered from two points of view: on the one hand, it is a description of the "type" of appraisal observed in real life, addressed to the economic world; on the other hand, in its unfolding, it is a system of duty applied to the economic world.

Earlier, we consistently took one or another point of view: first, we established the existence of the master's appraisal as a phenomenon; by collecting individual features scattered in reality, we constructed a "type". Then we elevated the created "type" into a "norm", the application and implementation of which can lead to the birth of the system of domain sovereignty. Although both stages are closely related to each other, theoretically they need to be distinguished and understood at the same time, so that the master's appraisal, equally as a type and as a norm, is addressed not to some "select few", but potentially to everyone.

This potential orientation does not exclude, of course, the fundamental, real difference between those who can and are fit to be a master in the fullness of their organizing functions, and those who cannot and are not fit.

We end our judgments with two series of thoughts pertaining to methodological issues. In the first row (A) we will try to establish the place of economic categories in the doctrine of "housekeeping"; in the second (B), to reveal new aspects in the very task of constructing such categories.

A. "Housekeeping" categories should form a special section of the study of economics; merely inserting them into the area of economic doctrine proper is unacceptable. Although the master's appraisal implies adherence to the economic principle, nevertheless, as has been repeatedly emphasized, in essence, the master's appraisal represents the expansion and transformation of this principle. It must be considered a methodological axiom that economic doctrine itself, as one (although not the only) element in the study of housekeeping, does not care at all about such expansion and transformation, just as it does not care about the master insofar as we imagine the latter as the bearer of the master's appraisal in its entirety. Economic doctrine is consistent, independent, great, and complete, precisely when it speaks of phenomena exclusively in the sweep of the economic principle and only from the point of view of economic man; it is nothing else than the limitation of the field of vision to economic man and economic principle that gives economic doctrine its logical force; in the name of the purity and originality of economic doctrine, everything that cannot be traced back to economic man and the economic principle must be placed outside economic doctrine, and "housekeeping" categories remain outside such doctrine. But can "housekeeping" categories form a separate, special department of the study of economics? Can't these categories be spread out into separate provisions from aesthetics, ethics, theology? Such an assumption can only be made by ignoring the reality of the master's appraisal. In the latter, individual parts that could be classified as aesthetics, ethics, theology, are welded into a particular unity. All the artistic, moral, religious elements included in it are specifically addressed, attributed, fitted to the economic sphere. Such appeal, reference, and fittingness compel us to consider this area as a specific and separate sphere - one that cannot be confused either with the economic proper, or with the aesthetic, ethical or religious environment. *Homini oeconomici*, the economic man of the economic sphere as a personal center and subject, corresponds in the sphere of housekeeping, a "kind", real, good master. And both the economic man and the "Good Master", according to what has been said above and as is not difficult to understand, are "ideal" types - in the sense of a certain consistent selection of elements, in such consistency and purity in real life not found or rarely encountered. And just as the determining principle in the psychology of the "economic man" is the economic principle, the same principle in the consciousness of the master is in the master's appraisal.

"Economic man" and "master" can equally be interpreted both from the point of view of present beings, as "types" of truly existing phenomena, and from the point of view of what should be. When interpreted from this second point of view, the "ideal" economic man, in his methods of valuing and actions will form the subject of applied teaching about domain economy as an acquisitive unity, the "ideal" master will be the bearer of that system of what is due in relation to the economic world, which we mentioned in the preceding.

In other words, "economic man" and "master" are both "type" and "norm". In the realm of phenomena accessible to human influence, each "type" can be elevated to a "norm"; and this is also outside the sphere of human-social relations proper. So, for example, the "type" of a forest community in its natural state, established by theoretical "forestry," is elevated in applied "silviculture" to the "norm" of reforestation. ("Forestry" and "silviculture" will be discussed in greater detail below.)

Of course, the justification for the "norm" in each of the cases under consideration will be specific: in one it is mainly technical, in the other it is ethical-ontological. Regardless of these justifications, the scheme of the relationship between "type" and "norm" remains the same.

B. The system of domain sovereignty, including at its core the public (sovereign) "conciliar" basis, posits a personal creative principle in "housekeeping" (in the above-mentioned understanding). In this regard, the system of domain sovereignty responds, among other things, to the voice of popular wisdom. The word "master" is pronounced precisely in the vernacular; it is the people's consciousness, turning to the master-personality, that puts the main emphasis on the role of the master; The positive content of the word "master" refers to none other than the master-personality. There is no need to exaggerate the vital significance of these contents. As is known, in the Russian folk element they did not result in either solid legal forms or even a stable worldview. The Russian folk element, as we know, did not provide sufficient resistance to anarchy and destruction. However, these positive contents themselves turned out to have a significant charge and, as it were, a force of resistance. Certain socio-political trends managed, for example, to make the word "bourgeois" a dirty word; from the point of view of these directions, it would seem to be of the greatest importance to make the word "master" the same dirty word. First of all, for ontological reasons - due to the repulsion of the theoretical statement, in any field, of the personal creative principle. After all, in the word "master", as in a formula compressed to the extreme, but all the more expressive, in this case lies the affirmation of precisely this principle for the field of domain economics. And while this word retains its positive content, the understanding and appraisal of the personal principle in the economy, at least instinctively and intuitively, is ineradicable from the people's consciousness; and without such eradication, the sustainability of many, many of the socio-political experiments currently carried out in Russia seems problematic. Can the degradation of the "rural master" into a "land user" and the master-industrialist into a "business owner" be considered assured when the elements are alive, claiming that there is no domain without a master's dominion, and the possibility is not excluded that sooner or later this element will take its toll? Moreover, socio-political considerations themselves seem to impel us to fight against this word. For in many cases the master is an owner and entrepreneur, often the peasant is an owner and small entrepreneur, and sometimes an owner and entrepreneur is even the master *par excellence,* for in cases of property and entrepreneurship the scope of the "master's will" is especially wide and there are especially many positive incentives for vigilance of the "master's eye". How could one not take up arms against such a word? Of course, they did indeed take up arms against it. But the charge of positive content invested in the word "master" in popular consciousness has so far proven to be stronger than the efforts aimed at discrediting it. And the social experimenters themselves are now inclined to rely on a "zealous master" - however, on a "master" whose master's will is subject to specific restrictions and in whom the impulses for the vigilance of the master's eye are "frozen." But the word lives, and in that word there is a lively, primal element. Completely independent of the circumstances just mentioned, purely abstract (scientific and philosophical) considerations force us to look for a concept that, in proportionate forms, would express the idea of the personal principle in "housekeeping", that would point to the executor of the domain's harmonious order. And such a concept is found in the idea of the "master". In the affirmation of the latter, the search for abstract thought meets the results of centuries of popular observation. Such a meeting is of the sort that can guarantee the vital influence of an idea. This is the meaning of the word "master". And one of the needs of the Russian future is that the thought of the intellectual heights of the people, using the methods of scientific and philosophical construction of concepts, forges from this popular word an independent and central category to designate the personal principle in housekeeping and throws it to the people, and so that the elements respond, and the people in this category recognize what they had instinctively put into their original usage of words.

If the identification of the personal principle in the economy, commensurate with the task, is carried out on the basis of the use of the folk word and the disclosure of folk ideas, this will not be the first such example in the development of Russian science. In a significantly different area, two scientific branches (creations of Russian genius) owe their terminology and to some degree even their emergence to folk language and folk ideas about nature; these branches are soil science, and the biosocial-geographical science of forestry, the pride of Russian geography created in the Russian environment (the latter considers the forest as a social phenomenon, as a "community," but a geographically determined community; the very name distinguishes it, as a theoretical science, from applied "silviculture"). The fate of Russian geographical science has given Russian geographers an understanding of the significance of folk terms in their field. "Being the result of the permanent local population's centuries-old observations of nature and the product of the creativity of such a brilliant team as the people," says V.V. Lamansky, "folk terms deserve the most careful attention by both philologists and, in particular, geographers. In their totality, folk terms can be called folk artisanal science. Artisanal sciences often consist of concepts that science masters only gradually and with difficulty, using complex research methods. Examples: moss [*pomkha*] and honeydew [*medvianaia rosa*], frazil [*donnyi led*] and hardened ice [*konovo*], the names for various soils and types of forests, etc." The famous, now deceased, Russian scientist G.F. Morozov, who quotes these words, adds: "soil terms such as *chernozem*, *solonetz*, *podzol*, *rudyak*, and *gley*, which have acquired the right of citizenship in science, are borrowed from folk language." "The value of folk terms," continues Lamansky, "for a scientific language is enormous. Constantly needing new words and expressions to denote various concepts, scientific language has in folk terms a ready-made stock of words in the spirit of the language, and some of these words fully correspond to the sought-after concepts, while others, although they do not fully correspond, can, however, be successfully used in the required sense; finally, folk terms are also important as a well-known example for the inevitable creation and composition of new words in scientific literature" (these quotations of V.V. Lamansky are taken from the printed theses of his report made at the Geographical Society in Petrograd in 1915.) Indeed, "nature leaves its mark on every manifestation of the spirit and human activity, including the artistic forms of folk art and scientific creativity, in addition to the consciousness of those who create spontaneously, and thereby imparts national characteristics to the products of creativity." G.F. Morozov continues: "And our young doctrine of types of plantings (in other words: the typological doctrine of forests is one of the foundations of the current science of forestry - P.S.), which first arose in the north, in its very first steps primarily took advantage of folk silvicultural terms." G.F. Morozov expands into scientific categories such folk concepts as *ramen'* ("spruce forests of high quality with a small admixture of pine and deciduous species... on loamy, well-drained, podzolized soils..."), *sogra* ("...spruce forests are always low-growing, the shape of the trunk is strongly tapered, much poorer density, with a greater admixture of deciduous species, with a lot of spruce windfall... drainage is poor... soil waters in the spring merge with groundwater"), *boron, subor*, etc. Morozov ends: "I have cited these examples in order to show the conveniences that stem from a successful term that makes it possible to combine in one word, in one concept, a whole sum of characteristics that would require a whole page to list. The same geographical individuals are hidden... also in such broader terms as desert, steppe, taiga and tundra."

The conveniences that Morozov points out do not relate only to geographical science. With our entire exposition, we have tried to show that the use and disclosure of the popular term "master" and others associated with it can also be important for the doctrine of "housekeeping". Only this time we have to put into folk terms the "sum of characteristics", the listing of which requires not one, but many pages.

Soil science, as we have seen, developed in the Russian environment upon, among other things, the basis of the scientific disclosure and processing of folk concepts. Subsequently, this science began to be cultivated as an independent science, following the Russian example, in other national scientific environments of the world. The development of Russian soil science led to the recognition of soils as a special (fourth) "kingdom of nature," that is, to the ultimate — in its kind and in its significance, "revolutionary" for natural science and geography — "act" of the Russian school. Today, Russian forestry is apparently on the verge of having a decisive influence on the forestry studies of the non-Russian world as well. Soil science and forestry are two new sciences, the fruits of the flowering of the Russian genius, growing on the primordial folk-historical tree. Their example is encouraging for other branches of knowledge, in particular for the study of agriculture. It should be noted: no matter how outstanding soil scientists and foresters Russia had, the creation of the sciences of soil and forestry was not anyone's sole endeavor; even Dokuchaev's influence was not singularly-determining. Soil science and forestry are both the result of the work of an entire school of scientists, several generations of them. It will be no different in the matter of establishing the housekeeping categories of domain management. In the field of housekeeping doctrine the Russian spirit will bloom and yield fruit – and so, too, will the cause of *sobornost'*.

***

THE MONGOL YOKE IN RUSSIAN HISTORY

George Vernadsky[133]

***

1.

One hundred years ago, in 1826, the Russian Academy of Sciences proposed the following question for scholars to deliberate: "What were the consequences of Mongol rule in Russia, and more precisely, what influence did it have on the political relations of the state, its form of governance, its internal administration, as well as the enlightenment and education of the people?" The deadline for submitting a response was set for 1 January 1829. By the appointed deadline, however, only one work — in German — had been submitted, and it was not considered worthy of any award.

A few years after this unsuccessful attempt, the Academy once again posed a question in the very same domain, but defined it much more narrowly. The new formulation of the task was put forth in 1832 and was expressed in the following manner: "Write a critical history of the Ulus of Jochi, or the so-called Golden Horde, on the basis of Eastern, especially Mohammedan, historians, monetary relicts preserved from the dynasty's Khans, as well as old Russian, Polish, Hungarian, and other chronicles found in contemporary European accounts." The deadline for solving this new task was also set at three

---
[133] Originally published in *The Eurasian Annals*, book 5 (Paris, 1927).

years (1 August 1835). This time, the Academy received another work in German, a large and significant one, but following reviews by the academicians Frähn, Schmidt, and Krug, a prize was not awarded to the work this time either.[134]

Decades have passed since then. Several generations of Russian scholars have labored on studying the questions posed by the Academy of Sciences in the early 19th century. Much has been researched and clarified. In addition to Arabic and Persian sources, Chinese sources have also been brought into consideration.[135]

However, if we are now getting closer to deliberating the second question (on the Golden Horde) posed by the Academy, then the first, more general question about the relative weight of the Mongol yoke in the history of the Russian people still remains unanswered in essence. Meanwhile, any resolution on this question still retains enormous significance for understanding the entire course of Russian history.

Russian history can be examined from two points of view: one can study the internal development of Russian life and the Russian people without regard for the peoples around it, or, on the other hand, one can strive to explain the development of Russian history against the backdrop of world history. Whenever Russian history has been viewed from the latter perspective, world history has habitually been taken to mean the history of the Western European world. Russian history is then, as it were, only an appendage to the history of Western Europe. The whole global significance of Russia over the ages is represented as merely a history of protecting Western European civilization from Asiatic "barbarism."

---

134 The work in question, *Geschichte der Goldenen Horde*, which was published several years later (1840), belonged to the pen of the famous orientalist Hammer-Purgstall.

135 Here it is necessary to note the outstanding role of our spiritual mission in Beijing (Hyacinth Bichurin in the first half of the 19th century and Palladius Kafarov in the second half).

The Mongol Yoke in Russian History

Outlining the provenance of the "Eastern question" during the Russo-Turkish War under Alexander II, the historian Solovyov wrote thusly:

> Our main character has an ancient and iconic origin... The Eastern question appeared in history as soon as European man became aware of the difference between Europe and Asia, between the European and Asian spirit. The Eastern question constitutes the essence of the history of ancient Greece; all the names familiar to us since childhood, such as Miltiades and Themistocles, are close and kin to us because they are the names of men who labored to solve the Eastern question and labored in struggle between Europe and Asia. A fierce struggle runs throughout all of European history, passing with varying fortune for the warring parties. At one point Europe takes the heights, elsewhere Asia does: now Xerxes' hordes flood Greece, then Alexander the Macedonian and his phalanx and Homer's *Iliad* appear on the banks of the Euphrates, then Hannibal is outside Rome, then the Roman eagles are in Carthage and its metropolis, then the Huns appear on the fields of Châlons and the Arabs near Tours, then crusading Europe shows up in Palestine, then the Tatar *baskak* rides through Russian cities and demands tribute, then the Crimean Khan burns Moscow, then Russian standards fly in Kazan, Astrakhan, and Tashkent, then the Turks remove the cross from the Hagia Sophia and spread their wild camp around the monuments of ancient Greece, then Turkish ships are burning by Chesma and Navarino, and the Russian army stands at Adrianople. All of this is one great struggle, all one Eastern question.

"But, of course," Solovyov added, "the Eastern question is of the greatest significance to those European countries that border Asia, with whom their struggle constitutes the essential content of their history. Such is the significance of the Eastern question in the history of Greece, and such also is its significance in the history of Russia, as a consequence of both countries' geographical position."

Of course, this element — the defense of Europe from Asia — has played a role in the historical weight of Russia. The indignation of Russian thinkers whenever Europe forgets this is also understandable. This Indignation was vividly expressed by Alexander Pushkin in his time, in 1834:

The Mongol Yoke in Russian History

> For a long time, Russia has been completely separated from the fates of Europe. Its broad plains have swallowed up countless crowds of Mongols and stopped their destructive invasions. The barbarians did not dare leave enslaved Rus' in their rear, and so they returned to the steppes of their East. Christian enlightenment was also saved by tormented and dying Russia, not Poland as some European journals recently claimed; but Europe has always been as ignorant as it is ungrateful towards Russia.

Without a doubt, this side of Russia's historical role also exists. For a number of centuries, Rus' was the border between West and East, between Europe and Asia. This aspect, however, is far from exhaustive of Russia's historical role in world history — that is, world history understood much more broadly than European history.

We are dealing with a distorted historical scheme of world history. Germano-Romanic Europe is presented as the backbone of the historical process. This notion was created by and large on the basis of the rapid growth of European culture in the 15th-19th centuries. Meanwhile, Europe's cultural hegemony — which, moreover, must be understood primarily in the limited sense of the development of the applied natural sciences, technology, and industrial, military, and political life — is a temporary phenomenon. How world life will take shape in the 20th century is a big question and a big mystery. New entities from among the Germano-Romanic peoples are increasingly coming to life, such as Anglo-Saxon America, but also Spanish-Portuguese America. Colossal shifts await the peoples of Asia and Africa — the Indians, the Chinese, the Japanese, the Mongols, the Turks, and the Negros.

In the past as well, we find a picture altogether different from the Romano-Germanic hegemony of the 19th-20th centuries. The so-called "fall of the Roman Empire" was an intersection between the Mediterranean, Greco-Roman-Syrian, and European and Arab worlds on the one hand, and the world of the Central Asian and Southern Russian nomads on the other. The seeming "regression" in the material culture of the Mediterranean world was, on the one hand, "progress" in the sense of a grandiose expansion of cultural-historical and cultural-geographical frameworks. The nomads that came in waves one after the other from the Black Sea steppes, from the depths of the continent, often turned out to be intermediaries between Mediterranean and Asian (Chinese and Indian) civilization and culture, not to mention the fact that the nomads themselves carried their own completely new culture, for instance in the realm of art. The material culture of the "Roman Empire" turned out to be impotent against the influx of the new "barbarian" peoples with their own culture.

But the spiritual upsurge of the medieval world associated with the new religion of Christianity by and large coincided with the raging historical elements. The Church was a link between the Mediterranean world and the "barbarian" world. Through the Church, many elements of "barbarian" civilization penetrated the life of peoples previously subject to the Roman sword. On the other hand, the Church brought the new "barbarian peoples" into the fold of its influence and organization.

The center of the Church's influence moved ever further to the East. The first ecclesiastical "Rome" was in the old Mediterranean Rome. The second, new Rome already found itself on the border between Europe and Asia, on the Bosphorus, in Byzantium. The third Rome was even further east, in the depths of Eastern, Mongol Rus' — in Moscow. Tsargrad, or Constantinople, Byzantium, was the center of Orthodox Christianity in the Middle Ages. This center's influence diminished in various directions as branches of Christianity spread laterally (from the point of view of medieval world history): Latindom reigned in the West, in the world of Romano-Germanic Europe, while Nestorianism took hold in the East, in the world of Iranian Asia and the Turkic and Mongol steppes.

The Mongol Yoke in Russian History

2.

The whole history of the Byzantine Empire was imbued with mutual relations with the steppic East. The same sort of relations colored the early centuries of Russian history and its "pre-Mongol period" of Kievan Rus'. The Pechenegs, Polovtsy, Torks, Berendei, and Black Klobuks — all of these predominantly Turkic peoples of the South Russian steppes came into constant contact with the Greek and Russian world, at times at enmity and at war with Tsargrad and Rus', and at other times, separately or in different combinations, entering into allied and friendly relations.

Russian civilization and culture gradually came to be permeated by elements from Byzantine (that is Greco-Eastern) civilization and culture on the one hand, and on the other, the civilization and culture of the steppe nomads, from whom it adopted clothing and weaponry, songs and fairy tales, its military structure and its way of thinking.

From this point of view, the Mongol invasion of the 13th century was not something fundamentally new. It was yet another deep continental wave, albeit one of extraordinary strength and hitherto unseen tension. Moreover, this wave completely overwhelmed the Russian world, or at least its Eastern half. This created a new basis for Russian-Eastern relations. Then began the political subordination of the Russian land to the East, to the "Mongol yoke."

3.

In our consciousness, the notion of the "Mongol yoke" is first and foremost associated with the Russian land being torn away from Europe. However, this circumstance also had another side. If the "Mongol yoke" contributed to the separation of the Russian land from Europe (and it remains a big question just how deep this separation was), then, on the other hand, the very same "Mongol yoke" also put the Russian land into the tightest bond with the steppe center and the Asian peripheries of the continental mainland.

The Russian land found itself within the system of a world empire — the Mongol Empire. For some reason, we still find ourselves insufficiently conscious of the global character of this empire. The Roman Empire of Trajan's time and its historical continuation in the Byzantine Empire of the era of Justinian and then Basil II were of world significance. The world empire of Byzantium was destroyed by the Latin crusaders in 1204. The medieval Latin empires — the "Holy Roman Empire of the German Nation" established by Charlemagne in 800 and the Constantinople Empire of Baldwin — could not have world significance. The "Empire of the German Nation" had only provincial European significance. The Latin Empire of Constantinople had no such significance.

The role that Rome and Byzantium played as unifiers of the cultures of West and East, of agricultural-maritime culture and nomadic-steppe culture, passed to the Mongol Empire at the outset of the 13th century after the fall of the Byzantine Empire. At the same time, however, the circle of lands and peoples covered by the Mongol saber was much wider than what had previously been demarcated by the Roman sword. The Roman Empire and later the Byzantine Empire had been built upon a systematization of relations between the Mediterranean hearth of civilization (which was agricultural and maritime) and the culture of the steppe nomads. The Mongol Empire early on seized the two centers of (agricultural-maritime) civilization: China on the one hand and the lands that made up the Byzantine Empire on the other (Asia Minor, the Caucasus, Crimea, the Balkans[136]). The center of gravity

---

136 After the death of the Bulgarian King Ivan Asen II in 1241, Bulgaria recognized Mongol authority and paid tribute to the khans of the Golden Horde for a number of years. Batu organized a review of his troops in Bulgaria in 1242 after the Hungarian campaign and the Dalmatian raid. Later, Bulgaria found itself dependent upon Nogai Khan (the usurper ruler of the horde in southern Russia), and in 1292 Serbia recognized Nogai's authority. It is quite possible that the Bulgarian kings of Tarnovo recognized the supreme authority of the Kipchak khans up until the Turkish conquest.

shifted from one type to another. The Byzantine-Roman Empire had been founded on the maritime-agricultural type and from this basis came into contact with the nomadic and continental type. The Mongol Empire had its center in the nomadic world, while the agricultural centers (China, Asia Minor, the Balkans) became its outlying branches.

The Russian land had cultural ties with one world empire — the Byzantine Empire. However, the political hegemony of Byzantium was rather weak in nature (with the exception of ecclesiastical relations). This link was completely shaken and weakened with the fall of Byzantium and the establishment of the Latin Empire of Constantinople in 1204.

As a result of the Mongol conquest, the Russian land ended up within the system of a different empire, the Mongol Empire, the sole exception being ecclesiastical relations, in which terms Rus' continued to be subordinate to the ecumenical patriarch, who, for most of the 13th century, resided no longer in Constantinople but in Nicaea (in Asia Minor).

Having submitted to the sovereigns of the house of Genghis Khan, the Russian land was politically incorporated into a vast historical world that stretched from the Pacific Ocean to the Mediterranean Sea. The political scope of this world is glaringly illustrated by the composition of the great Mongol Kurultais of the 13th century: these Kurultais were attended by (in addition to the Mongol princes, elders, and administrators of all of Central, Northern, and Eastern Asia) the Russian grand princes, Georgian and Armenian kings, Iconian (Seljuk) sultans, Kirman and Mossul atabeks, and others. People from all corners of the continent were drawn to the center of Mongol power to deal with various affairs — administrative, trade, and the like.

For Rus', the roads to the East were open. Russian military contingents marched alongside Tatar kings far beyond the Don, which the Polovtsy had previously blocked from "drinking with a helmet."[137] The "guests of Rustia" — Russian merchants — figured in large numbers in the Horde in the North Caucasus at the time of the murder of Prince Mikhail Yaroslavich of Tver in 1319. Throughout the North Caucasus at the time, one could find "Christian churches" where these merchants prayed. Russian military units also participated in Kubilai's troops in the conquest of South China in the late 13th century.

The Mongol Empire, completely unified under the first great khans, quickly began to break up into separate states — the Chinese, Persian, Chagatai, and the Golden Horde. Nevertheless, the individual Mongol states remained connected for a long time, and for a while vassal relations were maintained between the different Mongol sovereigns and the Great Khan, who resided in China since the time of the famous Kublai.[138] Thus, until the fall of the Mongols in China in the mid-14th century (1368), the unity of the entire imperial Mongol system was, albeit weakened, maintained. One glaring documentation of this imperial unity is a curious drawing of the Mongol Empire dated to 1331. On this outline, the Mongol Empire is divided into separate parts, but they all form an integral whole. These parts are as follows: (1) The main core was the Middle Empire (China) — the Tuoba-Timurid Empire; (2) Persia — the state of Bu-Sain (Abu Sa'id); (3) Turkestan — the Chagatai state[139]; (4) the Kipchak kingdom—the state of Yu-Ju-Bu (Uzbek).

According to this map, the Russian land ("*A-lo-sh*" in the transmission of the Mongolian draftsman — cf. Magyar *orosh*, Kalmyk *oros*, Caucasian *urus*) was the extreme North-Western corner of the great Asian world, comparable to the Byzantine

---

137 An interesting case is the Dagestan campaign, in which the princes of Rostov and Yaroslavl joined Mengu-Timur and took the Yassian (Alanian) fortress city of Dadakov in 1277-1278.

138 Nevertheless, the individual Mongol sovereigns often stubbornly fought amongst each other, such as the case of Hulegu, who ruled Persia, and Berke of Jochi.

139 Split into two halves in the early 14th century.

"ecumene" (οἰκουμένη). The Russian land did not figure as an autonomous member of this world, yet it was not directly subordinate to the Great Khan. Instead, the Russian land was part of the kingdom of Uzbek and the Ulus of Jochi.

4.

Among the Russian lands, North-Eastern and South-Eastern Rus' became part of the Ulus of Jochi for a longer time. The other half of Rus' fell to the West already in the mid-14th century. Although the Russian lands which became part of the Polish, Lithuanian, and Hungarian states largely retained their cultural elements, they lost their national-state culture.

The main line of the historical process of the development of Russian statehood lay not in Western Rus', which was conquered by Latindom, but in the Eastern Rus' seized by Mongoldom. The Eastern Russian lands also became part of a foreign — the Mongol — state. However, this state was a world empire, not a provincial power. This empire did not interfere in the internal cultural life of its parts, including that of the Russian land. Moreover, this empire waged war against its Western neighbors, Lithuania, Hungary, and Poland, and these neighbors were thus the adversaries of the Russian people. The Mongol-Tatar wave maintained the forward defense of the Russian people against the Latin West. When the Mongol Empire finally collapsed, the Ulus of Jochi, the Golden Horde, continued this traditional policy of fighting against the West.

Like Moscow, Sarai fought Lithuania. The historical role of Sarai on this front was not inferior. By attacking Lithuania, Sarai was defending Russian culture even while it was politically at odds with Muscovy. In 1380 at Kulikovo Field, Moscow openly challenged Sarai for the first time and held its ground. Whether it would have held its own against Lithuania

The Mongol Yoke in Russian History

without Mongol help in the same years is difficult to say. The strong Lithuanian Prince Vytautas increasingly expanded his possessions Eastward. It remains a big question how the matter would have ended up without Sarai's intervention, i.e., whether the center of Russian statehood would have been reinforced in Moscow or shifted to semi-Polonized Vilnius. Sarai settled the matter. In 1399, Vytautas' army suffered a terrible defeat at the hands of Edigu on the Vorskla River. Lithuania would not be able to recover from this defeat for a long time, and Latindom's push to the East was undermined. The historical significance of the Battle of Vorskla was no less than the battle fought by the Vorskla some 300 years later (Poltava in 1709). Even though Eastern Russian regiments did not participate in it, and Western-Russian forces fought on Vytautas' side, the Battle of Vorskla in 1399 was nevertheless one of the greatest events in Russian history. Moscow took historic advantage of Sarai's success.

5.

The common historical life shared by the Russian land and the Ulus of Jochi over the course of two centuries is of immense historical interest and great historical significance.

The Mongol Empire broke up into several powerful states. The greater part of them completely merged with the old states in which the new Mongol entities had arisen. The Mongol element simply became part of these states' history in the form of a certain dynasty. Such was the character of the period of the Mongol dynasty of Kublai and his successors in China (1260-1368) and the Mongol dynasty of Hulegu and his successors in Persia (1256-1334).[140]

A different historical fate awaited the Ulus of Jochi. We do not see it fully merging with Russian statehood. Instead,

---

140 Of equal significance was the formation of the Tatar Kazan kingdom on the land of the Volga Bulgar state.

it is as if we see two centers: Sarai and Moscow. The foremost significance of the former is the administrative-state life of the whole kingdom of the Golden Horde, although it was not the only center. Historically, this might be explainable in terms of how the Golden Horde was the successor of two state worlds at once: the steppe (the Polovtsian part) and the forest (the North Russian). It is no coincidence that the main center of the Golden Horde, the Jochid state, was established within the first zone, in the South Russian steppes, and was known in the East as the "Kipchak kingdom."[141] Within the second zone, in the North-Russian forests, arose another Russian center within the Jochid Ulus, Vladimir, followed by Moscow.

Theoretically, it is conceivable that the historical process could have further developed in these two veins, or, the internal importance of the Northern, Russian center, Moscow, could have gradually grown until it became stronger than the previous center, in which case a rupture, a split into two centers, would be inevitable. As we know, this is precisely what happened. When Sarai was weakened, Moscow gained in strength, and the Jochid kingdom was torn into two halves: the Golden Horde and the Grand Principality of Muscovy.

But the opposite phenomenon is also conceivable. The main center could have gained in predominant significance and gradually seized and transformed all of the internal and external forces of both halves of the Ulus of Jochi, the Tatar and the Russian. The Golden Horde could have become, if not directly Russian, then a Mongol-Russian state, just as there were Mongol-Chinese, Mongol-Persian, and Lithuanian-Russian states.

Of essential significance to such fusion between new Mongol states was the religious question. Cultural fusion was full and decisive once the ruling Mongol aristocracy accepted the faith of the majority of the population of the country in which it established itself (Buddhism in China and

---

141 Kipchaks = Polovtsy (and Kyrgyz).

Islam in Persia).[142] In other words, if the Mongol khans, the descendants of Jochi, would have accepted Orthodoxy, then Sarai, and not Moscow, would have become the spiritual and cultural center of the Russian land.

The notion that the Tatars and Mongols were long-since thoroughly Muslim is so firmly rooted in ordinary consciousness that the conversion of the khans of the Golden Horde to Orthodoxy might seem to be idle and empty fantasy. However, such fantasy came close to coming true on several occasions. Islam was by no means the original faith of the Mongol-Tatars.[143] None other than Batu's son, Sartak, was in all likelihood either very close to Orthodoxy or had already outright converted to Orthodoxy. We have testimony as to Sartak's Christianity from the conscientious Arab historian Juzjani, the author of the *Tabaqat-i Nasiri*. In the year 657 of the Muslim calendar (1258-59 AD), Juzjani saw Seyid Ashraf-ed-din in Delhi on a trade mission from Samarkand. The Seyid told the historian the following about Sartak and his death.[144] Sartak, who succeeded his father Batu after his death, had been a persecutor of Muslims. Upon ascending the throne, Sartak was supposed to pay respects to the Great Khan Möngke. On the way back, Sartak rode by the horde of his uncle Berke, but changed course without visiting him. Berke sent an envoy to inquire into the reason for such an insult. Sartak replied: "You are a Muslim, whereas I profess the Christian faith; to see the face of a Muslim spells misfortune." Berke locked himself in his tent, tied a rope around his neck, and spent three days crying and praying: "God, if Muhammad's faith is in accord with the truth, grant me revenge against Sartak." Four days later, Sartak died.[145]

---

142 It is easy to imagine the decisive significance for the Russians' historical fate if the Lithuanian princes would have firmly adopted Orthodoxy instead of Latindom.

143 See my article on St. Alexander Nevsky in the fourth volume of *Evraziiskii Vremennik*.

144 Sartak died in 652 according to the Muslim calendar (1254/5 A.D.).

145 According to another account (by Abu'l-Faraj), Sartak was even ordained as a deacon.

Sartak's successor, Berke, then opted for the reverse and officially adopted Islam. Berke's conversion did not, however, mean the Horde's final conversion to Islam. One of the next "horde kings," Tokhta (1291-1313), was a zealous admirer of shamanism and Lamaism. His successor, Uzbek, whose sister married the Prince of Moscow, Yuri Danilovich, was favorably predisposed towards Orthodoxy.[146] On Sarai coins apparently dating back to Uzbek's time, we find depictions of a double-headed eagle and what is likely the Virgin Mother of God (an image of a woman with an infant). Uzbek himself, however, converted to Islam. Our chronicles note: "Tsar Ozbyak went mad." Only from this time on (the beginning of the 14th century) was a final line in the sand drawn between the Golden Horde and Rus'. Yet, Uzbek himself and his immediate successors treated the Russian church magnanimously and gave "labels" guaranteeing the rights of Russian metropolitans and bishops; in the same spirit, they did not raise any obstacles to Mongol-Tatars converting to Orthodoxy.

6.

The two cultural centers of the Ulus of Jochi, Sarai and Moscow, were closely bound together by the structure of the greatest cultural force in Russian history: the Orthodox Church. Soon after the Mongol conquest, the leaders of the Russian church understood and realized the need to establish stronger contact with the new state center of Sarai. The Russian church went through a time of disorder. From the very beginning, the center of the metropolitan of Rus' had been Kiev. After the Mongol pogrom of 1240, Kiev lost its significance and would not recover for a long while. For a long time, the metropolitans took up their dwelling in North-Eastern Rus', in Vladimir on the Klyazma, and at the end of

---

146 Uzbek married a Byzantine princess who took the name Bailun. At the same time, he also maintained good relations with Rome.

The Mongol Yoke in Russian History

the 13th century they finally moved to Vladimir and then to Moscow.[147]

The metropolitan could not, however, ignore the main center of the Ulus of Jochi — Sarai. Every Russian metropolite of the 13th-14th centuries had to travel to Sarai frequently and reside there for a lengthy period. The idea behind this was clear: to build something in the likes of a permanent representation in Sarai. Such a representation came in the form of the Sarai episcopate founded in 1261 by Metropolitan Kirill.[148] The "Tatar Tsar" himself demanded that a "grand priest" be assigned to his capital. The Bishop of Sarai was, as it were, a representative of the Metropolitan of All Rus', just as the latter was the representative of the Ecumenical Patriarch of Tsargrad (Constantinople). The Bishop of Sarai served as an intermediary between the metropolitan and the Mongol khan on the one hand, and between the ecumenical Emperor of Tsargrad and the patriarch on the other. The bishop would travel to visit the Greek patriarch and emperor in Tsargrad with letters from both the Horde Tsar and the Metropolitan of All Rus'.

Thus, if there were two centers in the Ulus of Jochi — Sarai and Moscow —, then both served as the focal points of the ecclesiastical structure of Rus'. From the point of view of the state-administrative mechanism, the main center was Sarai, to which Moscow was secondary. In ecclesiastical terms, it was the other way around: the main center was Moscow, while Sarai was secondary.

That being said, if the above assumptions with respect to the Sarai khans' turn towards Orthodoxy are justified, then it is clear that the roles of Moscow and Sarai would have changed more quickly in ecclesiastical terms. The Metropolite of All Rus', upon losing its Kievan roots, would have ultimately rooted itself not in Moscow, but in Sarai. Various historical

---
147 The episcopal chair was still held in Kiev for a long time.

148 It is conceivable that Great Prince Alexander Yaroslavich (Nevsky) himself worked to have the Sarai episcopate instated.

traces of the Bishop of Sarai's claims to the leading role in the life of the Russian church have been preserved. The Bishop of Sarai constantly insisted on expanding his authority over the Russian lands. In the late 13th and early 14th centuries, there were constant disputes between the rulers of Sarai and Ryazan over the border parishes in the Ryazan lands (along the upper reaches of the Don). Metropolitan Theognostus resolved the dispute in favor of Sarai, and from then on the ruler was titled "Saraisky (later "Sarsky") and Podonsky" — even when disputed parishes were reattributed to Ryazan. One Sarai bishop, Izmail, schemed against the Metropolitan of Moscow, hence Metropolitan Petr of Moscow (later canonized) stripped Izmail of his rank and eparchy in 1312. The Sarai ruler's ambitions never became reality. Thus, the center of Orthodox statehood took root in Moscow, not Sarai.

The ecclesiastical-political significance of Sarai fell along with the decline of the Golden Horde until it finally collapsed. In the mid-15th century, Bishop Vassian of Sarai moved his see to Moscow and settled in Krutitsy, which from the end of the 13th century onwards served as the metochion of the Sarai bishops in Moscow. The Bishop of Sarai was then turned into the Krutitsy Bishop (and later metropolitan). The Krutitsy Metropolitan, vicar and right hand of the Patriarch of Muscovy and All Rus', is therefore an historical relic of deep significance. The Krutitsy Metropolitan, vicar of the Patriarch of Moscow, is a reminder of the unrealized historical possibility of a Patriarch of Sarai, for whom the holy leader of Moscow would have, conversely, been his vicar. The Krutitsy Metropolitan is a deep symbol of the Mongol influence on the development of Russian culture.

***

THE PHENOMENOLOGY OF REVOLUTION
(selected excerpts)

Lev Karsavin[149]

***

"What will happen next, professor? We expect an answer from you as a historian. When will this all end?" Such questions befell me quite often in the beginning of Bolshevik rule. Of course, I refrained from giving any precise chronological indications; nevertheless, in order to not let the authority of historical science fall in the eyes of those inquiring, I responded: "Sure, in 10 or so years everything will get straightened out." This proposed timeframe, just as unpleasantly long to me as it was to my interlocutors, has certain grounds and still has yet to be refuted by the turn of events. At the same time, however, I indicated such a timeframe out of my own inner indignation for my fellow scholars. Those few among them who once defended the idea of historical laws stubbornly shied away from specific forecasts or came out with obvious nonsense. The majority of them, with imperturbable complacence and indecent indifference to what was happening, repeated the stock phrases from textbook "methodologies" and "philosophies of history" (composed mainly along Rickertian lines), such as "There are no historical laws" and "History does not repeat itself." Meanwhile, half-educated columnists fearfully sought out analogies between Kerensky and Saint-

---

[149] Originally published in *The Eurasian Annals*, book 5 (Paris, 1927).

The Phenomenology of Revolution

Just (why exactly Saint-Just? I myself just read a column on this topic) — and on the basis of similar analogies they tried to prophesize about a future Bonaparte. In the end, prophets even appeared from the world of the natural sciences, who turned to analogies from the lives of animals and plants. The Bolsheviks themselves, of course, were the most confident of all when it came to constructing schemes for the future. But their constructions were only unsuccessful attempts to offer "scientific" expressions of their vague desires and hopes (after all, the Bolsheviks were the ones who respected "scientificness" the most). The reigning confusion is quite understandable if we recall that the elementariness of not only the Bolsheviks' theories, but of socialist theories in general, necessarily presupposes a corresponding elementariness of consciousness or, as Lenin might express it, the "physical power of thought."

Of course, history does not repeat itself in any sense resembling the "repetition" of natural-scientific "laws," and the historian who understands his work does not seek out any abstract formulas in the likes of such "laws." On the other hand, external analogy is a bad method, one which is long overdue to be left to theosophist feeblemindedness with its "astral cliché." However, and by no coincidence, historians do in fact use "general" notions, and the notion of revolution is one of them. The "similarity" between processes designated by this term — applying it in the very least to the "great revolutions" like the English (1640-1653-1660), the French (1789-1800), and both Russian ones (1598-1610-1613, i.e., the "Time of Troubles," and the one of 1917) — is not imaginary, but real. The phenomena before us are, without a doubt, of the same kind. If this is indeed the case, then the nature of revolution can be defined and a phenomenology of it can be presented.

"General" processes exist in historical reality. But they are not something special, abstracted from the sphere of being, as if abstract "laws" which govern being, restrict the freedom of historical subjects, and successfully find expression in conventional judgments. History is by and large a sphere of continuity and freedom. The historically general is the oneness of the manifold. The "general process" in history can be likened to the evolution of an organism (for example, the human) in relation to the evolution of a specific organism (for example, one given human being). After all, there is no abstract organism or abstract development, but rather all evolution comes about and exists only in the multiplicity of the individual organisms it encompasses. Of course, it is self-evident that "general" evolution in history does not contradict the evolution of the "general" (e.g., mankind) just as the evolution of the individual does not contradict the evolution of the species.

Evolution presupposes that something is evolving, which is to say that the subject of evolution in historical actuality is necessarily an individual. Moreover, evolution is not some kind of being in and of itself, but is the evolving subject (the evolving individual). In history, the subjects of evolution can be individuals as well as (in the case of "universal" evolution) collective, symphonic personalities (e.g., a group, a people, a culture[150], or even mankind). In the assumption that there are symphonic personalities, there is still no hypostasis of abstractions. For we do not presume that the symphonic personality has being outside of or "beyond" its individuations (i.e., that a culture or people is beyond the individuals that they comprise), yet we reject any equivalence between the symphonic personality and the arithmetic sum of its individuals. In exactly the same manner, in recognizing myself to be a personality that is coming about and that exists in all of my development, I do not thereby claim that there exists

---

150 To avoid any neologism, in this article we deliberately use the term "culture" in two senses. Culture is, firstly, the symphonic personality (the culture-personality, the culture-subject), which is close to Danilevsky's understanding of culture and to Spengler's use of the term; secondly, culture is the accomplished possibilities and products of the culture-personality, all that has, as it were, cooled down, hardened, and been emitted in the wake of the culture-personality — this coincides with the more common use of the term. No particular difficulties stem from this twofold meaning of the term "culture," for its meaning is always clear in context. Moreover, the products of the personality's activities are always organically connected to it.

my own abstract, "empty" "I" which would causally impact my development in any given moment.

Thus, the difference between the individual and the general boils down to a difference between the individual and the symphonic personality, where the former is the free self-individuation of the latter, and the latter is the unity and harmonious multiplicity of individuals at the same time. If this is the case, then it is necessary to presume the following: Christian culture, as a symphonic personality, comes about in the order of lesser symphonic personalities (Eurasian-Russian culture, European-Catholic culture, etc.), and these lesser orders of peoples are, as peoples, in the final analysis individuals. The symphonic personality manifests itself in states or actions, one of which is revolution.

We affirm the real unity and personal being of mankind and, within it, of Christian culture, but without an inkling of lapsing into advocating the so-called "universal historical point of view" (the name alone says it all!), and even less so without taking the side of the ideology of progress in all the absurdity and destructiveness it wreaks for the historian. By virtue of the unity of the personality itself, it is necessary to allow for all its "homogenous" states to be none other than manifestations of one state that is distributed in space and time. Thus, to express things paradoxically, there are no revolutions, but there is one diversely manifesting yet always identical Revolution. Therefore, Revolution manifests itself in any specific revolution, and in studying a revolution, for example the French one, we are therefore studying every other one, for we are studying Revolution itself. Hence why discussions attempting to understand and evaluate "revolution in general" are pointless. Modern nominalistic thought, although already significantly undermined, simplifies the fact of the state of "many-one," decomposing such into the affirmation of a multitude of specific and absolutely, essentially, disconnected revolutions and into the affirmation of the replicability of a certain general process, "revolution in

The Phenomenology of Revolution

general," within them. Hence positive sociologism or dumb, lifeless metaphysics.

Knowing the general historical process does not at all mean formulating something "repeating" in all specific discoveries, particularly in portraying the necessary course of any revolution. It is necessary to grasp the essence and inner dialectic of the process. And this dialectic, exhausting its possibilities within history, is expressible not in abstraction, but only by way of the historical description of its specific manifestations, which are altogether diverse and often apparently dissimilar. At the same time, in order to understand the essence of the process, it is often sufficient to have only one such manifestation. In any case, there is no need for pedantic picking of "analogous" material, for exterior generalization. Of course, there is practically no way to do without common words and thereby without the apparentness of something repeating itself. But it never follows that we ought to forget that these common words and apparent repetitions possess a purely auxiliary, instrumental significance.

Since roughly the middle of the past century, the doctrine of historical materialism has gradually gained in significance, much more than is commonly thought. The fundamental premise accepted equally by "materialists" as well as "idealists" is that the historical process can be understood in the likes of material-mechanical processes. The historical process is conceived as a sum of causally interconnected processes and, ultimately, immutable facts. The very notion and nature of causal connection is simply not a question for thought; likewise, the question of what exactly is a "sum" or "system" remains unanswered, or is answered by equating such a "system" with the natural-scientific "laws" which are interpreted only so far as natural science allows for them to be.

The origins of materialist-mechanical doctrine were already given in the Catholic religious and philosophical teachings on Providence (Bossuet), and later in deism. Here, the will of God is understood to be one of the components or one of the "factors" of evolution. The tenacity of this religious materialism is already altogether telling: on its basis, modern seekers of God have attempted to refute historical materialism while crookedly and obliquely arguing about history without any understanding of the fact that their premises are incompatible with its very essence.

By dialectical necessity, the basic premise of historical materialism gives way to clearer expression: formal materialism (i.e., the materialistic methodology or understanding for which historical being is a type of material) tends to put the material aspect of life in the forefront. Monism degenerates into materialism. The foundation of historical being is seen in material, "economic" processes, although it would seem to be completely clear that one cannot deny spontaneous generation and at the same time deduce anything other than matter from matter. Indeed, by dint of the real oneness of historical being, the latter can be recognized from the angle of any one of its manifestations, including the "organization of production." Hence arises the apparent credibility of various historical-materialist explanations, which would be even greater if only there were people with the best scientific education and critical sobriety of thought among the materialist historians. But this credibility will always be only apparent, because readers, as well as the authors themselves, do not take notice of a very simple fact: the real subject of their knowledge is not the material aspect of the process, but the nature of it that expresses itself within the material aspect of the process. Unfortunately, understanding this is psychologically difficult. In the very least, the opponents of historical materialism have fought against it by denying the very oneness of the historical process. The materialists have intimidated them, and they have striven only to prove the presence of other, immaterial "factors." But proposing "factors," even many of them, means rejecting the oneness of historical being in the way it is understood as material existence, i.e., they return to the basic premise of historical materialism only to make it pluralistic. Of course, it is some progress if a Marxist becomes a pluralist. However, pluralism is still far from the revival of historicism.

Just like its opponent, historical materialism's defender also comes around to revealing their pluralism. In reducing the primal ground of being to economic relations, he dismembers the symphonic personality into quasi-corporeal systems, and thereby denies the personality as such. The fundamental body is recognized to be class, i.e., the least organic of social units, which he elementarizes to the extreme. He comes to view not only the present as the history of class struggle, but also the past in which there were no such classes, and it therefore becomes necessary to identify classes in estates and castes that were completely unlike classes. In fact, it is inconsistent to stop at class. If there is no society, only a sum of classes, then what grounds are there for admitting the existence of class alone? From the point of view of a thoroughly reasoned materialism, class is only a sum of individuals. Would it be reasonable, then, to deny such symphonic personalities as the people, or even the individual personality, and instead believe only in the symphonic personality of class? Without a doubt, they do believe in the latter. Materialist historians speak, and they cannot help but speak, of class self-consciousness, which they hold to be the constitutive point in the notion of class, of class ideals, of class ideology, etc. And not only that: in outlining the ideal future (?) society, they equate such a society with a class (the former proletarians). Former people become future people — only there are no real people.

The hypothesis of the class structure of society and the absurd recognition of class struggle to be the essence of history are altogether symptomatic, for they reflect the real decomposition of modern Western society, the death of the personal element and the simplification of social relations. The rich diversity of personal life falls into the semi-animalian sphere and is simplified and concentrated in the primitive elements of jealousy, desire, and hatred. Poverty and wealth are made into the main, definitive categories of social being, the ideal of which is seen in expanding equality into the mental sphere. After all, it is natural and necessary that the real simplification of society corresponds to a simplified consciousness, which neither in the past nor in the future is capable of seeing anything complex. Vladimir Ilyin successfully brought both the atom and the head of the materialist socialist under one common definition: both are but a "little, round, absolutely inflexible body." However, the old still lives on in some socialist theories, and the problems of real life are partially even reflected. These theories are idealistic. They silently and unconsciously acknowledge symphonic-personal being, even if only as the class of proletarians. They endow this class with many, if not all, virtues, in particular the virtues of statehood. In other words, they deny themselves, just as the reality reflected within them denies itself, which is to say that it dies.

The only correct method of historical knowledge, justified by the experience of master historians, lies neither in materialization and mechanization nor in reducing the development of the personality to shifts in space and time. Of course, any historical personality is qualitative in different ways, and what is necessary is to distinguish its qualitative traits. But to hypostasize them, i.e., to regard them as personalities in themselves or — even worse — "factors" or "causes," is just as incorrect as establishing causal relations between a person's different psychic traits or between his nose and his heel. Any personality, individual or symphonic, lives its own economic, social, and political life; all of these, its qualities, are that personality itself. In each of its qualities, it manifests itself in its own specificity, albeit in different ways. These qualities ought to be distinguished, especially whenever a developing personality has gone beyond its "molten" phase of revolution, i.e., whenever the limitedness of the personality's manifestations are glaring in each of its qualities, when they are opposed to one another like ossified traditional forms, like the past is the bones of the present. But it never follows from such mutual contrasting of different qualities that one should forget their essential unity and raise the question of their causal interrelations otherwise than as a methodological convenience. Empirically, the symphonic personality expresses itself in its various qualities with unequal completeness and, depending on many factors, sometimes with more of one and sometimes more of another; sometimes primarily politically, sometimes economically, sometimes religiously, etc. Therefore, it is methodologically important to always proceed from that quality that is most telling precisely in the current period of development. For the period of revolution, the most telling quality is the political, and it is also essentially the most important, for the political pertains to unity. If the historical worldview has altogether suffered from neglecting problems of political history, then this is especially the case in the domain of the study of revolution.

Thus, at the basis of history we place the doctrine of the personality, and in particular we recognize the people and culture to be symphonic personalities. Whenever a symphonic personality exists in actuality, which is to say that it rises above its being in possibility, it necessarily possesses a form to its personal being. This form can be defined as a system of interrelations between the individuals actualized by a given symphonic personality, a system that clearly expresses their unity and distinguishes them from other similar unities (other "peoples" and "cultures").

The symphonic personality itself and the system that expresses it exceed the individual personality spatially and temporally. In the empirical life of any symphonic personality, its past is always present as tradition and its future is always present as its desires, hopes, and goals. But the fullness of the symphonic personality, or its very symphonic character and *sobornost'*, is empirically uncompletable. After all, the complete fulfillment of *sobornost'* implies that any act by the symphonic personality is the free agreement of the whole multiplicity of its individual acts which "constitute" and fulfill their own part in it. In its fullness, the symphonic personality is above spatial-temporal distinctions, beyond necessity and freedom, non-being and being. Such fullness is achievable within the Church, but not in empirical actuality. In empirical actuality, it is inevitable that *sobornost'* will not be completely fulfilled and that the particular personality and its freedoms will be limited. The passivity and oppression of some, the resistance and violence of others, and both consent and coercion, are empirically inevitable.

The principle of coercion, or powerful authority as such [*vlast'*], characterizes the system which empirically expresses the symphonic personality. The symphonic personality's consciousness and its will to be strive towards empirical expression and find such in its ruling stratum. The latter, of course, does not perfectly express the will and consciousness of the symphonic personality, as is evidenced by the ruling stratum's position of contrast towards the rest of society and its limitedness. It carries out the will that it understands to a limited extent by way of coercion. Between it and especially that "part" of it which is commonly called state power or government on the one hand, and the "governed" or "subjects" on the other, there is always some kind of tension that replicates itself in the internal conflicts of each individual consciousness, for instance in the battle between the "egotistical" motives and the "state" or "patriotic" motives that seize the individual.

In the political quality of this symphonic personality are complicit, to one degree or another, all of the individuals that constitute it, even if only in the order of passive obedience. But only the most consciously and actively "political" ones constitute the ruling stratum. Until the revolution, this ruling stratum in Russia included the whole so-called intellectual society, from the government to the most extreme revolutionaries. Out of the ruling stratum organically grows a government that empirically expresses a certain ontological fact: the real unity of the symphonic personality. In its ontological root, all powerful authority comes from God, for God creates every personality — individual, people, and culture. But the ontological origin of power and authority should not be confused with any particular empirical power. Empirical being is sinful being, and there can be no perfect empirical authority, for all down to the last are sinful. Transferring the Divine from the principle of power to its empirical reality, i.e., to a particular historical authority, is equivalent to the pagan deification of power. Such deification leads to recognizing authority to be unchanging and unerring: in the name of even the most ossified past, one can reject any novelty, any development, i.e., life itself.

It is fully understandable that people who have lived through a revolution's rejection of the very principle of authority and the wild destruction of everything old are ready to exaggeratedly emphasize the Divinity of power and confuse principle with fact. (Yet, can they really be said to have fully lived through the revolution when many of them still reject it, refuse to acknowledge the Bolsheviks' authority on the grounds that they are putschists, and oppose the real, albeit bad, power of the people in favor of an unreal dream of an authority that doesn't exist?). Such a mentality seems to me quite dangerous, especially as intellectual culture has undoubtedly declined. The crowds of readers do not distinguish between the philosophers who are conscious of their responsibility on the one hand, and writers who have the audacity to express their philistine thoughts in philosophical terms on the other. Even fewer are capable of figuring out notions that require precise distinctions and are not always accessible to the writers themselves. Hence, it is fair, although nothing new, that the justification of the Divine principle of authority and hierarchy are shifted to justify a given particular authority in a given particular hierarchy, and ultimately individual persons. However, one can hardly un-philosophize the facts and prove the Divine necessity of submitting to Rasputin or Lenin and respecting the unlearned youth.

The Phenomenology of Revolution

The Divine principle of hierarchy must be contrasted to the Divine principle of equality. If we are to dream of absolute hierarchy and the absolute exercise of powerful authority, then we must dream of absolute democracy and absolute equality. If we reconcile with the unfulfillment of equality and democracy, to which the anarchic period of the Russian Revolution came closest, then it would be right and consistent to reconcile with manifestations of the spirit of mutiny.

In perfect being, antinomies are overcome and merge into a harmonic whole without excluding one another. But one should not abandon metaphysical seeking out of fear of labor or error, i.e., clogging empirical actuality with foolish and harmful metaphysics by naively identifying the empirical with the absolute, the Divine principle of power with Divine authority. But if a particular empirical authority is illegitimately deified, then the old jams up novelty and the living stops and dies. The principle of fighting against the old is also Divine. But mutiny destroys both the old and the new. Empirical actuality is imperfect. Empirically, there is no power and authority without violence, and there is no life without mutiny. Empirical actuality can reconcile the old and the new only by way of half-baked and rather pitiable compromises, eternally balancing between dumb guardian-conservatism [okhranitel'stvo] and wild innovation. Of course, comparatively soft forms of struggle between the two principles are possible, and even desirable, but unfortunately they are rarely accomplished. Struggle itself is empirically ineradicable. Instead of soothing ourselves with rosy hopes for an ideal autocracy or ideal democracy, we need to recognize this empirical ineradicablity. If we want to create a state without sin, we need to conquer empirical reality. But then there would be no empirical sate, only the one perfect Church would be left. The path to this is known, except it is, like the perfectly Christian attitude towards authority and the world and the perfectly Christian life, equivalent to the empirical death of the individual, to self-sacrifice for the sake of peace. To this path pertains words of obedience to the "powers-that-be" (the "extant" powers, not only "legal" or "legitimate" ones) and the humility and need to be obedient to God more than to humans.

The symphonic personality does not possess its own personal being, which is to say that it empirically does not yet exist if it has no ruling stratum and government, if one of the latter does not spill over into a marked form of statehood. The fuller its personal being, the stronger its personal self-consciousness, the more marked and powerful is its state power. In the earlier, healthy period of the history of a given people, as well as in the period of the rise of its self-consciousness, state power externally appears to be unified and singular, even monolithic. Vice versa, the "dissipation" of statehood is always a symptom of a temporary oppression of the people, or even the dying of the people. We observed such a dissipation before the war and we are observing it now; it is the very same in monarchies as well as in so-called democracies. Utterly in vain are they trying to derive from the war arguments in favor of the latter. The war is far from over, and while it still has no victor, it has only the vanquished. The processes ongoing in France on the one hand and Russia on the other are simply incomparable. In Russia, the collapse of the ruling stratum was accompanied by the creation of a new one; in France, the hitherto parliamentary oligarchy is continuing its existence, and there is no new ruling stratum. It is no coincidence that the most talented politicians in France are people of venerable age.

In what way do the ruling stratum and government know and express the will of the people? Not by surveys and discussions of course. After all, not a single act of state power is fully intelligible to the majority of the people, and the majority of such acts remain unintelligible and even unknown to all. Many people do not understand the Treaty of Versailles; a person capable of understanding the new German *Aufwertungsgesetz* can safely be entrusted with interpreting the Apocalypse. Nor is the will of the people definable by means of electing a four-winged parliament. After all, parliament itself is part of the government and is recruited not even out of the entire ruling stratum, but out of a special group within it, from the milieux of professional parliamentarians, professors, and journalists. Parliament has no capacity to express the will of the people when the people are compelled to elect not from among themselves, but from "papers" (party programs); such papers contain nothing concrete (unless we count vague promises) and in the most critical cases (war) yield to the strength of members of parliament whose resourcefulness and wisdom are rarely known outside the institution itself. Moreover, the wisdom of a collegium is reversely proportionate to its quantity and undoubtedly diminishes the intellectual actuality of each of its members, as was beautifully expressed in the words of the Roman emperor: *"senatores optimi viri, senatus mala bestia."* On the other hand, *"scrutin de liste"* and direct elections are mutually exclusive things, and whatever comes out of various reforms remains to be seen. In any case, the Western European deliberations of *"solidarité"* are still philosophically poor.

Nor does a party facilitate connection between government and the people. The party is already part of the ruling stratum. Its ideology and program are worked out within its own walls and from above, not below. Parties can formulate the desires of the people only in cases when the party itself is organically tied to them. After all, socialist theory itself is not at all an expression of the class self-consciousness of the proletariat, but an invention of the intelligentsia. The intelligentsia invented and continues to "perfect" utopian theory. It would be entirely incorrect to call the cunning and abstract constructs of intellectuals, or the cheap and shabby literature of quasi-intellectuals, "proletarian self-consciousness." Socialist programs are a means of assimilating into the ruling stratum those rising up to it from the bottom, like newspapers. The fact that socialist programs are approved by many workers is no index at all. To the contrary, what is very indicative is how those workers who join the ranks of the quasi-intelligentsia or

The Phenomenology of Revolution

seize power and undertake struggle against capital (and not capitalists) begin to live and what they begin to carry out. The socialist movement is the purest impostor, very often a sincere one, but the False Dmitry was also an honest impostor. In addition, it is quite likely that the working class of modern society has the same attitude towards modern culture as the Roman slaves had towards Hellenistic culture. I want to say that the Western "proletariat" harbors some possibilities for a new, different culture. Some of these possibilities are being caught by "socialists," but the latter are also distorting them in unsuccessful "translations" into the language of "bourgeois" culture.

Reality is incomparable more complex, deeper, and more interesting than the graphics, or rather schemes, especially fashionable in Russia nowadays, with which they are trying to depict it. The "people," of course, is not a metaphor and matter of indifference, and not a "primal matter." A people is always defined by certain desires, aspirations, and ideas. But all of this only attains actuality in leading personalities, not in proclamations from the crowds, the masses, the voting population, nor in clear programs and formulas. Personalities carry out the national capacities that are neither exhaustive nor fully expressible in the language of abstract concepts. The result of the elections of the Socialist-Revolutionary Party did not express any popular will to the Constituent Assembly, whereas Peter the Great, Lomonosov, and Pushkin were genuine expressers of the will and spirit of the people. Some Kerensky speaking in the name of the people with the anguish of a tragic provincial did not express anything of the people, and Lenin, who oppresses Russians in the name of the International, did express something, as did General Kornilov on the other side.

Under normal circumstances, national capacities are carried out by the ruling stratum, which organically grows out of the people and expresses the people's cosmos in itself, like a microcosm. The ruling stratum carries out and shapes the people's capacities, and in so doing it carries out its own capacities. If such a normal correlation exists in general (and, given its empirical imperfection, it can exist only "in general"), then we are talking about the "national" policy of the government, about the "nationality" of one or another sovereign, statesman, or the "national" significance of one or another group, party, intelligentsia, etc. The ruling stratum and the government as a whole remain national as long as they abide in real and organic communion with the landmass of the people. The forms of this communion can differ greatly, as such connections can exist in despotisms as well as in extreme forms of democracy. The forms of communion depend on many conditions, yet the essence lies not in them alone, but in the organic connection that is not exhausted by rational formulations. If there is no organic connection, then a parliament expresses the will of the people no better than the most self-infatuated oligarchy or the most ludicrous despot; if there is a connection, then the unlimited monarch can carry out the ideals of the people faster and better than a technically perfected parliament. To put forth the essence of the matter, I do not mean to say that the forms of communion do not matter, that they should not be perfected, or that they do not wield different degrees of practical convenience and robustness. Rather, the point is that their expediency depends on their being organic and genuinely of the people. A popular English parliament that is organically connected with local self-governance would become an organ for distorting the will of the people in bureaucratic France. The Constituent Assembly is connected with the Russian people in spirit by way of the vulgar name *"uchredilka"*, i.e, the "little assembly." It is necessary to distinguish essence from form and to refrain from believing in the universally salvational potential of form, especially when it is most often alien and abstract. The main process should not be confused with its epiphenomena. The foremost crisis of modernity and our time is the crisis of power and authority, which lies in a rift between the ruling stratum and the government on the one hand and the people on the other, and in the impoverishment of the former. Thanks to confusions of the main process with its epiphenomena, this crisis of power and authority is believed to be a crisis of monarchy or a crisis of parliamentarism, etc., i.e., the form has been substituted for the content. Therefore, it is erroneous to hope to cure a sick monarchy by way of introducing parliamentarism imported from abroad, even by armored car, or to cure an impotent republic by means of dictatorship. All such attempts are the fruits of a naive rationalism which believes in a universally binding scheme of development and which, taking exterior forms for essence, does not understand organic processes.

We already know that the categories of rulership and subordination are necessary in the state being of a people. Along with this comes a fact that cannot be annulled by any forms: sooner or later the ruling stratum will break away from the people and close unto itself. In closing unto itself and losing its organic link with the people, the ruling stratum ceases to understand the people, quickly de-nationalizes, and degenerates, even though, out of the naïveté intrinsic to people, it might believe up to its very death that it is the expresser of the primal element of the people. This phenomenon is facilitated by the assimilation of the foreign ("Europeanization" in our case), which comes naturally whenever one outlives one's own. After all, what is foreign is assimilated in one's homeland only in an abstract form. Everything that is abstract in its imaginative clarity and lifeless simplicity is especially attractive to a decaying and rationalistic consciousness. The abstract is cosmopolitan and "sociological." It inclines one toward comforting faith in a universally binding path of historical development and towards taking an imaginary common good to be the good of one's own people. The evil of abstraction is deeper than our contemporary intellectuals think it is when they accuse socialists and Cadets of abstraction. After all, the very same intellectuals hold the logical idiotism of Leo Tolstoy's "religio-philosophical" creations to be a deep seeking, and they call his clumsy illustrations for the psychological textbooks of English empiricists knowledge of the human soul.

The further the rift between the ruling stratum and people grows, the deeper it becomes. Passing from the second to the first is increasingly bound up with losing national countenance and exterior attributes. As the assimilating force of the ruling stratum declines, so does its quality, which is diluted by the quasi-intelligentsia. Revolutionary pedocracy and the revolutionary prosperity of the self-taught only crown the long-running process that already appointed Nikolai Pavlovich Raev as Ober-Procurator of the Holy Synod, Generals Vannovsky and Glazov as Ministers of Education, and various homebred "sociologists" as professors.

The disconnect of the ruling stratum is the decline and decomposition of the symphonic personality of the people itself. But it is at once also the self-decomposition of the ruling stratum, a decomposition which is pompously deemed a struggle between society (even the people!) and the government. True, both sides — "society" and "government" — cite the people and consider themselves to be the expressers of its will. But both are equally wrong or, in the very least, are "exaggerating." Their hostility is an inner one, a family feud, for which the people care little. Both constitute one ruling stratum that consider the peasants to be *paysans* and sometimes even acknowledge their kinship, although only in hindsight and after a long time. Now Speransky's projects are being included in the honorary row of monuments to the fight against autocracy, and intellectuals are petitioning for 14 December to be a day of mourning for Emperor Nikolai I. The manners change, but the essence of the matter, that the intelligentsia belongs to the ruling stratum, remains the same.

During the period of its emergence, the ruling stratum might even be foreign — like the Varangians who established state power in Kievan Rus' or, if you wish, the Bolsheviks who arrived in armored train cars and took Russia out of anarchy. Sooner or later, the ruling stratum either assimilates and is reborn as one of the people, or, in the event that it is insusceptible to assimilation, dies and is replaced by a new one. In its heyday, the ruling stratum is neither an estate nor a class, just as state power in France under Henry IV and Richelieu, or even under Louis XIV, was not an estate. It is the rift and self-closing of the ruling stratum that really makes it into an estate or makes it merge with one or another estate or class. This doesn't yet mean the de-nationalization of the ruling stratum. However, along with the progressing degeneration, that which is national and of the people increasingly recedes into the background, leaving lifeless, abstract schemes which are easily filled with foreign content. "National" qualities are preserved longest of all in the domain of spiritual culture, that is in the most mature yet the most tardy fruits of development. The peak of literature and science often heralds the end of a culture that no longer recognizes itself in its own self-decomposition. Men of letters and scholars claim the role of leaders into the promised land. To this day, even such idle chatterers as Voltaire are widely held to be the forerunners of the revolution. In fact, Voltaire and Rousseau most of all reflect and comprehend the dying past, just as Beaumanoir in his time comprehended the already dying feudal life.

Typical of a degenerating ruling stratum is its detachment from the people — it is abstract, de-nationalized, and has turned into a closed social group, an "estate" or "caste." When the ruling stratum has degenerated into an estate, the estate as such has lost its organic character. Freed from its duties, it irresponsibly keeps its rights and privileges. If the real privileges of an estate, which no longer has, or even never truly had, any consciousness of its duties and "functionality" (as was the case in Russia, where "estatehood" was constituted by the "Gentry Charter"), are replaced with lusts for privileges, then we get what is called "class," which is the most elementary and typical unity of a dying culture.

The Phenomenology of Revolution

A degenerating ruling stratum dissipates into a weakened and stupefied government and a rowdy intelligentsia, one which likely calls itself such under the influence of association by contrast. But the rift between the ruling stratum and the people is also expressed at the bottom, among the "governed," for whom only a blind state element remains. Everything that rises up into the ruling stratum ceases to be of the people; it either assimilates or dies. The ruling stratum fatally weakens, yet the primal element of state power below can, under favorable conditions, demolish its rotten top in order to create or assimilate a new ruling stratum, but this requires a long period of time in any case. Such a favorable outcome presumes that the process of decomposition has not destroyed the vital forces of the symphonic personality, and that this process was either superficial or the reaction of a healthy body to some infectious disease.

The lengthy process of the ruling stratum's degeneration, the destruction of it by the primal national-state element, and the creation of a new ruling stratum, is what I call revolution. Revolution seems to me a dangerous disease afflicting the symphonic personality, one which might not lead to new statehood, but to death, turning the people into mere ethnographic material. In any case, revolution is an unpleasant and vile phenomenon, but, unfortunately, from time to time, it is inevitable. Revolution is a fact of political history and it bears being studied from precisely this point of view. However, in melting away the life of the people, revolution encompasses all of its spheres. It destroys the historically accumulated partitions between the properly political, the social, the economic, the everyday, etc., and it brings into the clearing of political being all the molten life of the people. In the era of revolution, politics is no longer writing papers, but the baking of bread. The established division of revolutions into political and social is even worse than their division into bourgeois and socialist. The illusion of the "socio-economic" process is created on the one hand by a lack of understanding of statehood and the form of symphonic being, a lack of understanding conditioned by the death of European culture, and on the other hand by the fact that revolution covers all spheres of life and exacerbates conflict between the poor and the rich. But the former might not profess the religion of Karl Marx.

The first phase of revolution should be defined as the degeneration and death of the old ruling stratum. This is essentially what is had in mind when historians speak of the "old regime." Yet they illegitimately narrow the problem. By "old regime" they mean partly the old forms of statehood (see above) and their corresponding social structure, and partly the personal composition of the government. The ruling stratum as a whole is not acknowledged. Thus, the struggle between the intelligentsia and the government is seen as a struggle between "the people" and the authorities (reactionary chauffeurs and traders who beat "students" are not counted among the "people," of course). The ideology of this intelligentsia (the Enlightenment ideology of the 18th century and Russian journalism) is taken to be the expression of the people's aspirations. The very same intelligentsia naively believes that its little ideas, whether invented or borrowed, formulate the ideas of the people, and that the people do not identify the intelligentsia with the government and are not using it as a temporary weapon.

They presume that the people, by way of their "vanguard," the intelligentsia, will powerfully (the intellectual very much likes to think of himself as "powerful") destroy the "fortress" of the old power and embark upon creative, constructive labor (mainly in the order of composing resolutions); but here, for some reason, the rabid and, of course, "dark" people displace the wise men of council and plunge into anarchy. In fact, no one destroys the old power as is usually imagined. Rather, the ruling stratum and its organ, the government, die in self-decomposition, and one of the manifestations of this self-decomposition is the struggle waged by the intelligentsia against the government. The intelligentsia's revolutionary ideology is a product of the decomposition of the old state ideology, the lean fruit of depleted soil. This is the self-determination of the ruling stratum and government ideology. All the dismal baseness and lifelessness of all pre-revolutionary and revolutionary projects, programs, theories, and "philosophies" merely serve to explain the death of the whole ruling stratum. The negligibility of the intelligentsia's ideology finds brilliant confirmation in the intelligentsia's own incapacity for statecraft when it "revolutionarily" seizes power. The Long Parliament, the French National Assembly in the revolutionary era, and the Russian Constitutive Assembly and Provisional Government are convincing and reproachful examples.

Of course, even in its self-decomposing, the ruling stratum might still to some degree express the will of the people and disclose specific national traits, only not the best ones, and rather the most politically negligible ones. State authority does not take into account the seriousness of the war that has begun, and society does not sympathize with this war. The diplomatic giftedness of the Russian man degenerates into the hypocrisy of the sovereign with his ministers. Instead of the elder who is the bearer of the religious ideal, there advances the red elder in literature (Gorky's Luka[151]) and Rasputin in the court. Of course, both sides in the struggle between the intelligentsia and the government put forth nationally important tasks, but these problems are posed either negatively or abstractly. The intelligentsia was right to protest ridiculous Russification policy, and the government was right to fight the politicking of youth. But there was little concretely and nationally important in Russian imperialism or "opposition to His Majesty" or parliamentarism in the English manner. Concern for one's younger brother, love for the people, and dreams of a just social system are beautiful things, and dreams

---

151 [Ed.] Luka is a character from Gorky's 1902 play "The Lower Depths". Luka is a tramp who offers the heroes comforting lies as solutions to their problems.

of the good of all mankind are even better. Both are intimately connected to the character of the Russian people. But faith in the implementability of an abstract dream does not testify to instinct for the concrete. The Cadets' program was far removed from Russian reality, as was confirmed by the course of events, and the "dreams of Vera Pavlovna"[152], that is the socialist program, were even further away from any reality whatsoever, for which no confirmation is needed.

In underscoring that the distinctive feature of revolution is the self-decomposition of the whole ruling stratum, we do not deny that it is essentially the people that replaces this stratum with a new one. The people destroy the whole ruling stratum as such, and it does so gradually and wisely, first by removing the government and then the self-decapitating intelligentsia. Only this destruction is not active, but rather comes from a refusal to support those who are killing themselves. The people destroy the old statehood while at the same time looking within itself for new people to bring forth out of its depths, or they pick fitting figures, albeit largely hesitant, from the old ruling milieux to either rework or eliminate once they no longer serve present need.

The revolutionary process makes itself felt above all in the disappearance of the ruling stratum's will to power. The reverse side of this is a lack of understanding of the real needs and tasks of the state and a loss of pathos for statehood... In the era of revolution, the ruling stratum has no sense of statehood or power. Therefore, it finds itself in a state of radical opposition to power without recognizing this opposition as a symptom of dying...

The death of the old statehood comes to fruition within the primal element of the people itself. But here — if the

---

152 [Ed.] Vera Pavlovna is one of the heroes of Nikolai Chernyeshevsky's 1863 novel "What Is to Be Done?" In Vera Pavlovna's fourth dream sequence of the novel, she has a vision of a future socialist utopia. This sequence was frequently utilized by the Soviet government as an example of what the communism they were attempting to build might look like.

revolution does not turn out to be a fatal disease — it is not the very essence of statehood, the will to power, that dies. The "revolutionary people" rejects the old forms primarily by being passive, by increasingly evading subjugation (cf. the proliferation of desertion in the army). But it actively destroys the old with riotous revolts and it opposes the old with its own self-proclaimed and self-organized authorities. Along with the political forms, the people shocks and destroys the socio-economic and religio-moral order, dissolving all in one stormy revolutionary stream. The people seeks a new powerful authority, and it seeks itself on the path of the most daring and wild experiments and active doubt. It shakes the foundations of everything in order to find the undoubtable and the unwavering so as to then establish itself thereupon. In this is revealed the final, religious meaning of revolution, for a healthy people's revolution is always religious in its source and always seeks truth yet takes lies for the truth, all the while as — and I am compelled to make this remark so as to avoid idiotic false interpretations of my thought — the whole agitated stream of revolution is sinful and vile.

Revolution reveals the nature of a people in its molten state. "Closest of all to the nature of power," Plato said, "is the power of the strong." It is clear that in its destructive struggle of elements, the new statehood can assert itself only with acts of the most elementary, cruelest violence.

In order for a revolution to happen, the decomposition of the ruling stratum is not enough. A corpse can float and sway on waves for a long time just like a living body. What is further necessary is for the last subject of statehood, the people, to be healthy, for it is a healthy body that most frantically reacts to a disease. If a people is healthy in its essence, then it still knows, no matter how poorly, the significance of statehood. Therefore, in order for it to overthrow its historical authorities, it is necessary for the latter to have not only clearly demonstrated their unfitness, but also threatened the people's state being and infringed upon the holy of holies that is its

The Phenomenology of Revolution

personal self-consciousness. In destroying the old statehood, the people is acting in defense of statehood. This explains every revolution's link to war (in England with the Thirty Years War and in relation to Ireland and Scotland, in France with the *grande peur* and the European wars, in Russia in the 16th-17th centuries with the Swedish and Polish wars and the fight to encompass the borderlands within the state)...

The first phase of revolution thus necessarily passes into the second, the period of so-called anarchy. "So-called anarchy" because the historical authority and ruling stratum self-decompose and disappear insofar as the latter itself in "anarchy" is not reborn into or does not merge with a new one. The old forms of statehood and the old political worldview are killed as they manifest their disjuncture with the primal element of the people. Everything becomes doubtful, and instinctive life everywhere displaces conscious living. But behind all of this flows a turbulent and creative process — the active aspiration of the state element to realize itself, the new ruling stratum's search for new authority and power, and their painful and slow birth.

The disappearance of state unity goes hand-in-hand with the disclosure of the egotism of the units that made up the state body. "Federalism" is the real enemy of the future statehood towards which a revolutionary people strives. But in the new political entities that complete the decomposition of the old statehood in the peripheries, the idea of the state lives on. If it cannot be realized, it is because the old has not yet separated from the new and there is yet no one who would be able to, no one who could grasp the new and serve as a new ruling stratum. In these "new formations" lives the idea of the whole. Their egotism, which degenerates into the conceit of "true independence," is attributable, on the one hand, to the share of good-for-nothing "last Mohicans" in the dying statehood, and, on the other hand, to the share of healthy instinct among the masses who feel that the greater whole can only be an organic whole and thus presupposes the integral functionality of its organs. If "federalism" in a rather specific sense (the Vendée, the Don Government, Ukraine, the Kuban Rada, etc.) is the enemy of revolution and state unity, then the federative structure, as an expression of the organic nature of the whole, might turn out to be the best solution to the problem for a large state. The departments and pupils of Richelieu who divided up France did not understand this. Yet, the Internationalist Bolsheviks turned out to be more attuned to the idea of the organism than the nationalists....

Characteristic of revolutionary "anarchy" is not that authority is unrecognized, but that everyone recognizes themselves to be the authorities and considers themselves to be the bearers of power. Statehood is atomized and individualized. Everyone sees statehood in themselves as the active elements of power. Like a feudal system taken to its extreme yet having lost the principle of hierarchy, revolutionary anarchy is not anarchy, but panarchy. No matter how egotistical the individual might be, the primal element of statehood lives on in his pretense to self-assertion and authority. It is not in vain that a wise Greek called man the "political animal."

None of this is to deny that sundry egotisms spill forth in revolutionary anarchy. This is how it must be in the moment of death of the old forms of statehood and the birth of the new. Egotistical aspirations are manifestations of the dying old outliving itself in the death of its statehood. On the other hand, this egotism is, as it were, a method for seeking out the state element in an environment that has seemingly lost it. This is the real *gnothi seauton* of the people, its terrifying experiment on itself. The essence of revolution lies in that all the nourishing fluids of the old statehood are poured into one festering abscess that separates the healthy tissues (*piemia saccata*) from the old ruling stratum and leaves the healthy tissues without the nourishing fluids of the state. The abscess bursts and covers everything in puss, and the healthy tissues must neutralize it and squeeze new juices out of themselves, which cannot be done without raising the temperature and without acute suffering. One good means for draining the wound is releasing the puss elsewhere in the form of emigration. The pleroma of the life of the people is left outside of the old statehood and is compelled, if it does not want to die, to replace the old in the shortest possible period....

And so, the will of the people for new statehood is found first and foremost in the manifestation of a stratum of rapists, ambitious individuals, and fanatics on the surface of the life of the people. This can be designated the third phase of revolution. Having lost its historical and religious sanctions, statehood manifests itself in the form of crude but thereby imposing force, once again dividing the people into "rulers" and "ruled." This division becomes even sharper than before, as the real and direct exercise of power is strengthened at the cost of the indirect and formally indeterminate rule of the intelligentsia. The environment that is the primary nursery for the new bearers of power consists of the old, active enemies of pre-revolutionary authority — revolutionaries in the likes of malicious, envious individuals, expropriators and rambunctious riskers, revolutionary fanatics and, to a significant extent, declassed and criminal elements, that is, generally speaking, the least moral and value-driven people, the bearers of the crude element of violence, or in the terminology of 16th-17th century Moscow, *vory* ["thieves."]

The revolutionary ruling stratum, almost coinciding with a new government, has no state experience and no state ideas, for the revolutionary intellectual's ideas are old, still pre-revolutionary, abstract, fruitless, and, as it would seem, prove their lifelessness. Meanwhile, it is not enough for the new state to have one will, even the most adamant. Every political act needs, if not conceptualization, then in the very least primitive ideological justification. One or another ideology is necessary as the exterior form of state consciousness and a comfortable means for justifying particular political acts. Ideology is especially necessary in the era of revolution, when everything is being destroyed by doubt and there is an acute desire to hold on to something. Ideologies, of course, albeit to different extents and always very imperfectly, reflect the people's worldview. Before and during the revolution, they often distort this worldview. In addition, they more often reflect the past, only projecting it into the future while simplifying and embellishing it. The present needs specific tasks and decisions which are often presented with equal success by contradicting ideologies. As a determination of future tasks, an ideology is possible only in the most general and non-obligating form. Every concretization, every time an ideology is turned into an obligatory principle of behavior, is dangerous and testifies either to an old mad phantasy or to infantile obliviousness.

Healthy statehood lives not in terms of schemes worked out down to the details by an ideology, and not by the "reforms" and "plans" derived from the latter, but in the face of the perils of the day, although this peril is always ideologically conceptualized... The evil of the Jacobins and the Communists is not so much the falsehood and limitedness of their ideology as it is in their doctrinairism and therefore in their inability to develop... I'll repeat: there can be no powerful authority, especially a revolutionary one, without ideology. But while recognizing the necessity of ideology, it is necessary to recognize its relativity, i.e., to more humbly evaluate one's mental capabilities and talents. For better or for worse, ideology still tries to press the absolute structures of a culture, a people, a state, and tries to map out cultural-national ideals and a mission. Every state should have these goals to which each ideology aspires. Let us at least call such "ideality"....

Natura non facit saltum — the process of finding revolutionary power proceeds with turbulence, but with consistency. The oppositional layers of the former ruling milieux arise to replace the fallen government, at times even replacing each other in bouts of growing radicalism... Through the fanaticism of the leaders once again peeks out the religious nature of revolution, and the fanaticism of rulers brings together a revolutionary ruling stratum out of which come Cromwells, Dantons, and Lenins.

By dint of its natural, internal development, revolutionary anarchy leads to the creation of a revolutionary ruling stratum[153] that bears and expresses the state element in its most primitive disclosures, and ideologically in the negligible epigone of the worst of the old intellectual ideologies. But, in order for revolutionary power to assert itself, it needs not only the people's awareness of such a necessity, but also an ideology that animates it and is to a definite extent close to the masses. It needs a simple and harsh organization, a "party," whose appearance testifies to the vitality of the new ruling stratum. This organization cannot be an institution of the state. After all, the old state organs that have survived and been merely renamed, or those which were not even renamed, as well as the new ones modeled after the likes of the old ones, do not in and of themselves wield sanction or power. They still have to grow into life and justify themselves. They are powerless in the face of the primal element of the people in whose name they wish to speak, and before the mutinous crowd and even the self-proclaimed organizations.... What is essentially necessary is a self-organization of the ruling stratum that would give it the opportunity to usher in and, if necessary, impose its will.

Such an organization is feasible in the form of a military dictatorship or an army-party (Cromwell). It is also feasible in the form of a cohesive, war-like party. The Jacobins and Communists organized themselves into such parties, and a similar party will probably be needed after Communism is overcome. It is unimportant whether the embryos of such a party exist before the revolution in the form of an underground or even emigrant organization, or if they arise in the process

---

153 We distinguish the revolutionary ruling stratum from the new ruling stratum as temporary and transitional in the sense that its ideology and its ideologically incompatible part disappear by the end of the revolution, and in the sense that the part of it that is the foundation of the future new stratum is in this period taking shape and coming into being.

of revolutionary anarchy. What is important is that the party at one point or another becomes the organization of the ruling stratum and the backbone of the new statehood. It coexists with the state institutions that constantly change their guise and grow into life while remaining de facto subordinate to the party... The dualism of a tyrannical party and state apparatus appears to be necessary in any "successful" revolution....

No matter what, the ideology and will of the ruling party will become concrete in the state apparatus, and they very often turn for the greater good of the state and the people into something completely opposite to their original design or impulse. On the other hand, it is mainly through the state apparatus that the concrete needs of life compel the party to respond and adapt to them... The old and the new are reborn into the ruling stratum of the near future that will sooner or later replace the revolutionary ruling stratum and form the basis for a new, post-revolutionary statehood...

Without going beyond the scope of our phenomenological study, we can only map out in general contours the sphere of problems connected to the new national-state ideas. First of all, the chaos of political relations must be ordered. In the current chaos, the old is mixed up with the new; the new is partly accidental and unnecessary and partly indicative of what is essential, but what is essentially new has been left fragmentary and unsuccessfully expressed. The task of bringing about order is not entirely correctly, and quite bombastically, called "reinforcing the conquests of the revolution." It is broader than what the notion of the "political" encompasses in normal circumstances. In revolution, after all, the whole of life and all of its spheres and aspects appear to be "political." Therefore, the consolidation of the revolution spreads to so-called socio-economic relations which, along with the cooling down of the primal element of the people, are once again differentiated and can be contrasted to political relations in the specific sense of the word.

Revolutionary power hitherto strove to define and assert a political and socio-economic system. But, firstly, it wrote its laws and codexes on the surface of a wave or coincidentally and unsystematically sanctioned whatever grew and gained in strength on its own. Secondly, it tried to slip the fragile and unneeded framework of its ideology into the emerging skeleton. It had no positive tasks. The problem of the new power should not be misunderstood, however: its task is not to create an unshakable system, but to find the grounds and open up the path for organic development, the very stopping of which led to the revolution in the first place. Political and social forms can still change considerably. The time of seeking has not yet passed; what has passed is only the time of experiments and fanaticism, and now the possibility has arrived for the new to be reunited with the traditional that has passed through the fire of revolution.

The political self-consciousness and self-determination of the people can only be internal: it should only then be directed externally, i.e., become the people's self-determination in relation to other peoples and states. Thus, every revolution is tightly bound up with international wars and upheavals. Revolution begins with war or ends in wars, and sometimes both. The new national-state ideology always in one way or another spreads to the sphere of international relations... Every people, as a living organism and organ, is part of something greater, something that is unsuccessfully called an "inter-national" unit, that is, a higher symphonic personality. Thus, the peoples and nationalities of Russia compose a culture-people which before the revolution was called Russia, and is more correctly called Russia-Eurasia. Europe, which consists of a number of nation-states, is another such symphonic personality. Not only has a Eurasian-European unity not become an actuality to the extent of a personal being, but neither has a European unity, i.e., such a unity has not poured forth into a form of statehood equivalent to Eurasia. Unity (even only European unity) is expressed here in the form of an unstable system of unions, ententes, and coalitions, sacred alliances and leagues of nations, which connect European peoples to each other to a greater extent than any one of them with Brazil. Nevertheless, this unity, this symphonic personality, wields a known empirical reality. Naturally, this unity makes itself felt in the era of revolutions. Albert Sorel has convincingly shown that the French Revolution was, properly speaking, a pan-European process which merely reached its culmination in France. Analogous is the relation between the English Revolution and the pan-European process of the Reformation, which ended with both the English Revolution and the Thirty Years War. The matter stands somewhat differently with the Russian Revolution, which is explainable in terms of the contrast "Europe vs. Eurasia." Being a state renaissance of Eurasia conditioned by pressure from Europe, the Russian Revolution is Russia's reaction to its Europeanization and the self-decomposition of European culture that took on especially acute forms in Russia.

Thus, in both the "external" and "internal" self-determination of the people, the problem is not the establishment of forms for its political and "international" being, and not the disclosure of the specific values of its statehood and culture. For a people's ideas to be fully grounded, they need to be comprehended as a special mission bestowed upon the people by God, a mission that is of value for other peoples and is an absolute value, being at once the individualization and the concretization of a human and Divine idea. It is to be understood that people come to know this especially in the era of revolutions just as well as do the revolutionaries themselves, albeit altogether imperfectly and abstractly. Hence the distortions of fundamental ideas, distortions like chauvinism, nationalism, imperialism, etc. Even revolutionaries derive the ultimate grounding of their ideology and their pathos from absolutely significant ideas. The French dreamed of blessing mankind with enlightenment, and the Bolsheviks linked this laudable yet naively haughty aspiration with the idea of the Russian people's sacrificial mission.

Overall, the development of Christian culture in the Renaissance and the Reformation seems to me to have been the time in which the heresy and doomed fate of Romano-Catholic culture was disclosed. Europe began settling down on an earth without God and took up arms against its religious foundation. Through the German mystics, Nicholas of Cusa, Eriugena, Irish-Scottish and early Gallic monasticism, the religious element was connected to the tradition of ecumenical Orthodoxy and could have expressed itself only in the flawed and heretical form of Germanic Protestantism. Seizing the weapons of the century under the pressure of Catholic-lay and Romanic culture, Protestantism tried in England to recreate European culture on true foundations that it itself did not understand. Failing to do so, it set about establishing a new life on the virgin soil of America. In the meanwhile, a second revolutionary explosion broke out in Europe as peaceable Catholic-Romanic culture attempted to establish its earthly kingdom by means which, so it seemed, had already been condemned by the experience of the 17th century. The beginning of the 19th century saw a new struggle to carry out Charlemagne's naive and even unconsciously sinful dream, and the beginning of the 20th century stood in the face of the terrible specter of the death of culture, a death that our fathers and grandfathers, having already gone headfirst into Kantian scholasticism and "scientific" materialism, did not foresee. The French Revolution, which many now consider "good" and beneficial for mankind, yielded the socialist International and pan-European war as its ripest fruits. Then the clash between European Catholic culture and Orthodox culture played out in the heart of Russia. After all, the de-nationalized Russian ruling stratum was "Europe in Eurasia."

In the midst of all this, revolution did not turn into a "creative" process. Revolution is one form of the historical process that is itself "creative" before and after revolution.

The Phenomenology of Revolution

Revolution as such brings nothing new: the historical process itself brings the new, which in the era of revolution is slowed down and all but runs in place. But it is because the subject of development, as it were, decomposes and melts in the era of revolution, that in many respects revolution better reveals the subject's nature and its contradictory tendencies which are otherwise not as sharply exposed and active in periods of peaceful development. In the moment of the death of the old and the birth of the new, the very nature of the symphonic personality and the absolute grounds of its being are exposed. What is the meaning of revolution, and in what conditions does it set in?

The symphonic personality comes to carry out its most difficult and fundamental tasks, which demand extreme tension and pertain to its very existence, or rather, with the existence of its given form, its given symphonic personality that is lesser than it itself as a whole but is precisely its individualizing character. After all, every culture and every people represents a certain order of changing symphonic personalities over the whole course of their development; in this sense, the symphonic personality should be likened not to an individual, but to a lineage. This is how we ought to distinguish Kievan Rus' from North-East Rus' and Muscovite Rus' and from Imperial Russia that began with the Time of Troubles and the new Russia being born. All of this is one symphonic personality that is analogous to, for instance, European culture, but its actual personality is a unity or "lineage" of the above-mentioned, lesser symphonic personalities. This is clear even from the ethnological point of view: we observe a corresponding order of ethnological substrates of development.

When the symphonic personality arrives at problems of life or death, it discovers its impotence to deal with them, which is often expressed in exhaustion and boredom in the commotion of external activity ("*Après nous, le déluge*" in France or Russia's "prime" before the war). The personality is incapable of knowing and realizing as a whole and in fullness the tasks presented to it. In its knowledge and in its activity, it disassembles and abstracts, and therefore it begins to decompose and become an abstraction, i.e., it dissipates. Instead of a genuine, integral, chaste tension, we are left with separate, uncoordinated, and shifting periods of prostration and "hysterical" outbursts. These produce an outward impression of turbulent energy and force, but they are in fact manifestations of impotence. This is the fatal sickness of the personality, its death. In moral terms, it is voluntary "carelessness" or "voluntary impotence," which is sin; in terms of dogma, it is heresy, the division and arbitrary selection of parts (the absolutization of the relative). But if revolution is the death of one symphonic personality (e.g., that of "old," "Tsarist" Russia), then out of the death of the old personality is born a new one, a new individuation of the higher personality, which itself does not die, but for which the revolution is a rebirth or a birth in the throes of a new self-expressing personality. Of course, the new might be stillborn, in which case revolution will mean the death of the higher symphonic personality, the death of culture.[154] The processes of death and birth occur in the individual and do not necessarily correspond with the physical death of the individuality. Thus, zombies can exist for a long time. Thus, the old dies in many, but the new is born just as many are "reborn" into the people of the new Russia, while others sometimes even become good examples of another culture, such as European culture.

Being a sin, heresy, and death, revolution is, in the empirical development of mankind, a delusion that sins and dies. But just as the sinfulness and limitation of man do not destroy his freedom even while diminishing it, so does the inevitability of a revolution not lead to historic fatalism.

In order to clarify the phenomenology of revolution, we should briefly touch on the nature of revolution (its ontology). The infirmity of the symphonic personality and its dying are

---

154 The death of culture is typified by features which were absent in the revolution but which are present in contemporary European reality. Cf. the Roman Empire of the 4th-5th centuries. We cannot touch on this question here.

the cessation of its personal being within empirical actuality. Personal being is in empirical actuality connected with its statehood, and its statehood is connected with its ruling stratum and government. Likewise, rebirth through death or healthy recovery presumes the birth of a new ruling stratum and new government, which is to say a new state existence. Since it is reborn to its own life, its own tasks arise to face it, and to ground them it must seek within itself, in its past and in its present, absolutely significant ideas that justify and comprehend its new life. Of course, the proximity to which it manages to come to know them and to express them in its ideology and in its activity can vary. This approximation is to a significant degree dependent upon the character of the final overcoming of the revolution...

Of course, it cannot be asserted with any confidence that the final overcoming of the revolution will not be complicated by the "coincidence" of a temporary restoration. This cannot be ruled out even though it is unlikely and — from the point of view of Russian interests — undesirable. If neither military dictatorship (empire and "Bonapartism") nor restoration are likely, then there should be some other outcome. It is possible that the current ruling stratum will evolve and there will appear in power people who are still unknown to anyone (whether as the result of a palace or party coup). The gradual character of such a transition would fully correspond to the state wisdom of the Russian people, which has to this day found brilliant confirmation in the whole course of the revolution. But there is the danger of a lack of ideality and the rotting of the new statehood... The best outcome should be regarded to be the emergence of a new governing "party"[155]

---

[155] The ruling, or one and only, party, the singular party, must be fundamentally and strictly distinguished from parties in the European sense of the word which are never, cannot be, and should not be the only ones. European parties are tied to the parliamentary, specifically European form of democracy. They are incompatible and inconsistent with the Soviet system and cannot arise on its soil. A certain analogy for such a singular party is represented by Italian fascism, which has so joyfully been welcomed among emigre restorationists, and it is quitecharacteristic that it pushes for a new form of democracy. However, the Italian case differs from

which, accepting the fact and positive results of the revolution, would dissolve the revolutionary party and put forth a new ideational content that comprehends the now established statehood.... In order for the new power to be a power of the

> the revolutionary party first and foremost in its secondariness to the state problem, which threatens rationalistic solutions, whereas in Russia there is an original, organic link between statehood and the singular party, even though the latter evolved out of a party of the old type. Moreover, fascism is a modern European phenomenon, and therefore it lacks an absolutely grounded and significant "religious" ideology. It is therefore fraught with the danger of a Napoleonic empire, i.e., the replacement of absolute imperatives with external ones, namely imperialist policies. Let us offer a few more words in response to the hysterical defenders of the idea of democracy (European, of course) who accuse us of defending dictatorship. The existence of a ruling stratum is sociologically necessary. It can be disorganized, as in modern Europe, but in such a case it disempowers itself, and life itself leads such a ruling stratum, whenever it attempts to organize itself, to differentiate itself into hostile "parts" or "parties," which calls to life parliamentarism. We believe the most expedient to be its unified organization on the grounds of undisputed starting ideas and tasks which are not partial, whether to party or "class," but statewide, which means definitively and finally rejecting the class hypothesis of the state. Such a unified organization necessarily leads to one ruling part which, in distinction from the European parties, is perhaps better called none other than a council or union [*soyuz*]. Would this be a dictatorship? In the ordinary sense of the word, dictatorship presumes: (1) the arbitrariness of the ruler(s), (2) the absence of any firm norms binding the ruler(s), (3) exercising governance out of one's own will, not the will of the people, and (4) the absence of so-called subjective public rights. But we do not affirm the arbitrariness of the singular party (1), we affirm that the party will carry out the unconscious will of the people (3), and we believe the absence of any firm norms (2 and 4) to be a sign of the revolutionary process as such, which disappears along with the "consolidation of the revolution." In our understanding of these norms and "subjective public rights," we base ourselves not on the individualist precepts of European jurisprudence, but on our ability to distinguish the theory of law from the art of statecraft. A fundamental demarcation between the state and the individual must exist, and it cannot but exist in a healthy state. But, firstly, we should not rule out dynamism and struggle in the interrelations between the state and the individual; secondly, in concrete and empirical terms, the spheres of the state and the individual (as well as other social groups) cannot by their very content be demarcated absolutely, once and for all. Their concrete demarcation is always relative to the domain of the technical aspects of the state. We are decided enemies of snappy phrases and sentimental formulas on whether it is necessary to engage in a common cause. Therefore, we want a strong, powerful authority for Russia, not a new, temporary government, and not European forms of democracy. If our opponents nevertheless wish to accuse us of striving for dictatorship in the manner of those that have existed in Europe, then we will calmly treat such accusations in the same way as we would false — but likely in accordance with European democratic rules — attributions of sympathy for Communism or anti-Semitism.

people, and not a collegium of salesmen managing without a boss, a new ideology is needed. Thus, the political process of the creation and affirmation of a new power must bring the revolution to a close in accompaniment with the process of ideational creativity, that is the recognition and definition of the ideals of the people and their religious explanation and justification.

Great Napoleon was a great deceiver, one who deceived even himself. His rightful disdain for "ideologues" (doctrinaire-ideologues) hindered him from understanding the significance of absolute ideas and turned himself into an "ideologue." He became a national hero because, in affirming the "conquests of the revolution" internally, he proclaimed tasks that were pleasant and attractive to every Frenchman and in their grandioseness resembled something absolute. Ever since then, to this very day, France lives by the "ideas" of Napoleon, out of humility calling them "natural borders," leagues of nations, and defending human rights, which are interpreted in relation to degrees of geographic connection. If we look into the leading ideas of France after the revolution and to the ideologies that arose out of its soil, we will easily be convinced that they are impossible to realize or implement, for they are lifeless. It is all doctrinarian, abstract phraseology covering up an altogether practical, specific, and relative aspiration of an egotistical will to dominance and "bourgeois" self-aggrandizement. Boring.

The English Revolution ended the religious history of Europe, although religiosity continues to be the true foundation of European development and the European revolutions — it is merely not recognized as such, and is instead identified with dumb relativistic phraseology. They deny God only so as to hold idols as gods (without even naming them so).

Due to its incapacity to discover the absolute foundation, i.e., to reveal the questions and worldview of Orthodoxy, Russia fell into the Time of Troubles, which made possible the forced Europeanization that began under Peter and reached its apogee in Communism.[156] Thus, the Russian Revolution once again raised the problem posed and left unresolved by the first Russian Revolution, meaning the Time of Troubles: Russia's "to be or not to be" is to be consciously religious, to be or not to be its own special world (Eurasia), i.e., briefly and simply, to be or not to be at all.

Firm conviction as to the exceptionally gifted statehood of the Russian people and its vitality leads me to respond in the affirmative to this question and allows me to hope that the Russian people will escape both the Scylla of monarchical restoration and the Charybdis of "Bonapartism." In its revolution, the Russian people remains a most religious people. This statement has always seemed to me self-evident and unambiguous, and so it would seem to be now if not for efforts which are more fiery than intelligent, to see in it some kind of "mystagogy of evil." For, the personality (both individual and symphonic) being created by God cannot be evil, and evil cannot be a personality (an "evil personality" does not equate to "a personality of evil"). Evil is not a personal being and does not exist in itself, but is the sin of the personality or, in the terms of the holy fathers, its voluntary carelessness. Of course, the Russian people is sinful, and sin is an inextricable aspect of its revolution — whether revolutionary or counter-revolutionary, the hatred of man is not something we would choose. But in its sin, it remains religious, even if it has not recognized this and does not know European languages well, and has therefore translated its religiosity as "atheism." Its revolution is religious not because of its "positive" tasks which are put forth by its "leaders" and carried out like a fratricidal massacre and fight against the Church, but because in both red and white ideologies is distorted that which "is being in evil."

---

156 This is not intended to deny that Peter and even the entire quasi-imperial period furthered Russian national development. National development continued and achieved great successes despite Europeanization. But it achieved ever less lasting successes than it could have without Europeanization. To distinguish between the false and the true in Peter does not mean to reject Peter. This means only one thing: to not be a doctrinarian (revolutionary) and to not engage in idolatry.

The very force and terror of the whole people's sin testifies to the force of the religious nature and religious tension within the Russian people.

Thus, the foremost task of the moment we are living through is the development of a new religious-national worldview. A new structure and a new ideology are needed, even if, as is the case with any ideology, it will express the "ideality" of the new Russia in a limited, imperfect, and at first even primitive manner. If one relates to it in the correct way, this will be no great misfortune. A correct relation to it means overcoming the revolutionary-doctrinairist mindset, overcoming the revolution within ourselves as Russia herself overcomes it. Of course, this new religious-national worldview must not remain in the sphere of abstract principles. It should lead to a definitive, concrete program built upon the grounds of acknowledging what the revolution has clarified as positive. Thus, this program should include the foundations of the "Soviet system" and the resolution of the socio-economic problem in the sense of acknowledging such to have its properly functional significance, which is as far from the idea of holy property as it is from socialism. Here, Russia's internal problem turns out to be its historical mission.

We are therefore going beyond a "phenomenological" study, for we are posing the question of the meaning of the revolution and of all Russian history. What is phenomenologically important is only pointing out the significance of ideology. Every ideology is doomed to unreality if its appearance and development are not accompanied by the creation of a new governing party, one which must come to take the place of the Communist Party as the axis of the already created, new ruling stratum.

***

www.ingramcontent.com/pod-product-compliance
Lightning Source LLC
Chambersburg PA
CBHW070047080526
44586CB00013B/951